Edward Elgar, Modernist

The first full-length analytical study of Edward Elgar's music, this book argues that Elgar was a modernist composer, and that his music constitutes a pessimistic twentieth-century assessment of the nature of human being. Focusing on Elgar's music rather than his life, Harper-Scott blends the hermeneutic and existential philosophy of Martin Heidegger with music-analytical methods derived from Heinrich Schenker and James Hepokoski. In the course of engaging with debates centred on duotonality in musical structures, sonata deformations, meaning in music, the nature of tragedy, and the quest narrative, the book rejects poststructuralist and literary-theoretical interpretations of music, radically interprets Schenkerian theory, and tentatively outlines a new space – a Heideggerian 'clearing' – in which music of all periods can be perceived to operate, be experienced, and be understood. The book includes a detailed glossary which provides the reader with clear definitions of important and difficult terms.

J. P. E. HARPER-SCOTT is Temporary Lecturer in Music at Royal Holloway, University of London. He studied at the University of Durham and at Magdalen College, Oxford. His essays on Elgar have been published in *19th-Century Music* and *Music Analysis*, and he is a contributor to *The Cambridge Companion to Elgar*. He is the co-editor, with Julian Rushton, of an essay collection, *Elgar Studies* (Cambridge University Press, forthcoming). This is his first book.

Music in the 20th Century

GENERAL EDITOR   Arnold Whittall

This series offers a wide perspective on music and musical life in the twentieth century. Books included range from historical and biographical studies concentrating particularly on the context and circumstances in which composers were writing, to analytical and critical studies concerned with the nature of musical language and questions of compositional process. The importance given to context will also be reflected in studies dealing with, for example, the patronage, publishing, and promotion of new music, and in accounts of the musical life of particular countries.

Recent titles

The Music of Conlon Nancarrow
Kyle Gann

The Stravinsky Legacy
Jonathan Cross

Experimental Music: Cage and Beyond
Michael Nyman

The BBC and Ultra-Modern Music, 1922–1936
Jennifer Doctor

The Music of Harrison Birtwistle
Robert Adlington

Four Musical Minimalists: La Monte Young, Terry Riley, Steve Reich, Philip Glass
Keith Potter

Fauré and French Musical Aesthetics
Carlo Caballero

The Music of Toru Takemitsu
Peter Burt

The Music and Thought of Michael Tippett: Modern Times and Metaphysics
David Clarke

Serial Music, Serial Aesthetics: Compositional Theory in Post-War Europe
M. J. Grant

Britten's Musical Language
Philip Rupprecht

Music and Ideology in Cold War Europe
Mark Carroll

Polish Music since Szymanowski
Adrian Thomas

Edward Elgar, Modernist
J. P. E. Harper-Scott

Edward Elgar, Modernist

J. P. E. Harper-Scott

CAMBRIDGE
UNIVERSITY PRESS

CAMBRIDGE UNIVERSITY PRESS
Cambridge, New York, Melbourne, Madrid, Cape Town, Singapore, São Paulo

CAMBRIDGE UNIVERSITY PRESS
The Edinburgh Building, Cambridge CB2 2RU, UK
Published in the United States of America by Cambridge University Press, New York

www.cambridge.org
Information on this title: www.cambridge.org/9780521862004

First published 2006

Printed in the United Kingdom at the University Press, Cambridge

A catalogue record for this book is available from the British Library

ISBN-13 978-0-521-86200-4 hardback
ISBN-10 0-521-86200-0 hardback

for my family

Song is existence

... To sing, truly to say worldly existence, to say out of the haleness of the whole pure draft and to say only this, means: to belong to the precinct of beings themselves. This precinct, as the very nature of language, is Being itself. To sing the song means to be present in what is present itself. It means: Dasein, existence.

(Martin Heidegger, 'What are poets for?')

Contents

Preface

This book grew from a belief in meaning, and the desirability of discovering it, in musical works and human life. It was written to satisfy a perceived need for musical criticism that retreats neither into conservative, narrowly formalist analysis nor into poststructuralist hermeneutics guided by nihilistic Foucauldian or Derridian dogma; a criticism which does not allow for a potentially tendentious location of musical works in scores, psychological states, political ideologies, socio-historical constellations, or mere physical reverberations, but acknowledges that music is, before we make it anything else, *itself* – a distinctive entity with its own ontology that can be unveiled, understood, and relocated within the world (and not just a musicologist's favourite part of that world). It is intended as a challenge to old *and* new orthodoxies.

But more than that or anything else it is intended as an analysis of Edward Elgar's music. Its focus on his music, not his life, makes this book an unusual contribution to Elgar scholarship. And the particular critical attitude adopted in writing it deserves clarification, for which words written to open another book may serve.

> To study the lives of great artists is often a positive hindrance to the understanding of their works; for it is usually the study of what they have not mastered, and thus it undermines their authority in the things which they have mastered . . . Even if the works of art show characteristics closely resembling the faults of the author, we have always to remember that the business of the work of art is to be itself, whereas neither the science of ethics nor the structure of society can thrive for long on the denial that it is the duty of a man to improve himself. A sense of duty imposed upon a work from without is artistic insincerity. Whatever goes into the work of art must belong to it.[1]

So Donald Tovey opens his unfinished monograph on Beethoven. Had he lived another half century and read the vast biographical literature that has grown up (and shows no signs of going to seed) around Elgar, he might have said the same again. Carl Dahlhaus thought that the principle

---

[1] Donald Francis Tovey, *Beethoven* (London: Oxford University Press, 1945), p. 1.

of reading musical meaning off a composer's biography had died out by the beginning of the twentieth century.[2] He was wrong.

What is Elgar's place in musical history? What are his musical preoccupations, his view of form, language – or meaning? After a hundred years of Elgar studies,[3] detailed responses to those questions, and questions like them, are still quite thin on the ground. What we have in place of rigorous musicological discussion of Elgar's music is a vast and ever-increasing biographical literature which, with a few worthy exceptions, has been the favoured way to write a lengthy study of him. Several of the contributions to this literature have been of outstanding quality.[4] But this book does not add to their number.

This book draws on twentieth-century philosophy and music-analytical theory among other things, makes connexions between different pieces of music, and draws hermeneutic conclusions – literally (the word comes from the Greek messenger Hermes), conclusions about the 'messages carried by the music' – which educe from the works under discussion meanings relating to human existence. It cannot aspire to be a work of what the last century called the New Criticism, but insofar as such a thing is possible these days when fewer and fewer people believe in 'the music itself', a savour of that tradition still lingers in its critical attitude. That is the attitude of (if one could adopt it properly) 'the perfect critic' who – like a phenomenologist or, as T. S. Eliot notes in an early essay on the subject, like Aristotle – looks 'solely and steadfastly at the object',[5] a writer identified ideally as an individual critic (initials and surname) rather than an individual personality (forename and surname). However much it wanders, in whatever direction, it maintains a tenacious propinquity to discrete musical works, and wanders only to bring experience to bear on analysis and understanding of them. Seeing an object steadily and seeing it whole means seeing its place in the world and humankind's place alongside it: but the world must not obtrude on the analysis; and whatever

---

[2] Carl Dahlhaus, *Foundations of Music History*, trans. J. Bradford Robinson (Cambridge: Cambridge University Press, 1983; orig. edn 1967), p. 17.

[3] The first book on the composer was Robert J. Buckley's biography, *Sir Edward Elgar* (London: The Bodley Head, 1905).

[4] Among these contributions Jerrold Northrop Moore's vast and mythic *Edward Elgar: a Creative Life* (Oxford: Oxford University Press, 1984) still dominates, but excellent alternative interpretations are offered by Michael Kennedy, who has written two quite different but equally superb biographies: *Portrait of Elgar*, 3rd edn (Oxford: Clarendon Press, 1987), and *The Life of Elgar* (Cambridge: Cambridge University Press, 2004).

[5] T. S. Eliot, 'The perfect critic', in *The Sacred Wood: Essays on Poetry and Criticism*, 2nd edn (London: Faber and Faber, 1997; reset from 1928 edn), p. 9.

meaning is claimed to subsist in a work must be rooted absolutely and solely in its inner workings.

Elgar's modernism has not had a sure ride through the critical chicanes. Apart from the often incisive contemporary assessments of his position in musical history, his place in early modernism has often been doubted in the eighty-odd years since his wife's death (a date which has, as part of the later interpretation, been considered overly significant).[6] But that does not make this book's impassive critical attitude any less essential for a study of Elgar; indeed it is likely that the assumption of a critical position closer to a tenor of modernism (an early exponent was T. S. Eliot) will reveal aspects of his music which the more Romantic, and generally biographical, accent of the vast majority of the Elgarian literature to date is by nature ill-attuned to grasp. Any findings of the present study will inevitably be provisional and partial, but if they provide a counterweight to the differently orientated findings of other studies, they could do some good.

Of course nobody is a perfect critic; nobody quite manages to sacrifice the individuality signified by his or her personal name even when it hides behind initials: and although this study attempts to concentrate attention steadfastly on the works it discusses, drawing on larger ideas only insofar as they aid in detailed, note-centred critical engagement with the texts, it risks slightly distending the works' frame when discussing their possible meanings. (Eliot would call this a 'tolerable avocation'[7] for a critic.)

It is a failing of critics that they take from their reading only what confirms their own insight, and excoriate other ideas which left alone might spoil their party. So although the argument of Chapter 5 Section 1 is not intended to dismantle the apparatus of poststructuralist theory – it would be an inadequate weapon with which to attempt that task – it *is* a rigorous attempt to distance my views and my critical method from aspects of contemporary writing with which they might, to my discomfort, otherwise be associated. But not all misunderstanding can be avoided. I shall inevitably distort or misuse even the work of writers whose views I think I hold, and by arguing without sufficient clarity will leave open room for interpretation that I do not intend. However that

---

[6] Several contributors to the *Cambridge Companion to Elgar*, ed. Daniel M. Grimley and Julian Rushton (Cambridge: Cambridge University Press, 2004) argue for Elgar's modernity with renewed vigour, however.

[7] T. S. Eliot, 'Studies in contemporary criticism', *Egoist* 9 (1918), p. 113, cited in A. David Moody, *Thomas Stearns Eliot, Poet*, 2nd edn (Cambridge: Cambridge University Press, 1994), p. xix.

may be, the book must stand on its own feet, in the hope that they provide a sufficiently sturdy support – at least until the last page, if no further.

Some technical points should be dealt with here. When using Heideggerian or Schenkerian terminology I follow the usual practice in the relevant traditions of philosophy or musicology: so 'Dasein' (which cannot be avoided in discussion of Heidegger) is set in roman, but '*Ursatz*', '*Urlinie*', '*Augenblick*', '*Ereignis*', etc. (which *can* all be avoided in discussion of Heidegger and Schenker, and so remain 'foreign') are italicized. Musical pitch is indicated in the form C–B, c–b, c^1–b^1, c^2–b^2, etc., where c^1 is middle C. Scale degrees and keys are written in abbreviated form, so that '$\hat{3}$/a' indicates scale degree 3 within the key of A minor and '$\hat{5}$/F' indicates scale degree 5 within F major. Other conventions are introduced in the text. A glossary of hard terms (most of them Heideggerian) is found on p. 231.

I acknowledge with heartfelt thanks the help of Magdalen College, Oxford, Jeff Lincoln, and the Arts and Humanities Research Council, without whose generous financial support I could not have written this book at all. I am grateful too to the staff at Oxford's libraries, especially the Music Faculty Library, the Music Reading Room of the Bodleian Library, the Philosophy Faculty Library, and Magdalen College Library. I also thank staff and students at the Universities of Oxford, Nottingham, Liverpool, and Royal Holloway, University of London, for giving me something profitable and enjoyable to do with my time while writing, expanding, and tinkering with the text, and Penny Souster and (especially) Vicki Cooper for steering the book to publication with care and generous encouragement.

I could not have been more fortunate in my D.Phil. supervisors, Nicholas Marston and Suzannah Clark, without whose advice I could never have proceeded in the right direction. But others also aided in the gestation, and I can only mention by name a few of the most important. Without the use of Bill Ives's keyboard, my analysis of Elgar's music would have been almost impossible. Julian Rushton has been a sage support, guide, and friend throughout the process. Daniel Grimley's generous response to and help in focusing my work is greatly appreciated. Furthermore I am indebted to Robert Anderson and Michael Kennedy, inspirations from my boyhood on, for (among other things) writing so beautifully and insightfully on Elgar and British music that I felt I wanted to join in, and to Jeremy Dibble for evangelizing so strongly that in the end I could do no other. I thank Raymond Monk for years of encouragement, and for providing the cover photograph from his private collection. While writing and revising I have benefited from the criticisms and suggestions of Robert Bailey, John Williamson, Max Paddison, Julian Johnson, Aidan Thomson, Arnold Whittall, and an anonymous reader (to whom must go credit for the idea of a glossary). Heideggerian discussions with Michael Inwood have done much to shore up my doddering arguments. But naturally no one except me is responsible for any unobliterated nonsense.

My family have kept my emotions on track throughout, and the book is dedicated to them. Among friends, thanks for many favours both academic and amicable must go to Duncan Ferguson, John Livesley, Peter McCullough, and Michael Piret. Frederick Hodges, Peter Anthony, and Andrew Petiprin were always on hand to help with German, and Russell Dewhurst introduced me mysteriously to Heidegger. Without them, this study would have been very different and might never have been completed.

1 Styles and ideas

1.1. Aims and context

This book advances five closely interconnected but wide-ranging theses. 1: Elgar was a modernist composer. 2: His music carries meanings that can be discovered by analysis. 3: Schenkerian voice-leading analysis is a useful preliminary to the hermeneutics – the study of meaning – of all kinds of tonal music, but its foundations and presuppositions need to be examined and reworked in this case. 4: The philosophy of Martin Heidegger can at the same time aid in three tasks: the useful reformulation of Schenker's phenomenology, the understanding of music's ontology, and the hermeneutics of musical works. 5: A work of music, being an intentional object with a supratemporal form, is a mimesis of humankind's lived temporality, and lights up for us the structures of our own existence.

All of these theses are controversial to a greater or lesser extent. Few Elgarians or academic musicologists would instinctively accept thesis 1. Of those who sense *something* of the modernist in him, he has been compared, not entirely to his favour, with contemporaries: after noting that his conservatism need not rule out a kind of progressiveness, Arnold Whittall adds, echoing Adorno's view of Debussy, that 'the fractures and ambiguities characteristic of modernity are . . . less likely to be found in Elgar than they are in other tonal symphonists of the time, such as Sibelius, or, in particular, Mahler'.[1] And on the surface – the place where fractures are generally seen – he is entirely right. But James Hepokoski may be counted among those who still feel bound to call Elgar 'modernist',[2] and until it is proven through thorough analysis of his music, as opposed to an instinctive response to it, by however learned a listener, that that music has little to do with his historical situation, then Dahlhaus's characterization of the years 1890–1914, and therefore the heart of Elgar's mature music, as a modernist period of musical composition also still

---

[1] Arnold Whittall, *Musical Composition in the Twentieth Century* (Oxford: Oxford University Press, 1999), pp. 16–17. He quotes some of Adorno's words on Debussy on p. 10, and quietly rebuffs them on p. 26.

[2] James A. Hepokoski, 'Elgar', in *The Nineteenth-Century Symphony*, ed. D. Kern Holoman (New York and London: Schirmer, 1997), pp. 327–44 and *Sibelius: Symphony No. 5* (Cambridge: Cambridge University Press, 1993), p. 2.

holds, and its value as a descriptive category for Elgar's music should be examined.[3]

Theses 2 and 3 are supported in part by Adorno's opening remarks on Mahler: 'Inadequate as is thematic analysis to the content of Mahler's symphonies – an analysis which misses the music's substance in its pre-occupation with procedure – no more sufficient would be the attempt to pin down, in the jargon of authenticity, the statement put forward by the music.'[4] Thesis 2 points to the suggestion (in Chapter 2), through arguments put forward by Roman Ingarden and Martin Heidegger, that it is only through analysis that a work's substance may be grasped. Adorno would agree that neither an 'analysis which misses the music's substance in its preoccupation with procedure' nor a hermeneutics which has no basis in close textual analysis is an adequate approach to musical criticism: the two must be combined, and this book is an attempt to do that. It may even be argued that Elgar's mature music is, taken as a whole and in its parts – and here his modernist credentials shine out – a powerful negative dialectic so subtle that it largely goes unnoticed even now, when musicologists are on the alert for such things, one which takes apart and reconstitutes musical concepts of form, tonality, and structure, and by extension reconstructs human, existential notions of self.

I shall not balk from using 'the jargon of authenticity' (the Heideggerian tradition which Adorno distanced himself from) where it serves useful methodological or hermeneutic ends. One of the book's intentions is to establish an adequate situation for Elgar in European intellectual history, and since it is basic to the nature of his compositional procedure to argue through and with a musical tradition that stretches back to the beginning of the Enlightenment, the 'jargon' is a useful way of situating him with some precision in the intellectual development that Robert C. Solomon has called 'the rise and fall of the self'.[5] It should come as no surprise that Elgar's ideas were bang up to date.

It seems this project is not, except in terms of its ideology, terribly different from Adorno's; it might even turn out to be a differently

---

[3] See Carl Dahlhaus, *Nineteenth-Century Music*, trans. J. Bradford Robinson (Berkeley, CA and London: University of California Press, 1989; orig. edn 1980), Chapter 6. The author of a big new history of Western music seems to think that Elgar does not warrant *any* place in musical history: see Richard Taruskin, *The Oxford History of Western Music* (Oxford: Oxford University Press, 2005). But this is an extreme and polemical position.

[4] Theodor W. Adorno, *Mahler: a Musical Physiognomy*, trans. Edmund Jephcott (Chicago and London: University of Chicago Press, 1992; orig. edn 1960), p. 3.

[5] Robert C. Solomon, *Continental Philosophy Since 1750: The Rise and Fall of the Self* (Oxford: Oxford University Press, 1988).

grounded way towards achieving certain of his interpretative ends. After all, Adorno's pronounced revulsion to technical analysis was probably only a self-defensive façade. As Max Paddison admits, Adorno 'was interested by Schenker's work . . . although his understanding of it seems to have been somewhat limited'.[6] The result is that Adorno's analyses rarely convince or even grip the reader qua technical analyses, but that the conclusions he draws from the hidden analytical processes of his mind are usually fascinating and compelling. Viewed alongside Paddison's codification of Adorno's dialectical model of music criticism, my approach appears as a combination of the first and third of three interpretative strands, i.e. 'immanent (including technical) analysis' and 'philosophical–historical interpretation'.[7]

Adorno defines immanent analysis straightforwardly. 'Technical analysis is assumed at all times and often disclosed, but it needs to be supplemented by detailed interpretation if it is to go beyond mere humanistic stock-taking and to express the relationship of the subject to truth.'[8] My analysis is more detailed and more fully presented for scrutiny than

---

[6] Max Paddison, *Adorno's Aesthetics of Music* (Cambridge: Cambridge University Press, 1993), p. 170.

[7] Ibid., p. 59. I have no interest in the second category, 'sociological critique', since I am not persuaded by Adorno's claim that all art is ideological: that claim seems rooted in Adorno's historical and cultural situation to an unhelpful degree. I am more persuaded that our *readings* of artworks may be ideological (and are becoming more so, ironically, the more Adorno is read), at least until reconstructed, and I shall propose a reconstructive way round some entrenched musicological ideologies in the course of this book.

By 'Adorno's historical and cultural situation' I mean not merely that of a German of Jewish extraction during the rise of fascism, although it would be difficult to overstate the importance of that, but rather his self-styled role as the philosophical voice of artistic (and especially musical) modernism. Dahlhaus's critique of Adorno's view of history – he suggests that Adorno 'reconstrue[s] aesthetic norms into historical trends to form a basis for a pre-history of the twelve-note technique' (Carl Dahlhaus, *Foundations of Music History*, trans. J. Bradford Robinson (Cambridge: Cambridge University Press, 1983; orig. edn 1967), p. 31) – strikes at the heart of what I call Adorno's 'ideology', which is in one sense a verbal equivalent of the famous duck-rabbit image. It is either because he believes in the fragmentation of society and the individual that he gives the tenets of musical modernism control over his entire philosophy or, conversely, because he holds that the tenets of musical modernism disclose world-historical truths that he believes in the fragmentation of society and the individual. It doesn't matter which conviction came first – they probably came together, *Einfall*-like – but the combination of the two leads him to argue for the necessity of sociological critique. I see neither duck nor rabbit, and will argue for a different form of critique.

[8] Theodor W. Adorno, *Philosophy of Modern Music*, trans. Anne G. Mitchell and Wesley V. Bloomster (London: Sheed and Ward, 1973), p. 26.

Adorno's, and the connexions between different stages in my hermeneutics are therefore more clearly visible and more easily assessed. In place of Adorno's neo-Marxian approach I set a Heideggerian philosophical–historical interpretation, and so Adorno's sociological critique becomes for me an existential–ontological critique.

This study begins with relatively abstract methodological questions, progresses to very detailed analyses of two individual works, introducing along the way more general methodological concerns of a philosophical nature, then offers a hermeneutics of the works thus analyzed, before concluding with new, relatively abstract methodological observations which result from the process.

Chapter 1 outlines the aims and context of the study, and begins to flesh out the first thesis, to be developed at greater length in Chapter 6.

Chapter 2 problematizes Schenkerian phenomenology, addressing hermeneutic and methodological problems at its heart. Schenkerian theory is reformulated in the light of ideas borrowed from post-Husserlian and Heideggerian philosophy, chiefly, but not exclusively, in relation to the way Heidegger's *Augenblick* affects our conception of Schenker's *Ursatz*. The intention is to sever Schenker's theory from its restrictive association with Beethoven's heroic style, thereby making possible a richer hermeneutics. This is probably the most complex chapter and the least easy to read, and furthermore its relevance to the book's overall argument (which builds incrementally through each chapter) only becomes fully clear in Chapters 5–7.

During an analysis of the First Symphony in Chapter 3 an important Elgarian fingerprint is uncovered: his 'immuring–immured' tonal structure, in which an opening and closing key, posing as 'the tonic' but not necessarily in a convincing manner, immures another, perhaps more 'viable' key which, however, Elgar turns his back on. In this case the immuring tonality is A♭ and the immured tonality D. Elgar's use of a static *Kopfton* (another fingerprint) throughout the symphony helps to prolong through the entire structure a single four-movement *Ursatz*. Significant thematic, tonal, and contrapuntal problems in each of the first three movements negate a satisfactory sense of closure, and a single coherent argument is carried on through the work. It is demonstrated that the final, very delayed, closure of the *Ursatz* in the very last bar of the symphony, which on the face of it seems orthodox, is unconvincing in terms of purely musical grammar and rhetoric, and deliberately so. Another general question, related ultimately to the same hermeneutic impulse, is also confronted: why do multi-movement works have as many movements as they do, and in a particular order?

Chapter 4 discusses the nature and function of Elgar's 'symphonic study', *Falstaff*. It draws on James Hepokoski's argument that symphonic poems hold text (music) and paratext (non-musical image) in meaningful inter-connexion, and that the listener or analyst must always pay attention to both. But Elgar explicitly writes in his analytical note on the work that 'the composer's intention' (his words) is to write a piece of musical Shakespearean criticism; he quotes quite extensively from critics as early as Maurice Morgann (1777). This 'meta-paratextual' content makes *Falstaff* perhaps unique among symphonic poems or 'studies', and adds another facet to the work which must be grappled with in an analysis. Its meta-paratextual content is examined through the Shakespeare critics Elgar cites and their subsequent development in much later critical writing. Of particular importance is Morgann's notion of narrative and psychological 'inference', which has recently been picked up by Harold Bloom, and which forms the theoretical basis for Elgar's addition of the Dream Interlude, a crucial part of the work.

Through an analysis of Elgar's use of associative tonality – he associates keys with Falstaff, Hal, and the Kingship of England – a window begins to open up into a hermeneutic of the work's existential content, in terms of its analysis of Falstaff in particular and humankind more generally. The relationship between Falstaff's C and Hal's E♭ is the central interest, and the ultimately destructive role played by the Kingship's E is closely examined. The analytical technique is a mixture of Schenkerian and Hepokoskian methods, especially the 'non-resolving recapitulation deformation' and 'rotational structures', but the emphasis is principally on tonal association and the insights gained from a modified Schenkerian approach, rather than on the mechanics of undertaking one. I therefore focus on more outward-looking implications of the phenomenology, to encourage a more extensive exploration of extramusical meaning.

Chapter 5 outlines my theory of musical hermeneutics, placing it alongside Lawrence Kramer's in many ways, setting itself a little against his in others, principally because of my Heideggerian focus and insistence that music is a mimesis of human temporality, which itself leads into a broader consideration of human being and Being as such, not merely into musical hermeneutics. The second half of the chapter develops my conception of music's mimetic nature through a comparison with the quest narrative in literature. These hermeneutic and mimetic conceptions are grounded on Heidegger and Gadamer, and set apart from (Derridian and Foucauldian) poststructuralist musicology.

Chapter 6 offers an interpretation of the 'data' garnered in the analyses, drawing on Chapter 5 and the refinements of Schenkerian analysis in

Chapter 2, to establish Elgar's modernist credentials and point to new challenges for musical hermeneutics. It examines a possible existential meaning of the temporal unfolding of the First Symphony and *Falstaff*, characterizing it as a kind of failed quest narrative which rejects the Beethovenian heroic paradigm while – and this is a typically modernist move – ostensibly but disingenuously repeating it. Suggestions are made there and in Chapter 7 of ways in which we may read off Elgar's modernist music an incisive and distinctively twentieth-century commentary on human nature and the possibilities for human being in the future. In conclusion the significance of the study's findings is discussed.

1.2. A musicological context

This study will draw on and open up new areas for debate with several contexts which range from challenging new ideas in musical analysis through studies of reception history to works on hermeneutics and the philosophy of music.

In the last twenty years a number of Schenkerians have been persuaded by Robert Bailey's rejection of the classic monotonal view of the structure of neo-Romantic and early modernist music, and his proposal that it may be better understood in terms of the prolongation of a 'double-tonic complex'. 'Directional tonality' and 'associative tonality' may also have an important part to play in the overall structure of movements or works.[9] As yet, there is no consensus among Schenkerians as to how these tonal structures, especially the first two, are to be assimilated into Schenker's explicitly monotonal conception of music's unfolding. It is one of this book's concerns to show how this is possible. By regarding prolongation of and resolution into 'the tonic', understood as the governing key in a monotonal hegemony, as a *possibility* rather than a *necessity* we may see secondary keys, whether in a double-tonic complex or in a directional-tonal structure, as choices to be made rather than difficulties to be overcome. This requires a fundamental

---

[9] The most recent 'duotonal Schenkerian' studies are the essays in William Kinderman and Harald Krebs (eds.), *The Second Practice of Nineteenth-Century Tonality* (Lincoln, NE University of Nebraska Press, 1996). Like Patrick McCreless's *Wagner's 'Siegfried': Its Drama, History, and Music* (Ann Arbor, MI: UMI Research Press, 1982), Christopher Orlo Lewis's *Tonal Coherence in Mahler's Ninth Symphony* (Ann Arbor, MI: UMI Research Press, 1984) and Warren Darcy's *Wagner's 'Das Rheingold'* (Oxford: Clarendon Press, 1993), they are greatly influenced by Robert Bailey's 'An analytical study of the sketches and drafts', in *Richard Wagner, Prelude and Transformation from 'Tristan und Isolde'* (New York and London: Norton, 1985), pp. 113–46 and 'The structure of the *Ring* and its evolution', *Nineteenth-Century Music* 1 (1977), pp. 48–61.

reformulation, but not a corruption, of Schenker's phenomenology, one which makes sense of a significant change of emphasis.

Schenker's contention, as I wish to formulate it, is that each 'present' moment of a piece of music, each point along the unfolding of the *Ursatz*, holds within itself the entire 'past' and 'future' of the work in a meaningful union: his conception is on a 'retentive–protentive' model familiar to the philosophical school of phenomenology, and as such is basically identical to the Husserlian and Bergsonian understanding of time-consciousness which is the basis of the thought of Ingarden and Heidegger.[10] At each stage, we know what has passed and predict what is to come. Yet Schenker insists that we *know* what is to come, i.e. the closure of the *Ursatz* and the reaffirmation of 'the tonic'. After Scott Burnham's reading of Schenkerian theory in the light of nineteenth- and twentieth-century reception history, it is clear that this claim – reasonable enough in its historical context, given the fact that many nineteenth-century composers seem to have held this view themselves – points not to necessity but merely to possibility. We cannot now agree that the closure of the *Ursatz* in 'the tonic' is a necessity. And that is the fundamental change to Schenker's conception which allows for the reconciliation of his monotonal outlook with the duotonal outlook of more recent scholars. His retentive–protentive model is not smashed, but merely opened up and made more pliable. We know at each musical moment that it 'protains' *a* future, but we are open to the possibility that it might not be a heroic Beethovenian future. The reasons for this will be more fully explained in Chapter 2.

Here duotonal Schenkerian analysis and Hepokoskian Sonata Theory may join hands. Daniel Harrison has pointed out Bailey's and Hepokoski's implicit, shared Heraclitean ancestry:[11] for all three (as well as for Heidegger), everything flows. Since the early 1990s, James Hepokoski has been developing an increasingly rich and vivid way of thinking about early modernist structures and the meanings they may carry.[12] His discussions

---

[10] In Chapter 2 I shall say more on studies by phenomenologists of music – but this book is not a phenomenology of music; it is merely a combination of my interpretation of two different but (I think) related phenomenologies: those of Schenker and Heidegger.

[11] Daniel Harrison, 'Nonconformist notions of nineteenth-century enharmonicism', *Music Analysis* 21 (2002), pp. 115–60.

[12] Hepokoski's largest study is his *Sibelius: Symphony No. 5* (Cambridge: Cambridge University Press, 1993), but other important ones are 'Back and forth from *Egmont*: Beethoven, Mozart, and the nonresolving recapitulation', *Nineteenth-Century Music* 25 (2001–2), pp. 127–54, 'Beyond the sonata principle', *Journal of the American Musicological Society* 55 (2002), pp. 91–154, 'Fiery-pulsed libertine or domestic hero? Strauss's *Don Juan* reinvestigated', in *Richard Strauss: New Perspectives on the Composer*

of sonata deformations and rotational structures are in important respects similar to my refined Schenkerian methodology, with its emphasis on the choice of whether to be 'another heroic Beethovenian piece' (compose out an orthodox *Ursatz*), and, through a more explicitly Heideggerian formulation of music's goal-directedness, on the teleological thrust towards the end of all possibilities – the close of the piece, whether that be monotonal or duotonal in implication or in fact.

The two central Hepokoskian categories to be drawn on in this book require brief introduction now: sonata deformations and rotational structures. Hepokoski has recently defined a sonata deformation as

> an individual work in dialogue primarily with sonata norms even though certain central features of the sonata-concept have been reshaped, exaggerated, marginalised or overridden altogether . . . The appropriate formal question to be asked of such a piece – more often, of one of its movements – is not the blunt, reductive one, 'Is it in sonata form?', but rather, 'Are we invited to apply the norms of the traditional sonata in order to interpret what does (or does not) occur in this individualised work?'[13]

He discusses three kinds of deformation in Elgar's symphonies, of which a complicated form of the 'non-resolving recapitulation' also reappears in *Falstaff*.[14] In this deformation, 'a sonata's "second theme" (or any theme that is used to bring the exposition to a non-tonic close) is not permitted to resolve satisfactorily to the presumed "tonic" in the recapitulatory space, thus creating a sense of unease, alienation, futility, recapitulatory failure, or the like'.[15] As we shall see in Chapters 2 and 3, the 'failure' of the First Symphony's and *Falstaff*'s recapitulations to provide the necessary

and His Work, ed. Bryan Gilliam (Durham, NC: Duke University Press, 1992), pp. 135–75, and 'Structure and program in *Macbeth*: a proposed reading of Strauss's first symphonic poem', in *Richard Strauss and His World*, ed. Bryan Gilliam (Princeton, NJ: Princeton University Press, 1992), pp. 67–89. He has recently summarized many of his ideas in 'Beethoven reception: the symphonic tradition', in *The Cambridge History of Nineteenth-Century Music*, ed. Jim Samson (Cambridge: Cambridge University Press, 2001), pp. 424–59, and in collaboration with Warren Darcy is completing a very substantial book explaining Sonata Theory: *Elements of Sonata Theory – Norms, Types, and Deformations* (New York and Oxford: Oxford University Press, forthcoming).

[13] Hepokoski, 'Beethoven reception', p. 447.

[14] He observes deformations mostly in his First Symphony analysis: see Hepokoski, 'Elgar', esp. pp. 328–36.

[15] Hepokoski, *Sibelius: Symphony No. 5*, p. 94, n. 17; he discusses the usual pattern of resolution in such cases, which usually comes in the coda space, in 'Back and forth from *Egmont*'.

tonal resolutions for the exposition themes is crucial to their semantic content. Elgar thematizes, by engaging in explicit, intricate 'play' with, three interrelated traditions:

1. The multi-movement 'narrative' form, found in several of Beethoven's symphonies and works inspired by them, which often charts a course *per aspera ad astra*.[16]
2. The fused multi-movement form frequently used by Liszt and Strauss (the source probably being Schubert's *'Wanderer' Fantasy*), which had by Elgar's time a strong pedigree of use in symphonic music.
3. Sonata form itself, with its generic implications of statement, development, and (resolute) restatement of a definite, identifiable, central idea.

Composers had deliberately played with generic conventions throughout what Dahlhaus calls the 'second age of the symphony',[17] but Elgar's play was particularly advanced, and he was manifestly aware of it himself, as we shall see in later chapters.

The other Hepokoskian concept to be introduced is the rotational model that has been identified particularly with Bruckner and Sibelius.[18] A rotational form is a progression of varied strophes,

> a series of differentiated figures, motives, themes, and so on (which . . . may also be arranged to suggest such things, for example, as a sonata exposition). The referential statement may either cadence or recycle back through a transition to a second broad rotation. Second (and any subsequent) rotations normally rework all or most of the referential statement's material, which is

---

[16] Robert Bailey observed some time ago that by the time of *Tristan und Isolde*, 'the major and minor modes [had] . . . become equivalent and interchangeable, so that either one can substitute for the other' (Bailey, 'An analytical study of the sketches and drafts', p. 116). This is unquestionable, and an important theoretical point, but should not be taken to imply that the difference between major-feel and minor-feel music has been eradicated, which would be a nonsense, even in the first movement of Mahler's Ninth Symphony, whose post-*Tristan* modal mixture is perhaps uniquely asseverative. Despite 'interior' post-*Tristan* modal mixture in many of his themes, Elgar makes a deliberate and careful distinction between major- and minor-'feeling' music, and for that reason I shall continue to refer to 'C major' etc. not ignorant of Bailey's observation, but aware of its limitations. This is a crucial point: it allows Elgar to play more clearly with the *per aspera ad astra* narrative.

[17] Dahlhaus, *Nineteenth-Century Music*, pp. 265–76.

[18] Hepokoski, 'Beethoven reception', p. 451. The forthcoming *Elements of Sonata Theory* promises to explain the eighteenth- and early-nineteenth-century origins of the process.

now elastically treated. Portions may be omitted, merely alluded to, compressed, or, contrarily, expanded or even 'stopped' and reworked 'developmentally'. New material may also be added or generated. Each subsequent rotation may be heard as an intensified, meditative reflection on the material of the referential statement.[19]

Expressed in these terms, the concept might seem unmanageably vague, with themes that may or may not return or be alluded to and so on, but Hepokoski is careful to say that a rotational structure is a process, and not an architectural formula. In Elgar's music the sonata deformation and the play with fused/actual multi-movement 'narrative' structures provides the scaffold for the work, but it is pulled across this scaffold in variable strophes, or 'rotations'.[20]

In terms of musical hermeneutics, this work enters a debate centred on Lawrence Kramer's *Music as Cultural Practice*.[21] It accepts his proposal of three 'hermeneutic windows' into musical works, but owing to the assertion, based on Ingarden and Heidegger, that music is a mimesis of human temporality, suggests the opening of a fourth, 'mimetic window', which allows the philosophy of Heidegger to illuminate the discussion.[22] This philosophy, as it has been argued in two recent monographs by Julian Young,[23] establishes strong existential and even ethical reasons why music's meanings ought to be grappled with. Not the least of these is Heidegger's startling contention that we are, as moderns, oblivious to the complexity of our own Being, and that artworks, and in the view of this study the human mimesis of music in particular, can wake us up to ourselves, to our responsibilities in the face of our own existence, and to our place among other human beings and in the world.

1.3. Elgar the progressive

The titles of this chapter and this section are, of course, stolen from Schoenberg, a contemporary of Elgar's (a fact easily forgotten). The

---

[19] Hepokoski, *Sibelius: Symphony No. 5*, p. 25.

[20] As I apply these ideas in the course of this book I shall expand on them further; for the moment this brief introduction should suffice.

[21] Lawrence Kramer, *Music as Cultural Practice, 1800–1900* (Berkeley, CA and London: University of California Press, 1990): see esp. Chapter 1.

[22] 'Mimesis' is a word with ancient associations and modern meanings in musicological discourse. I shall clarify my use of it (and other terms) in Chapter 2.

[23] Julian Young, *Heidegger's Philosophy of Art* (Cambridge: Cambridge University Press, 2001), and *Heidegger's Later Philosophy* (Cambridge: Cambridge University Press, 2002).

section title has already been used by Hans Keller, who also acknowledges the debt to Schoenberg.[24] But I wish to argue a case for Elgar as 'the first English progressivist'[25] that differs quite considerably from Keller's, and contradicts an assertion – clever as it is – made in the same centenary year (1957) by another Britten aficionado, Donald Mitchell, that Elgar's 'conservatism' was a result of his English (i.e. *not* European) historical situation. Mitchell writes:

> The fact . . . that he did not emerge from a [musical] tradition increases our understanding of the make-up of his convention, especially its relative orthodoxy when compared with Mahler's or Strauss's . . . [They] lived at the end, the tail-end, of a great tradition: they inherited, in part, an exhausted convention. To develop new trends, new forms, new sounds, was an obligation: they had, in a very pressing sense, to originate, and originate hard, if they were to survive as independent voices. Elgar, on the other hand, was encumbered by no tradition. He could handle his more conventional convention with all the enthusiasm of an early starter; the convention simply had not aged for him as it had for his contemporaries in Europe. The oddity of his English situation spared him the necessity of composing, as it were, with history at his elbow.[26]

This penetrating observation nicely accounts for Elgar's late start, but not for the circumstances that led to what amounts to a stylistic turn after *Falstaff* (1913). In the final section of Chapter 6 I shall argue for an Adornian definition of Elgar's 'progressiveness'; but for that, detailed analysis of two representative works of Elgar's early modernist full maturity in Chapters 3–4 is a prerequisite. In the interests of sharpening the critical cross-hair before the analysis begins, I shall suggest a more superficial but no less important way of identifying and examining his modernist tendencies.

---

[24] Hans Keller, 'Elgar the progressive', *The Music Review* 43 (1957), pp. 294–7.

[25] This was Richard Strauss's assessment in 1902, after a German performance of *The Dream of Gerontius* (see Jerrold Northrop Moore, *Edward Elgar: a Creative Life* (Oxford: Oxford University Press, 1984), pp. 368–9).

[26] Donald Mitchell, 'Some thoughts on Elgar', in *An Elgar Companion*, ed. Christopher Redwood (Ashbourne: Sequoia, 1982), pp. 279–90 at p. 289. The article is reprinted from *Music & Letters* 38 (1957), pp. 113–23, and is reprinted in Mitchell, *Cradles of the New: Writings on Music, 1951–1991*, selected Christopher Palmer, ed. Mervyn Cooke (London: Faber and Faber, 1995), pp. 255–68. Mitchell used precisely the same argument to explain Walton's musical style in an article which predates this on Elgar by five years. See Donald Mitchell, 'Some observations on William Walton, I', *The Chesterian* 26 (1952), pp. 35–8 at pp. 36–7.

First a note on a contemporary. James Hepokoski has given a concise evaluation of Sibelius's stylistic 'periods':

> Once past his training as a student, his compositional development took him through three interrelated but distinguishable phases. The first, lasting from the early 1890s through around 1902 or 1903, is indeed an emphatically Finnish political phase marked by his immersion into and gradual emergence out of the exclusively local and national. This phase ranges from the early, massive 'symphonic poem' (with voice) *Kullervo* (1892) and the subsequent suite of Kalevalaic tone poems, *Four Legends* (1895–96, actually something of a programmatic symphony in E♭ major) to the First and Second Symphonies. In the second phase, from around 1904 to 1912, Sibelius shifted to a 'modern-classical' strategy that strove to engage a larger public, that of the central musical marketplaces of Europe. To this end, he forged a modern musical language of renunciation and compression, one clearly evident in the Third and Fourth Symphonies. The third phase, from around 1912 to the early 1930s, was triggered both by his realization of the inevitable market-place failure of the second and by the unforeseen emergence of the aggressive cultural politics surrounding the dissonant New Music of a younger generation. This final phase, which saw the compression, severity, and 'strangeness' of his style pushed to their limits, is one of disillusioned withdrawal into a private world of symphonic meditation and nature mysticism. Its monuments are the Fifth, Sixth, and Seventh Symphonies and the tone poems *Luonnotar, The Oceanides,* and *Tapiola.*[27]

The developmental parallels between the composers should not be pressed more than is reasonable, but Hepokoski's analysis is too good to pass over, especially since Elgar's and Sibelius's stylistic development did broadly run side by side. The major difference is that Elgar's third phase was rather less spectacular, if no less 'modern', than Sibelius's; but a tripartite division of Elgar's compositional maturity is still possible.

Elgar's mature stylistic development begins around the time of his first highly educational move to London and the composition of *Froissart* (1890) with a neo-Romantic phase, which culminates in the *'Enigma' Variations* and *The Dream of Gerontius*, and – it could be argued – drags on with little further development through the first two parts of the proposed oratorio trilogy. Then follows an early modernist phase, whose musical characteristics and meanings are the main interest of this study. After a socio- and musico-historically motivated stylistic 'turn' comes a

---

[27] James A. Hepokoski, 'Sibelius', in *The Nineteenth - Century Symphony*, ed. D. Kern Holoman (New York and London: Schimer, 1997), p. 418.

third and final phase, which could be designated 'second-stream mature modernist' for reasons which will become clear later.

Elgar's neo-Romantic phase is a vibrant and lusty one, as masterly as the two which followed, and unduly neglected in its own right. Robin Holloway's self-confessedly 'contentious' and passionate defence of the early choral works strikes the exact right note in this respect.[28] Apart from its energy and the high quality of its invention and spontaneity, the salient characteristics of Elgar's neo-Romantic phase are what one might expect of a Wagnerism only gradually digested (and there are still remnants on the surface of Weber and Mendelssohn, which disappear later). Leitmotiv, tonal dualism, and associative tonality have a critical function, especially in the oratorios. But as Elgar settled on an individual voice he developed distinctively Elgarian fingerprints which would be inflated to magisterial proportions in his modernist phase. Chief among these are the static *Kopfton* and the immuring–immured tonal structure.

The first was developed insouciantly in the *'Enigma' Variations* (1898–9), where the *Kopfton*, unexpectedly, does not descend during the course of every movement, and the *Ursatz* does not close.[29] There is no dramatic or hermeneutic significance to this: the variation form, so brilliantly and characterfully used by Elgar, leaves the listener with no question as to the essential autonomy of individual movements; but nevertheless Elgar seems to have been experimenting with multi-movement *Ursätze*, which he would make profound use of in the First Symphony. There are, conceptually, four *Ursätze* prolonged through the work. Their structural significance is nil: the final arrangement of the variations was reached only after much reshuffling, and Elgar clearly did not write the work with the intention of making multi-movement units an important part of the design.[30] Nevertheless, the contrapuntal unfolding of the *Variations* is unusual, even if it does not threaten musical cohesion or demand serious hermeneutic reflexion, and as an experiment in Elgarian unorthodoxy it was to result almost immediately (in *The Dream of Gerontius*, 1900) in an important innovation, the immuring–immured structure. I shall adumbrate this sketchily here, before the fuller and clearer presentation in Chapter 3.

---

[28] Robin Holloway, 'The early choral works', in *The Cambridge Companion to Elgar*, ed. Daniel M. Grimley and Julian Rushton (Cambridge: Cambridge University Press, 2004), pp. 63–80.

[29] This curious behaviour, here presented without explanation for brevity's sake, will be discussed more fully in Chapter 2.

[30] Julian Rushton tabulates Elgar's changes of heart: see *Elgar: 'Engma' Variations* (Cambridge: Cambridge University Press, 1999), p. 59.

Again the fingerprint does not at first take control of the work – the immuring–immured structure is only operative in its fullest sense in Part I of *Gerontius*, where a single, 'immuring' key opens and closes the Part and another is 'immured'. But it nevertheless carries great narrative weight, and is even worked into Part II in a less obvious but no less potent form. Elgar combines a use of associative tonality (D for Judgement, major or minor depending on whether it is good or bad; C for Angels; and E♭ for prayer or other longing for God) and the static *Kopfton*. Both are tied together into a tonal scheme which first immures one tonal area (E♭) between two solid walls of another (D), then in Part II progresses from one double-tonic complex (C/E♭, eventually reached after a long pre-paration that begins on F major) to a final resolution in the original D, thereby forming a two-part immuring–immured tonal structure that architecturally (if not experientially) holds the whole work together.

The narrative significance of this combination of structural tools is straightforward. John Henry Newman's poem, the basis of Elgar's oratorio, is about a worldly man who, after his death, sees a blinding vision of God which persuades him that he is still too tainted by his worldiness to enter into full communion with his Lord. He commits himself to Purgatory, although the Angel that has guided him from the point of his death to the edge of the 'judgement court' assures him that his stay there is 'not for ever'. Naturally Elgar could not end such a work with a simplistically positive outcome. The attainment of a key associated with God would be out of the question, so he ends in D major, the positive mode of the Judgement tonality. Since after his death nothing at all becomes clear until The Soul's encounter with God, the stasis of the work's *Kopfton* over such a stupendously large stretch of time in Part II is entirely convincing, and the precise coincidence of its descent with the words 'take me away!' is inten-sely moving. Being-towards-God, the E♭/B♭ movement in Part I ('Kyrie' to 'Sanctus fortis'), or the C/E♭ pairing of Part II (Angels joining in a vast hymn of praise), remains locked away between the iron walls of the Judgement that prevents the human soul from reaching its destiny within the confines of the work. These broad Elgarian brushstrokes are calcula-ted with such brilliance that a powerful and overarching hermeneutic statement permeates every moment of the work.

The Dream of Gerontius is the high point of Elgar's neo-Romantic phase (the later biblical oratorios make no significant stylistic advances), and in it he sets himself on a course that would lead into the critique of human and musical history that constitutes his modernist phase. For although the work ends with hope – Purgatory is not Hell, after all – the hope is not certain to be fulfilled. Nothing in the immuring–immured structure absolutely compels an ultimately optimistic interpretation: we cannot be *certain* that The Soul will end up with God, however likely it seems. And that is a central Elgarian move: the broad gestures of his tonal structures do not point to the kind of absolute truths, attractive to the nineteenth-century mind, that can be found in the thought of Hegel, Marx or Freud, or the music of Beethoven's heroic style. Certainly Elgar's structures point onwards, but it is not entirely clear in which direction they are going, or whether any larger force is guiding them. An exploration of this Elgarian move will take up a large part of Chapters 3–6.

In his neo-Romantic phase Elgar also developed a peculiar (and very subtle, perhaps *too* subtle) gift for what some might call irony, and is at the least an invitation to contradictory interpretations. It is demonstrated clearly in *Caractacus* – a kind of Elgarian *Kullervo*, but with a distinctly ambiguous tone. The point of chief critical interest is the closing chorus of Scene VI, which provokes disagreement between commentators; in fact potential for disagreement within the circle of Elgarians is so intense that Michael Kennedy's discussion in his recent *Life of Elgar*, which closely paraphrases that in his sleeve notes to the 1977 Charles Groves recording of the work, actually espouses two critical positions.[31] A few pages after hinting that Elgar's finale may be ironic (i.e. obscurely anti-imperial), he comes down firmly against those, including himself in his *Portrait of Elgar*, who wish to defend Elgar against charges of jingoism, quoting two letters of Elgar's which make his case for him.

> There was a slight *contretemps* in June [1898] when the German-born Jaeger [Elgar's publisher] objected to the truculent reference in the final chorus of *Caractacus* to 'menial tyrants'. Elgar replied: 'Any nation but ours is allowed to war whoop as much as they like but I feel we are too strong to need it – I *did* suggest that we should dabble in patriotism in the Finale, when lo! the *worder* (that's good!) instead of merely paddling his feet goes and gets naked and wallows in it.' He followed this up in July with: 'I knew you would laugh at my librettist's patriotism (& mine). Never mind. England for the English is all I say – hands off! There's nothing apologetic about me.' [Does he mean not a semblance of the conciliator, or not a semblance of the propagandist, in him?] Nothing tactful either, but there it is. Efforts to claim Elgar for liberalism are in this instance doomed to failure. He went fox-hunting, too. But he changed 'menial' to 'jealous'.[32]

---

[31] His *Portrait of Elgar* quotes some of the same material but forgoes comment on it. See Michael Kennedy, *Portrait of Elgar*, 3rd edn (Oxford: Clarendon Press, 1987), pp. 65–7.

[32] Michael Kennedy, *The Life of Elgar* (Cambridge: Cambridge University Press, 2004), p. 58.

One could speculate on how much the tone of the second letter is a reaction against Jaeger's response to the first. Furthermore, the language of the first seems to deplore imperial patriotism as a mild form of exhibitionist sexual perversion (and a Freudian would probably be on Elgar's side). If read as a disdainful comment on the text, it suggests that Elgar had a lighter patriotism in mind for the finale: one for an England of lichen-covered willows dangling their leaves into little rivers, not necessarily the England of the British East India Company and sweaty North-Indian summers; that is the England of the Woodland Interlude in Scene III, not the patronizing and culpable mismanagement over centuries of millions of foreigners.[33] The second letter is typical of Elgar's emotive response to criticism, and in the case of Jaeger – a German who had lived in England since the age of eighteen – he surely felt he was on strong ground in this instance.

The meaning of the recall of music from Scenes I and II in the final chorus of Scene VI ('The clang of arms is over') seems unmistakable. The text proclaims the numinosity of the empire on which the sun does not presume to set, and the zest of Elgar's support for imperial expansion is clear from the music's vigorous gesturing (even if we cannot be certain what kind of 'imperialism' Elgar found appealing, or indeed whether his conception of imperialism was anything but a superficial liking of its smart outfits and ceremony). But Elgar's thematic and structural technique creates a kind of ambiguity which is grist to the mill of the anti-imperialists.

His thematic recall brings back the British bivouac's anxious 'watchmen, alert!' on the eve of disaster and the Arch-Druid's 'fatheaded'[34] travesty of the gloomy augury (which he converts into a prophecy of

---

[33] Another 'jingoistic' piece from this period, *The Crown of India*, invites comment because of its use in some movements of a crude 'Oriental' topos (as well as for the words of the masque it was written to accompany). Like the Orientalism of Rimsky-Korsakov's *Sheherazade*, the topos is thoroughly inauthentic (to the East; but authentic to the West's view of it). But the modern PC (postcolonially correct) critic misses a trick here. As is evidenced by Borodin's contrapuntal treatment of the 'Russian' and the 'Eastern' tunes in his *In [the Steppes of] Central Asia* (commissioned for Tsar Alexander II's silver jubilee, in circumstances like Elgar's *Crown of India* commission), there is one happy result of the nineteenth century's Westernized view of the East: if their representative tunes can be made to fit together harmoniously, what might that suggest about the ordinary man's view of Oriental people? Perhaps that 'they are the same as us, but different'. And that is the view held by the modern, liberal society from which critics of centuries-old musical Orientalisms seek to embarrass admirers of dead composers. The sentiments are crass, yes: but that need not spoil our enjoyment of this music.

[34] Michael Kennedy says his motives are left ambiguous in the text, so that 'we do not know if he is a villain or just a fathead' (CD liner notes to EMI CMS 7638072, p. 11).

unabated British glory), 'Go forth, O King, to conquer'. By the simple expedient of giving old music to old and disproved sentiments, Elgar ensures that the concluding words

> Britons, alert! and fear not,
> But gird your loins for fight.
> And ever your dominion
> From age to age shall grow
> O'er peoples undiscover'd,
> In lands we cannot know;

sound, to listeners alert to this ambiguity, potentially as fatuous as the Arch-Druid's rose-tinted vision of Ancient Britain's might in Scene II. Yet the opposite interpretation is also always valid. Barking at Kennedy's de-imperializing reading of this scene, Jeffrey Richards writes that

> of course [this scene] was not ironic, nor was the choice of theme in the least incongruous. Firstly, the final paean was a clear and unambiguous statement that the Druid's prophecy *would* be fulfilled in due course and that Britain *would* in the end triumph . . . Secondly, heroic defeats are part and parcel of Britain's self-image: the charge of the Light Brigade; the sinking of the *Birkenhead*; Gallipoli; Dunkirk . . . Kennedy's interpretation is absurd; but it is an absurdity typical of anti-imperial Elgarians.[35]

The point is well taken: it *is* difficult to ignore such elements in Elgar's music, even sometimes in music which does not explicitly advert to Empire. But it is an unresponsive interpretation of Elgar's music which irons out all the creases and claims the cloth is wholly imperial. In fact it is a bizarre interpretation which reaches that conclusion. Furthermore, many (though not all) of Elgar's imperial moments are coloured by a flighty kind of ambiguity that it is not always possible to resolve, and which it would therefore be foolish to pronounce definitively upon.

Whether or not he intended ambiguous presentation of pro-/anti-imperialist views, Elgar certainly had a genius for giving people what they wanted on occasions like this. Yet hiding behind the appearances (which can seem almost banal in his third compositional phase), we must always be receptive to what could be a cunningly disguised irony. On this single

---

[35] Jeffrey Richards, *Imperialism and Music: Britain 1876–1953* (Manchester and New York: Manchester University Press, 2001), p. 50. He enjoys barking at Kennedy, and later pointedly *sics* him for a strictly incorrect use of 'comprise' (when 'compose' would have been unimpeachable). See ibid., p. 57.

matter of the interpretation of *Caractacus*, Kennedy's argument (in *Portrait*) is probably just trumped by Richards's. When a composer of Elgar's gifts – and so well-versed in Wagnerian thematic recall – brings back an old theme, it is with the intention of resurrecting and nuancing some element of its earlier appearance. Richards's assessment of the new nuance as the eventual fulfilment (after two thousand years) of the Arch-Druid's prophecy is persuasive. Even so, it's a curious person who takes pleasure from the reflexion that goals can only be achieved after two millennia; weren't the most fervid imperialists rather of the opinion that progress could be made *now*? On balance, the imperial interpretation of the scene is a little stronger than the anti-imperial one – but this passage *is* still ambiguous, and only reasoned reflexion after the event can make clear sense of its likely meaning, and so eradicate the ambiguity felt while it is heard.

In other works, like the symphonies, Elgar is not always true to the superficial imperial 'meaning' of such passages, and for critical listeners willing to dirty themselves in the admittedly grotesque surface sentiments of some (*extremely* little) of Elgar's music it will not be difficult to discern a more subversive voice speaking from behind the imperial moustaches. And these were, in fact (speaking metaphorically), probably grown only under the influence of his wife.

There is no space here to properly develop an argument to account for Elgar's imperialism, but in a nutshell my view (which is explored more fully elsewhere, and has much in common with Bernard Porter's) can be expressed in the following way. First, since there was no such thing as a single 'British society' in the nineteenth century, it is deeply ambiguous to assert, as postcolonial critics like Richards do, that 'British society was rank with imperialism'. Such a statement is as logically problematic as the assertion, made in a world where the French live in a republic, that 'the present King of France is bald'. Second, since nobody in the youthful Elgar's social position – the lower middle classes – would have either the family background or the education to take up an interest in empire (pro-imperial propaganda did not take off until a generation after Elgar had left school), and especially not in provincial Worcester, there can be no *a priori* grounds for reasoning that Elgar could have caught the imperial bug. That he manifested a limited interest in empire later in life is clear, but there is no documentary evidence in his music or his letters to suggest that he was at all interested in it until he married Alice – who was, not coincidentally, born into a family recently steeped in imperial involvement. That Elgar wrote no masterpiece of imperialism, and in fact devoted virtually no time to vamping the crumbling edifice in his music, further supports the view that his imperialism was only tweed-deep. It therefore follows, third, that Elgar's late-adopted imperialism was superficial, not very enthusiastic, and brought on through his wife's influence; had he married an anti-imperial wife he might never have written *The Crown of India*. In short, nothing about Elgar's imperial music supports the postcolonial critic's view of it.[36]

Turning back to the historical overview of Elgar's stylistic phases, one could argue that the second phase of Elgar's mature composition, the modernist phase, was not, as in Sibelius's case, an attempt to please a broader public. That had been the goal of his neo-Romantic music (witness the attempted evangelism of the oratorio sequence), which came on the back of the enormous success of numerous tub-thumpers, the *'Enigma' Variations*, and 'Land of Hope and Glory'. Rather, the public became progressively less receptive to his music between 1904 and 1914.

His modernist phase begins with a bang and ends with a whimper. The bang is the opening rhetoric of his *In The South*, comparable to that of Strauss's *Don Juan* (both are musical gestures suggestive of rampant male virility), which Dahlhaus cites as one of the two pillars supporting the ceremonial entrance to musical modernism.[37] The whimper is the quiet and perfunctory final chord of *Falstaff*, a stark tombstone bearing many names (see Chapters 4 and 6). Detailed comments on his early modernist style, his greatest contribution to musical history, will come in Chapters 3–7. But his later music may also profitably be used to help one understand this central part of his work.

Elgar's style after *Falstaff* is the least well understood of all, but it is motivated just as strongly as the others by historical circumstances. By 1912 the King for whom Elgar wrote the *Coronation Ode* was two years in the grave, and under Asquith England's Liberal politics were inimical to

---

[36] On this rather uxorious view of Elgar's imperialism see Bernard Porter, 'Edward Elgar and empire', *The Journal of Imperial and Commonwealth History* 29 (2001), pp. 1–34, reprinted as 'Elgar and empire: music, nationalism and the war', in *'Oh, My Horses!':* *Elgar and the Great War* (Rickmansworth: Elgar Editions, 2001), pp. 133–73 and my 'Elgar's deconstruction of the *belle époque*: interlace structures and the Second Symphony', in *Elgar Studies*, ed. J. P. E. Harper-Scott and Julian Rushton (Cambridge: Cambridge University Press, forthcoming), and also Chapter 6, the present book. A broader context for this reading of Elgar's imperialism, which swims against the current Richards is happy to drift with, is given in Bernard Porter, *The Absent-Minded Imperialists: Empire, Society, and Culture in Britain* (New York: Oxford University Press, 2004).

[37] The other is Mahler's First Symphony. See Dahlhaus, *Nineteenth-Century Music*, p. 330. Note that Elgar's *Don Juan* came in 1904, not 1888: it is well known that Elgar was a late starter.

Elgar. The Second Symphony had been received coolly – the audience 'sat there like a lot of stuffed pigs'[38] – and *The Music Makers* fared no better. Elgar's last modernist work, *Falstaff*, was premiered in 1913, the same year as *Gurrelieder*, and its reception was as cool as Schoenberg's was warm. In retrospect we can identify an ominous augury: the public was abandoning the *echt*-Edwardian composer.

It was a crucial period in musical history, and its significance for the generation of early modernists born around 1860 (which includes Elgar) is nicely encapsulated by James Hepokoski:

> the premiere in Dresden of Strauss's *Der Rosenkavalier* on 26 January 1911 and the death of Gustav Mahler on 18 May 1911 . . . ceded the Austro-Germanic sphere of *avant-garde* authority to expressionism and the Schoenbergians. A parallel story could be told of Paris on 13 June 1911, where as part of the Summer Ballets Russes offerings Stravinsky's *Petrushka* would take command of the musically new, decisively overtaking the Debussy style, not to mention that of the more orthodox D'Indy and Dukas. (Ravel's glitteringly hedonistic – and coolly mechanistic – *Daphnis et Chloë* would follow in 1912; Stravinsky's *Le sacre du printemps* in 1913.)[39]

He also calls attention to Henry Wood's premiere of Schoenberg's *Five Orchestral Pieces* on 3 September 1912, an event with a special English significance. If, then, we are to identify a creative 'turn' in Elgar's music, it should be with the death of Edward VII and the first performances in England of avant-garde music, and not with the death of his wife in 1920. He reacted to his change in fortune by turning to a different audience, in the theatre, and paid little further attention to the concert hall, which had remained largely empty for *Falstaff*'s early performances, till his last years.

The specious but traditional view of Elgar's creative life, an Oedipal and uxorious one, states that his artistic flourishing and his marriage were coeval and inseparable, but this will not quite do. It is seldom admitted, but although Elgar wrote most of his good music during his marriage to Alice, he wrote most of the bad music then too; and he sketched some great symphonic music after her death.[40] Beguiling as it is, the traditional interpretation must therefore be rejected. It springs from oversensitivity to Elgar's personal situation and understatement of the extraordinary

[38] Robert Anderson, *Elgar* (London: Dent, 1993), p. 102.
[39] Hepokoski, *Sibelius: Symphony No. 5*, p. 15.
[40] Diana McVeagh makes a similar point in *Edward Elgar: His Life and Music* (London: Dent, 1955), p. 213.

musical changes taking place between the First Symphony and *Falstaff* which, contra Mitchell, I say Elgar was not impervious to. We may still need to remind ourselves that Elgar was a 'modern' composer in 1913. The fact that he never emancipated the dissonance is immaterial; as Dahlhaus has said, comparing Brahms's and Wagner's neo-Romanticism, 'The spirit of an age, insofar as there is such a thing, is to be found in questions rather than in answers'[41] – and the same musical questions that troubled Schoenberg also troubled Elgar.[42]

But by 1914 the mode of discourse, even in insular England, had seen profound changes, and Elgar's war-time theatre music was his first reaction to them, in terms of both style and practical necessity: he could no longer fill concert halls. It would set the tone for the late Cello Concerto, i.e. a retreat into more or less undiluted diatonicism. Indeed, perhaps the most immediately striking fact about Elgar's theatre music and the music which followed is the (ostensibly) 'untroubled simplicity' of its diatonicism. Although one would be surprised to hear complex modernist chromaticism in some of his lightweight war-time pieces there is no immediately obvious reason why some of the more substantial works like *The Starlight Express*, the chamber music, or the Cello Concerto should be composed of such 'antiquated' musical materials.[43] Elgar's sudden shift after *Falstaff* from opaque to transparent musical language is obvious and remarkable, but we should beware of drawing swift conclusions about it.

Elgar's diatonicism, often remarked upon, is still not fully understood. In none of his stylistic phases is it ever merely fogeyish musical atavism or an extension of his 'popular' style, although both play their part. In fact in certain cases it is a pungent twentieth-century mode of musical cynicism. Elgar's language is diatonic in an essentially chromatic post-Wagnerian 'language game', as Wittgenstein might have called it; and although there may be quantitatively more of the diatonic, 'Nimrod'-style writing in Elgar's oeuvre than the complex chromaticism of the First Symphony's exposition, nevertheless this more involved style is the basic one: one might

---

[41] Dahlhaus, 'Aesthetics', in John Deathridge and Carl Dahlhaus, *The New Grove Wagner* (London: Macmillan, 1984), p. 99. He makes the same point in greater detail in 'Issues in composition', trans. Mary Whittall and Arnold Whittall, in *Between Romanticism and Modernism: Four Studies in the Music of the Later Nineteenth Century* (Berkeley, CA and London: University of California Press, 1980), pp. 40–78 at p. 48.

[42] I shall return to this below, and propose a simple dialectical view of mature-modernist music.

[43] 'Antiquated' is Elgar's own word: see below, in connexion with *Falstaff*'s first interlude.

characterize Elgar's preference for diatonic music as symptomatic of a typically English understatement.[44] Yet an Englishman often means more than he says, and Elgar's diatonicism presupposes more chromaticism than it resonates. It is as Carl Dahlhaus notes with respect to *Die Meistersinger*: when chromaticism is 'expunged from the consciousness . . . what is denied is always present, even though unexpressed'.[45] In common with that of many nineteenth-century composers, much of Elgar's 'diatonic' music actually prolongs two keys, not one: he writes in 'double-tonic complexes'.[46] But he also reserves a 'pure', monotonal diatonicism of the sort Beethoven might have written in 1820 for crucial moments, and it becomes more meaningful as a result of its special emphasis. Even in Elgar's largely accessible language such moments stand out, and they are among the most significant in his music. This meaningful opposition of diatonicism and chromaticism was learnt from Wagner, but Elgar makes the technique distinctively his own.

The classic case of Elgar's idiosyncratically pure diatonicism is in *Falstaff*, perhaps the last monument to the first wave of musical modernism. Falstaff's second reverie is interrupted sharply by Hal's unexpected entrance on E major (he is usually associated with E♭), and the resulting 'breakthrough' initiates a spectacular tonal collapse which calls the concluding C major seriously into question.[47] This sudden dyscatastrophic turn of events is closely related to the *peripeteia* of classical drama, which Jung identified as the third and defining section of a dream.[48] A similar focus on dreams and sudden realizations is essential to the

---

[44] Strauss and Mahler, whom we more happily and naturally consider 'modern' nowadays (although that was not the case in Mahler's own time), aid comprehension of their modernism in a way which Elgar does not, by their predilection for acidic harmonies and the insertion of passages which sail close to 'atonality'. But we should not allow ourselves to be confused by this. A great revolutionary may do his work even if he prefers outmoded forms of public utterance. An enemy's skull may, for instance, just as satisfactorily be smashed in with one of *Homo erectus*'s primitive cudgels as with a modern fire extinguisher. Outdated means may still achieve modern ends.

[45] Dahlhaus, 'Works', in *The New Grove Wagner*, p. 158. He adds parenthetically that 'this applies to John the Baptist's scenes in *Salome*', and if his opinion of English music had been more generous, he could have added Elgar to the bracket.

[46] We have already seen, in rough outline, how Elgar uses them in *Gerontius*. A particularly destructive and characteristically Elgarian form of the double-tonic complex is critical to the structure of *Falstaff*: see Chapter 4.

[47] See Chapter 4 of this book for a detailed analysis of the work. On the idea of 'breakthrough' see Hepokoski, 'Fiery-pulsed libertine or domestic hero?', p. 149.

[48] Carl Gustav Jung, 'On the nature of dreams', in *Dreams*, trans. R. F. C. Hull (London: Routledge, 1985), pp. 67–83 at pp. 80–1.

war-time incidental music for *The Starlight Express*, but there Elgar's purest, most heavily pregnant diatonicism permeates the entire work, drawing everything into the dream world of the story. Falstaff's dreamy A minor, 'simple in form and somewhat antiquated in mood',[49] is the template for much of the later – some might say postmodern – music.

The nature of Wagner's influence may be inferred from Dahlhaus's note on dramatic irony in *Parsifal*. 'In her search for absolution, [Kundry] yearns for Parsifal's embrace, but if Parsifal succumbs to her as Amfortas did she will only plunge even deeper into the damnation from which she is trying to escape.'[50] Elgar goes a stage further. Since for him redemption comes from regression (e.g. an immuring-to-immured tonal structure; a chromatic-to-diatonic trajectory; a move from adulthood to childhood), he builds into each goal the awareness of its future failure. It is not just a regression, but an *infinite* regression: once locked into the cycle there is no escape. There is in his conception something of the Schopenauerian–Nietzschean Eternal Recurrence. Certainly he is not more optimistic than those philosophers.[51] One difference between Wagner and Elgar is therefore that in *Parsifal* dilemmas are personal, while in Elgar's work they are universal. For instance, it is perfectly conceivable that Amfortas's *Weltschmerz* could be cured by a love affair (that panacea of *Weltschmerzen*), although Kundry cannot choose that lemma if she is not to be utterly destroyed. The problems are therefore personal. But in Elgar's music, as I hope to demonstrate in Chapter 6, the problems are universal.

Is Elgar's third-period music in a postmodern idiom founded on affected simplicity? Yes and no. We should not be afraid to admit that the term 'postmodern' is awkward and counter-intuitive, and perhaps a better alternative can be found. It seems to me that there are two streams of late or 'mature modernism', both radically different in style but both proceeding in logical stages from the early or 'fledgling modernism' of the years 1890–1914. The different styles of mature modernism represent different answers, not different questions, and in that sense it is imprecise to call one 'modern' and the other 'postmodern'.

---

[49] Edward Elgar, 'Falstaff', *Musical Times* 54 (1913), pp. 575–9 at p. 578.

[50] Carl Dahlhaus, *Richard Wagner's Music Dramas*, trans. Mary Whittall (Cambridge: Cambridge University Press, 1979), p. 145.

[51] Julian Young notes that the doctrine of the 'eternal recurrence of the same' originates with Schopenhauer, although Nietzsche made it famous. See Julian Young, *Nietzsche's Philosophy of Art* (Cambridge: Cambridge University Press, 1992), p. 157, n. 13.

Moreover, in the dialectical development of musical material one may find thesis and anti-thesis forged into a new synthesis in the neo-Classicism and resurrected and transformed neo-Romanticism of some later music. Elgar's form of mature modernism is similar to Strauss's, and both are set in opposition to Schoenberg's. But it is unpersuasive to grant one kind the artistic high ground simply because it tastes more exciting and seems (superficially) more innovative than the other. That is simply jumping on the band-wagon, and an inspiration for snobbishness. And in any case, without the dialectical explanation for the development of a 'synthetic' form of musical material later in the century, the mature-modernist 'argument from dissonance' cannot account neatly for the fact that there are composers who write like Robin Holloway, Colin Matthews, Oliver Knussen, or Mark-Anthony Turnage – to consider only a few contemporary English examples. Nor, on a less ambitious scale, can it quite explain the new stylistic turn, a synthesis of his second and third phases, which Elgar seemed on the verge of beginning with his Third Symphony.

The truth as I see it is that Elgar was never cut off from musical history and he never turned his back on it. He was a product of his times not only in his location vis-à-vis empire and habit of wearing starched shirts and spats exquisitely beneath a preposterous moustache – if that was all one could say of his historical situation, he would be uninteresting and perhaps (depending on one's viewpoint and way of interpreting the imperial element in his music) deplorable – but also because his assessment of the hopes for human progress and the nature of the self place him right in the middle of the intellectual climate of the early twentieth century.

I conclude with a final word on my aims in this study. At the end of the first chapter of *Music as Cultural Practice* Lawrence Kramer makes a touching confession about his own objectives:

> It is scarcely a secret that the extraordinary value ascribed to music, and to the arts in general, during the nineteenth century has lost much of its credibility; not much survives except a certain quantity of impoverished rhetoric. Professional students of all the arts have been increasingly confronted with a sense of cultural marginalization, an unhappy awareness that their work is tolerated rather than encouraged by the academy and society at large. One response to this state of affairs has been a retreat into ever more arcane languages of inquiry and ever more exclusive specialities . . . Yet there has also been a more affirmative response, particularly among literary critics. This has taken the form of developing communicative languages of inquiry that empower and even demand the breaking of

disciplinary barriers, and of using those languages to (re)open – to discover, construct, provoke – a dynamic, dialogic relationship between cultural processes and cultural products. The growing interest in musical hermeneutics, without which this book could scarcely have been written, is a sign of this same affirmative development struggling to be born in humanistic studies. My purpose here is simply to assist in the birth.[52]

There is some hope that the infant will survive, since it is nursed by so many Anglophone musicologists; but – bearing in mind Ingarden's and Heidegger's combined philosophies of art, music, and human being (Chapter 2), and Auden's and Tolkien's analyses of the quest narrative and fairy-stories (Chapter 5) – it is my hope that among the baby's first words we might hear: 'Music "is" us!' There are strong social, intellectual, and even ethical reasons for this, which Dahlhaus's telling observation on the role of music in the nineteenth century will illuminate:

> Early nineteenth-century music could be said to be romantic in an age of romanticism, which produced romantic poetry and painting and even romantic physics and chemistry, whereas the neo-romanticism of the later part of the century was romantic in an unromantic age, dominated by positivism and realism. Music, *the* romantic art, had become 'untimely' in general terms, though by no means unimportant; on the contrary, its very dissociation from the prevailing spirit of the age enabled it to fulfill a spiritual, cultural, and ideological function of a magnitude which can hardly be exaggerated: it stood for an alternative world.[53]

The arts are now all 'untimely', being 'disclosive' in the Heideggerian sense of that word, to be explained in subsequent chapters, in a 'destitute', 'forgetful'(-of-Being), godless age. Their spiritual, cultural, ideological – i.e. ontological, and therefore ethical[54] – function can hardly be exaggerated:

---

[52] Kramer, *Music as Cultural Practice*, p. 20.

[53] Dahlhaus, *Between Romanticism and Modernism*, p. 5.

[54] For Heidegger, ontology and ethics are the same. 'He who truly knows human beings [and therefore knows Being in general] knows what he wills to do in the midst of them' (Martin Heidegger, 'The origin of the work of art', trans. Albert Hofstadter, in *Basic Writings: Martin Heidegger*, ed. David Farrell Krell (London: Routledge, 1993), pp. 139–212 at p. 192).

they open up our world, which we seek always to view within 'the enframing' and, ultimately, to destroy.[55] And in the particular case of music, the ethical imperative seems even stronger: it opens up human beings. We are well advised to try and understand it.[56]

[55] The concept of 'the enframing' will be discussed in Chapter 5. On Heidegger's account, artworks are the antidote to the destitution of modernity, capable of reinvesting the world with numinosity (the only value which would compel us not to destroy it) and preparing a place for the gods to return to. This is Heidegger's philosophy of art, very crudely expressed. For an infinitely more nuanced presentation, see Young, *Heidegger's Philosophy of Art* and *Heidegger's Later Philosophy*, Chapter 3, and Hubert L. Dreyfus, 'Heidegger on the connection between nihilism, art, technology, and politics', in *The Cambridge Companion to Heidegger*, ed. Charles Guignon (Cambridge: Cambridge University Press, 1993), pp. 215–39. Gadamer's philosophy is hardly less pro-artistic. He basically holds Heidegger's view of the artwork as a 'happening' of truth, but whereas Heidegger believed in the epochal potential of the artwork, to create a basically new world order founded on German poetry, as the old world order had been founded on Greek poetry, Gadamer believes that the happening of truth in the artwork leads to a renewal of the truth-claims of the past in the more broad *European* tradition. Another difference between the two is that Gadamer 'is not just a profound thinker but also something of a stylist. Unusually among modern philosophers, he is a pleasure to read' (Paul Gorner, *Twentieth Century German Philosophy* (Oxford: Oxford University Press, 2000), p. 132).

[56] Several themes of this section, as well as many more, are discussed lucidly and at times provocatively in Julian Johnson, *Who Needs Classical Music? Cultural Choice and Musical Value* (New York and Oxford: Oxford University Press, 2002).

2 A Heideggerian refinement of Schenker's theory

2.1. Analytical preliminaries

This book, with its focus on the First Symphony (1908) and *Falstaff* (1913), addresses a number of problematic issues in the analysis of early modernist music. Chief among them is the difficulty of finding a way into an analysis at all. Which methodology is best to use as a basis for analyzing music that is neither classically common-practice tonal nor yet post-tonal, and which therefore inhabits a troublesome gap between idiolects that many people believe we have come to grips with? Post-tonal theories will inevitably miss the predominantly tonal surface and larger-scale architecture of much of this music, but an orthodox Schenkerian approach is always at risk of skirting round surface ambiguities for the sake of exegetical expediency, and its contrapuntal dependence on a form-generating opposition of tonic and dominant may be anachronistic in a style which has long since discovered other possibilities for structural tension. Section 2 will offer a methodological framework for the analysis of early modernist music in general and Elgar's music in particular.

I want to suggest that a modified Schenkerian approach is the best way to pursue our investigation, because the kinds of difficulties we (viz. Anglophone musicologists) face when attempting an analysis of early modernist music invite us to think in terms of voice-leading and contrapuntal prolongation. When confronted, for instance, with a passage without any obvious cadence, we still search for contrapuntal configurations suggesting recognizably functional chords that we hear prolonged. If, like me, an analyst was trained in the tradition, then instinct will draw him or her to a Schenkerian approach even before it has been decided that a piece opens in a given key; and having been drawn thus far into the method, there is no obvious reason why Schenker should be sidelined, unless there are further objections. Nor is there reason, yet, to step outside our musicological tradition, for reasons to be given below (Section 4). A final supporting reason is that Elgar considered himself part of the tonal tradition, so at the very least we should take his claim seriously and assess *after* an analysis whether he is justified in it. That means analyzing from within the tradition, rather than without.

But a good objection to the extension of Schenker's chronological scope is, as Scott Burnham argues so compellingly in *Beethoven Hero*, that his theory is based paradigmatically on Beethoven's goal-orientated heroic style: the *Ursatz* is, on this view, the most refined theoretical ossification of Beethoven Hero.[1] Although early modernist music demonstrably functions at least superficially in a tonal language, there are no grounds for claiming a priori that its structural syntax is Beethovenian–Schenkerian. While an analysis of early modernist music, in this case Elgar's, may profitably proceed along Schenkerian lines, the analyst must be wary of the risk of twisting the music to fit the theory; and if the Beethovenian syntax of the *Ursatz* is eventually deemed unsuitable for Elgar it is probably because another syntactic structure is more appropriate. One of the principal challenges of analyzing Elgar is, then, the need to wait till the analysis is complete before divining his *Satz*. Yet the *Ursatz* may still have a role to play, even if it can no longer be presumed to be the driving force of the piece: it is conceivable that the articulation of the *Ursatz* may in some way act as a structural support while some other, less Beethovenian force pulls the material of the work along and over it.

Burnham's analysis forces us to ask whether music is all just footnotes to Beethoven. The answer is, or surely should be, *no*; yet how can we talk about music at all if, as Burnham suggests, all our illegitimately conceived discourse is bound up with him, as if a Big-Brother Beethoven had bastardized our language till all we have left is a mouldering rump of *Heldensprache*? This is the kind of question a poststructuralist critic might seem well equipped to answer, but why argue, as a poststructuralist might, that we cannot escape from Beethoven's knowledgeable/ powerful grip without utterly rejecting him? Such a conclusion would only make Burnham's important insight seem terrifying rather than thrilling, and compel music departments either to shut up shop or remarket their degree as a 'BA in Beethoven'. Instead of this, after acknowledging that our basic understanding of music depends on Beethoven's heroic style, we may work with that prejudiced understanding, take it to bits (or as we must say these days, 'deconstruct it'), and put it back together, after a little reshuffling and realignment, in a form that will free us from this too-pleasant straitjacket.

For this reconstruction of an analytical and hermeneutic methodology I shall draw on the phenomenological analysis of music undertaken by Roman Ingarden, the philosophical hermeneutics of Hans-Georg Gadamer,

---

[1] Scott Burnham, *Beethoven Hero* (Princeton, NJ: Princeton University Press, 1995), especially Chapters 3 and 5.

and, primarily, Martin Heidegger's philosophy of Being (in all its periods). I shall reconstruct the two interrelated methodologies in two broad sweeps, each of which will apply my reconstruction to criticism of two pieces of Elgar's modernist music. The analytical techniques will be reconstructed and reapplied in the next two chapters, the hermeneutic method in Chapters 5 and 6. It may appear at times during Chapters 3 and 4 that the ascent of the Heideggerian mountain which is about to begin has served no immediate purpose. Many of the important ideas that emerge during this chapter do not return until Chapter 5, and it is there that the full power of Heidegger's thought begins to break its chains. The only really critical notions for Chapters 3 and 4 are those connected in some way with the *Augenblick*, which will be introduced below. But in the structure of the book the early introduction of Heidegger is essential, because the philosophical basis for the hermeneutics of Chapters 5–7 also undergirds the changes to Schenker's method which are essential for the data-garnering of Chapters 3 and 4. So although the emphasis of the next two chapters is different from those which surround it – being more exclusively focused on close analysis of intramusical details – this does not mean that Heidegger has slipped from view. On the contrary, although we pause during the ascent of the mountain, it is only so that we can collect provisions for the much more challenging and ultimately vista-opening progress of the second stage.

My modifications to Schenkerian theory will depend largely on considerations of 'authenticity', both musical and existential, and since that word and its cognates are very much in use in musicological discourse, the sense in which it will be used throughout this book must be made clear at once.

Heidegger's usage of 'authentic' in *Being and Time*[2] and elsewhere has a basis in the *Oxford English Dictionary* which distinguishes it quite clearly from other commonly understood usages of the word. The pertinent meaning is a combination of senses 7 and 8 in the second edition: (7) 'Belonging to himself [sic], own, proper', and (8) 'Acting of itself, self-originated, automatic'. Peter Kivy, who also begins his philosophical study of authenticities by referring to the *OED*, calls the dictionary an 'unimpeachable source',[3] but this is too deferential. The *OED*'s 1989 edition suggests that sense 7 of the word is obsolete (its most recent citation is from Milton in 1649), and it is a little odd that its researchers should have missed an entire century of existentialist discourse. But regardless of the *OED*'s purblindness, Heidegger is careful to disambiguate

[2] Martin Heidegger, *Being and Time*, 7th edn trans. John Macquarrie and Edward Robinson (Oxford: Basil Blackwell, 1962; orig. edn 1927).

[3] Peter Kivy, *Authenticities: Philosophical Reflections on Musical Performance* (Ithaca, NY: Cornell University Press, 1995), p. 4.

the term by calling it *Eigentlichkeit*, literally 'own-ness' or 'the way most one's own' (Adorno, who also uses the term but wishes to distance himself from 'the jargon of authenticity' as promulgated by Heidegger, opts for the more usual and ambiguous *Authentizität*). Authenticity for Heidegger is personal authenticity, authenticity to self, 'the other authenticity', as Kivy calls it.[4] It has something of the meaning of sense 8 insofar as Heidegger also lays stress on the authentic individual's self-propulsion through existence, but sense 7 is its basic meaning. It is therefore markedly different from other prevalent *OED* (and modern) senses:

> Of authority, authoritative (*properly* as possessing original or inherent authority, but also as duly authorized)

> Entitled to acceptance or belief, as being in accordance with fact, or as stating fact; reliable, trustworthy, of established credit. (The prevailing sense; often used in contradistinction to *genuine* . . .)

> Really proceeding from its reputed source or author; of undisputed origin, genuine. (Opposed to *counterfeit, forged, apocryphal* . . .)[5]

There is no sense in Heidegger's usage of the word of a controlling 'authority' which commands awe and respect.[6] The other two senses, especially relevant to uses of the word 'authentic' in historical performance practice (perhaps the most popular usage of the term in musical discourse), are also basically unrelated to Heidegger's use, although in the sense that each human being is the 'author' of his or her own life, there is something of the final sense given above – as a metaphor.

Because the term has such wide applicability, it is entirely possible to be authentic and inauthentic at the same time but in different senses. An example might be Rachmaninoff's recorded performance of the funeral march from Chopin's Second Piano Sonata.[7] The gradual crescendo from *p* to *fff*, evoking an approaching cortège which recedes into the distance, certainly has nothing to do with Chopin, and so is 'inauthentic' in the sense of not being what the author 'intended', so far as his dynamic markings communicate 'intention'. But it is nevertheless authentic to Rachmaninoff, and to a performing tradition of the late nineteenth and early twentieth centuries. Richard Taruskin diagnoses this essential

[4] Ibid., esp. Chapters 5 and 9.
[5] These are senses 1a, 3a, and 6 from the *OED*.
[6] For this reason alone his early philosophy is wholly at odds with life under a dictator.
[7] RCA Victor Gold Seal 09026 612562.

difference between composers and performers, which has relevance to Heideggerian 'authenticity'.

> I wish to . . . suggest that in many if not most instances composers do not even have the intentions we would like to ascertain. And I am not even talking about what are sometimes called 'high level' versus 'low level' intentions, that is, specific intentions with regard to individual pieces as opposed to assumptions based on prevailing conditions the composer took for granted.[8] No, I mean something even more fundamental: that composers' concerns are different from performers' concerns, and that once the piece is finished, the composer regards it and relates to it either as a performer if he is one, or else simply as a listener.[9]

He gives examples of what he means, one of them taken from some words of Debussy's.

> He said to George Copeland on their first meeting that he never thought he'd hear his piano music played so well during his lifetime. No question then that Copeland's playing realized the composer's intentions to the latter's satisfaction. On another occasion, though, Debussy asked Copeland why he played the opening of *Reflets dans l'eau* the way he did. Copeland's response was that old performer's standby, calculated to make any musicologist see red: 'Because I feel it that way'. To which Debussy replied that as for himself he felt it differently, but that Copeland must go on playing it as he, Copeland, felt it. So once the pianist's credentials as a Debussy performer were established, his performances were accepted by the composer as being no less authoritative than his own.[10]

Part of Heidegger's analysis of the relation between human beings and the society by which they are shaped and of which they are part may be seen in this musical analogy. The 'composer' of a script for a particular way of life is a gigantic syndicate of all members of society. The 'performer' of the existential script is an individual human being, who may choose to interpret that script in any way. The 'performer' may choose to enact the

---

[8] Here he has in mind Randall R. Dipert's analysis of 'The composer's intentions: an examination of their relevance for performance', *The Musical Quarterly* 66 (1980), pp. 205–18. For Dipert, 'low-level intentions' would be considerations of the kind of instrument used, the kind of fingering to be employed, etc.; 'middle-level intentions' would concern the intended overall sound; 'high-level intentions' would be 'the effects that the composer intends to produce in the listener' (p. 207).

[9] Richard Taruskin, 'On letting the music speak for itself: some reflections on musicology and performance', *The Journal of Musicology* 1 (1982), pp. 338–49 at p. 340.

[10] Ibid., pp. 340–1.

script such that it is 'authentic' to him- or herself, even if not strictly 'authentic' to the intention of the 'composer'. The 'composer' may provide a script for being, say, a chartered accountant; the 'performer' may choose to interpret that script in a surprising and 'authentic' (-to-self) way, perhaps by becoming a chartered accountant who manages the finances of rock bands.

That is the main Heideggerian meaning of 'authenticity' in rough outline. Richer nuances will be drawn out in the discussion of the *Augenblick* in the next section and in Chapter 6.

2.2. Temporality and the *Augenblick*

Heidegger's name probably still has the power to cause worry, especially because of his political beliefs. There is insufficient room here to give this issue the discussion it deserves, but the nettle must be grasped. As is well known, on 27 May 1933 (two months after the opening of Dachau; a Jewish businessman was killed there on that day), at Heidegger's inaugural address as Rector of Freiburg University (a job he had been given by the Nazis), the 'German Greeting' ('Heil Hitler') was used and the 'Horst Wessel Lied' was sung. But in 1933 Nazism had not yet publicly shown the abhorrent core of its nature, and by 1935, in a lecture entitled 'Introduction to Metaphysics', Heidegger was already voicing disapproval of the way the Party was abusing what he credulously saw as the real philosophy of the movement. 'The works that are being peddled about nowadays as the philosophy of National Socialism . . . have nothing whatever to do with the inner truth and greatness of this movement (namely, the encounter between global technology and contemporary man).'[11]

The criticism seems stupidly mild now, but was bold then. Heidegger was, at bottom, a bucolic conservative: he longed for a Germany full of farms and 'family values', and some of the early rhetoric of Nazism – the veneration of 'blood and soil' – appealed to him. Yet his vision of the new Germany did not exclude Jews. Many of his personal friends and students were Jews; he forbade the posting of anti-Semitic materials in his university; at a meeting in Rome in 1936 he 'described Julius Streicher's rabidly anti-Semitic *Der Stürmer* as "pornographic"'.[12] His conservatism was, as Julian Young lucidly demonstrates,[13] *völkisch* (spiritual, philosophical) and not

---

[11] Martin Heidegger, *An Introduction to Metaphysics*, trans. Ralph Manheim (New Haven and London: Yale University Press, 1959; orig. edn 1935), p. 199.

[12] Julian Young, *Heidegger, Philosophy, Nazism* (Cambridge: Cambridge University Press, 1997), p. 38.

[13] Ibid.

racist (biological). Although usually laughable, right-of-centre naivety is hardly evil, and it is largely irrelevant to the abstract considerations drawn upon here: the entirely apolitical fundamental ontology in *Being and Time*, which addresses the mode of Being of all human beings, regardless of sex, race, or gender identity.

This is a philosophy of intense interrogation of the verb 'to be', and via Roman Ingarden's phenomenological study of the musical work, it can be shown to bear not only on human Being but on musical Being too. Ingarden holds that our appreciation of music, the nature of music itself, while being somehow determinative of the time of its own unfolding, actually transcends the particular time of a particular performance and so is 'supratemporal'. That is, although it is not tied down to a specific time in a specific performance, the work of music, which he believes is an intentional object,[14] still has in essence a temporal form of some sort.[15] We experience a piece of music from a particular temporal aspect in some way or other dictated by the piece: no matter how fast or slow a performer may play, certain parts of the music always come before or after, and are therefore defined by, others. That is, in any given present, we 'retain' the past and 'protain' the possible or likely future of the music. There is an important and unavoidable temporal shape to our appreciation *imposed* on us by the music in a way that is not the case, on Ingarden's view, with the other arts (although there is an argument to be had about theatre). This is music's 'supratemporality'.

Ingarden's is not the only, and not even the most detailed, analysis of musical temporality, but it is probably the most philosophically accomplished one of recent times. As such, and more strongly than other recent discussions of musical temporality (some of which are mentioned below), it invites comparison with Heidegger's much more ambitious analysis of human temporality. One recent study which constructs a model of musical temporality based on the 'projection' (a decidedly Heideggerian form of Ingarden's Husserlian 'protention') of musical metre through a piece is Christopher Hasty's *Meter as Rhythm*.[16] Hasty disdains 'the transcendental and idealistic bias of classical phenomenology',[17] but his project has distinctively phenomenological undertones, and his model of musical time-consciousness, although expressed in different terms, comes close to Husserl's and therefore Ingarden's. Its stress on the 'decision' behind

---

[14] The implications of his view of intentionality will be discussed in Section 4.

[15] Roman Ingarden, *The Work of Music and the Problem of its Identity*, trans. Adam Czerniawski (Basingstoke: Macmillan, 1986; orig. edn 1958).

[16] Christopher Hasty, *Meter as Rhythm* (New York: Oxford University Press, 1997).

[17] Ibid., p. ix.

projections, with its connotations (which he does not draw out) of 'authenticity', also places it quite close to my own existentially tinged conception of musical time-consciousness.

Although the present book is concerned with analysis and hermeneutics, it takes as its basis this widely held insight about musical temporality which phenomenologists of music have taken in a variety of different philosophical–theoretical directions which are only of tertiary importance (behind Elgar's music and Schenkerian analysis) to this study. In the present context, Ingarden's (by Hasty's standards) limited Husserlian analysis is useful for showing the similarities between the temporal existence of music and the 'ecstatically temporal' existence of Heidegger's human mode of Being, Dasein.

There is only space here to give a sketchy outline of Heidegger's notion of the *Augenblick*, but little needs to be said to illuminate my figurative appropriation of it as a controlling influence in Elgar's music, and I shall clarify things further in Chapter 6, in the course of the hermeneutics in that chapter.[18] Heidegger takes up Husserl's retentive–protentive model of time-consciousness, but gives it an existential tinge with his conception of 'authenticity'. He defines the *Augenblick*, 'the moment' which changes our perception of ourselves, as the 'authentic' mode of the 'ecstasis' of the present. 'Ecstases' are not static and ungraspable 'nows', which are like the lines on a mathematical diagram (conceptually without thickness); ecstases are active, lived time, in which we do things towards certain ends: 'thick' moments of time, so to speak.[19] There are three 'ecstases': past, present, and future. All may be 'authentic' (*eigentlich*), i.e. in some sense

---

[18] The Heideggerian–Schenkerian method proposed by this book is not limited to Elgar, or even merely to early modernist music; the modifications of the theory hold for music of earlier periods too, and complement the Hepokoskian refinement of sonata theory, with which they share a common Heraclitean ancestry. The evolutionary 'missing links' in Hepokoski's case are Adorno and Dahlhaus; in mine they are Heidegger and Schenker. But my method's applicability to earlier periods does not mean the refined method is *required* for analysis of music on the Bach–Brahms axis. I only seek to draw out what I believe is implicit in Schenkerian theory, examine it, and reinsert it into the theory in a refined form which allows for analysis of music after the 'common practice' period.

[19] Henri-Louis Bergson's image of the sort of time Heidegger is *not* talking about is that of a cinematic film, where images are all separate, individual 'nows'. Nevertheless this concept of durationless 'nows' is central to the scientifically orientated metrical theory of Fred Lerdahl and Ray Jackendoff, *A Generative Theory of Tonal Music* (Cambridge, MA: MIT Press, 1983). In his more recent, more philosophical, work on metre, Christopher Hasty emphatically denies, as would a phenomenologist, that durationless instants are part of musical appreciation. It is this denial which places the reinstatement of metre as an active, projective part of musical experience, rather than a basically atemporal construct

true to the nature of an individual Dasein, or 'inauthentic' (*uneigentlich*), i.e. caught up in the expectations of convention, 'the One' (*das Man*).[20] Dasein 'stands forth' ('ek-sists') by holding these three ecstases in meaningful relationship, rather than just tripping meaninglessly along a succession of 'nows'. Heidegger introduces the *Augenblick* into his discussion of Dasein's temporality in typically cryptic and lapidary fashion.

> Everyday concern understands itself in terms of that potentiality-for-Being which confronts it as coming from its possible success or failure with respect to whatever its object of concern may be. Corresponding to the inauthentic future (awaiting), there is a special way of Being-*alongside* the things with which one concerns oneself. This way of Being-alongside is the Present – the 'waiting-towards'; this ecstatical mode reveals itself if we adduce for comparison this very same ecstasis, but in the mode of authentic temporality. To the anticipation which goes with resoluteness, there belongs a Present in accordance with which a resolution discloses the Situation. In resoluteness, the Present is not only brought back from distraction with the objects of one's closest concern, but it gets held in the future and in having been ['having been' is the authentic past]. That *Present* which is held in authentic temporality and which thus is *authentic* itself, we call the 'moment of vision' [*der Augenblick*]. This term must be understood in the active sense as an ecstasis. It means the resolute rapture with which Dasein is carried away to whatever possibilities and circumstances are encountered in the Situation as possible objects of concern, but a rapture which is *held* in resoluteness. The moment of vision is a phenomenon which *in principle* can *not* be clarified in terms of the '*now*' [*dem Jetzt*]. The 'now' is a temporal phenomenon which belongs to time as within-time-ness: the 'now' 'in which' something arises, passes away, or is present-at-hand. 'In the moment of vision' nothing can occur; but as an authentic Present or waiting-towards, the moment of vision permits us *to encounter for the first time* what can be 'in a time' as ready-to-hand or present-at-hand.[21]

(or at least a construct which conceives of time as a container), at the heart of his work – and into the title of his book. I subscribe to his theory on this crucial point that time as experienced (as opposed to time as codified) has no durationless 'nows'.

[20] Heidegger's conception of 'authenticity' and 'inauthenticity' is, as already noted, bound up with the adjective *eigen*, or 'own'. Every Dasein is to some extent 'inauthentic' (i.e. 'not-his-own') insofar as it acts in certain ways because 'one does'; but at the same time, Dasein can *choose* to act in ways 'one does' (say, by writing in English instead of Dutch), and so make the action its 'own'. I shall argue that the same distinction between authentic and inauthentic choices holds for musical works, although in each case the 'choices' are made by the composer, since the music is not Dasein and cannot choose for itself.

[21] Heidegger, *Being and Time*, pp. 387–8; punctuation modified.

What does all this mean? In the *Augenblick*, the resources of the present (historical, temporal) 'Situation' are focused in such a way that the authentic future may be *aimed towards* rather than just *waited for*, and individuality may be attained. The *Augenblick* makes the present active, not passive: in it Dasein takes its future into its own hands. Heidegger uses the term 'repetition' for this authentic appropriation of the past, in which its crucial role as shaper of the present situation is acknowledged creatively. Authentic projection of past possibilities is thus for Heidegger an *anticipating* repetition, an active rather than a passive repetition, that holds fast to a moment of vision. Dasein focuses its past and all the possibilities it contains for personal development in an *Augenblick* that discloses how things should be if *this* Dasein is to be as *this* Dasein ought to be. If such a disclosure is worked with through the rest of Dasein's existence, with past possibilities 'repeated' in a creative way, then it will have been 'authentic'. Heidegger stresses that the *Augenblick* is not a 'now', or a single clarion call to stir a sleepy Dasein, but rather the authentic mode of the present – i.e. an ecstasis, a 'standing-out' from a preoccupation with immediate concerns.

Hubert L. Dreyfus clarifies further:

> The moment of transformation from falling to resoluteness Heidegger calls the *Augenblick*, literally the glance of an eye. This is Luther's term for what the King James Bible calls the 'twinkling of an eye', in which 'we shall be changed'. For Kierkegaard, the *Oieblik* is the moment that an unconditional commitment comes to define my world and redifferentiate the content of my past and future. For Heidegger, it is the moment of the total gestalt switch of Dasein's way of being-in-the-world from inauthenticity to authenticity.[22]

A simple example from ordinary life may clarify the term by making it concrete. In the week before an *Augenblick* a girl may go to the cinema with her friend, share popcorn and a drink with him, and have some physical contact in funny or scary parts of the film. They are friends, and the content of the evening is understood on those terms, within that miniature horizon of understanding. But then in the *Augenblick* which follows the night out she catches a glimpse, from the future, of her friend and herself as lovers. From that point she looks on her past and her present entirely differently. Possibilities from the past ('he finds this funny'; 'he doesn't like me to wear leather shoes'; 'ice cream is his favourite') take on utterly new significance as she acts resolutely on the realization in the *Augenblick* that she is in love and that her way of Being-with her friend has undergone a total gestalt

---

[22] Hubert L. Dreyfus, *Being-in-the-World: a Commentary on Heidegger's Being and Time, Division I* (Cambridge, MA: MIT Press, 1991), p. 321.

switch. The *form* of their relationship has therefore changed, but the *content* remains the same. Whether they become lovers depends on her friend also experiencing an *Augenblick*, and if he does, on his *Augenblick* (his 'authentic present', his 'owned present') revealing to him a future which he can project himself into and which includes being with her as a goal. But not everyone crosses the Hellespont: it is possible for an *Augenblick* to reveal a way of Being which, while being definitely one's 'ownmost' way of Being (the way of Being most one's own), still ultimately leads to pain and the shedding of hubristic tears. It discloses the course of a life, but does not guarantee a happy ending.

There is an interesting parallel between this account and later Heidegger's conception of the work of art, which he says discloses the nature of other entities.[23] As he puts it, in words redolent of *Being and Time*, 'The establishing of truth in the work is the bringing forth of a being such as never was before and will never come to be again.'[24] In a work of art, we 'leap' into an encounter with truth. Heidegger plays here with the word *Ursprung*, which in everyday German means 'origin'; he gives it his wonted hyphen, changing it to *Ur-sprung*, 'primordial leap', and so re-expresses the 'origin' of the work of art as the 'primordial leap' into truth, which for him is the disclosure of the complex Being of an entity.

In Heidegger's famous example, van Gogh's *A Pair of Boots* discloses the physical nature of the shoes, their history, and the life of their wearer. The picture is different from the shoes it represents because it is 'only in the picture that we notice all this about the shoes. The peasant woman, on the other hand, simply wears them. The equipmental being of the equipment consists indeed in its usefulness.'[25] To put it another way, the equipment's material (i.e. the shoes' leather) 'disappears' into its usefulness, and becomes invisible to the peasant woman who wears them. The shoes may indeed bear a leathery trait, but she wears them because of their usefulness and 'reliability':[26] their leatheriness is secondary to her, and so 'hidden' from her, but in the work of art it is revealed. The example is simple, but makes a complex point. On Heidegger's view works of art

---

[23] There are 'two' Heideggers. Following a 'turn' in his thought in the 1930s, he abandoned the phenomenological analysis of Dasein in favour of 'meditative thinking' on artworks and Being as such. This book blends ideas from both Heideggers, with a slight accent on the later Heidegger. The only important early text referred to is *Being and Time*.

[24] Heidegger, 'Origin of the work of art', trans Albert Hofstadter, in *Basic Writings: Martin Heidegger*, ed. David Farrell Krell (London: routledge, 1993), p. 187.

[25] Ibid., p. 160.

[26] Heidegger's location of our primary understanding of things as 'ready-to-hand', i.e. 'handy', is discussed at great length in Division I of *Being and Time*.

show up the hidden sides of things in a way we might not otherwise notice. This is not to say that they simply offer a different, but still obvious, interpretation of a thing from a different aspect: artworks actually open up entirely unexplored aspects of the Being of entities. This is what he means by the 'primordial leap'; and since this leap constitutes 'the bringing forth of a being such as never was before and will never come to be again', it is in the nature of art to reveal the truth of an entity *for the first time*.

Hence, although it functions differently from the *Augenblick*, art still fulfils the same basic purpose that is common to all human activity: to disclose something of the truth of an entity. The *Augenblick* discloses Dasein's authentic Self in a 'moment'; the artwork discloses the Being of an entity in its *Ur-sprung*. It is very easy to see that van Gogh's painting of boots will very likely disclose the Being of the boots it represents, but not quite so easy to say what sort of Being music discloses. Heidegger himself makes no helpful suggestions, yet what is certain is that music does not primarily disclose the Being of sounds, or of musical forms.

It is, on Heidegger's view, as difficult and unusual to listen to 'a pure noise' or a strict formal organization of pure noises as it is to attend to grammar or the sonorousness of consonants and vowels when someone cries: 'Help! Drowning!' He gives an urbane example. 'What we "first" hear is never noises or complexes of sounds, but the creaking waggon, the motor-cycle . . . The fact that motor-cycles and waggons are what we proximally hear is the phenomenal evidence that in every case Dasein, as Being-in-the-world, already dwells *alongside* what is ready-to-hand within-in-the-world; it certainly does not dwell proximally alongside "sensations"; nor would it first have to give shape to the swirl of sensations to provide the springboard from which the subject leaps off and finally arrives at a "world". Dasein, as essentially understanding, is proximally alongside what is understood.'[27] We see things and hear things as referring to other things; and the reference doesn't leave us lagging behind with the assertion: we run on to what is being referred to, and find ourselves 'alongside' it. In the case of sounds, the particular physical concatenation of reverberations in a given instance is irrelevant to everyday understanding: we do not 'hearken' to them. We simply hear the cars outside or Mozart's 'Jupiter' Symphony. It is artificial to do otherwise. Thus the sounds of music do not indicate themselves: they take us beyond themselves, to something they are calling our attention towards. What that 'something' is is the object of this enquiry.

[27] Heidegger, *Being and Time*, p. 207.

Since Ingarden's retentive–protentive model of music's supratemporality bears very close resemblance to Heidegger's ecstatically temporal model for Dasein it does not seem unreasonable to work from the hypothesis that in some way music discloses the Being of Dasein. To put it another way, it is a mimesis of our temporal existence; or, conversely, 'you are the music / While the music lasts'.[28]

2.3. Mimesis and disclosure

'Mimesis' is another word with a wealth of implications ranging from Ancient Greece to (among musicologists) Carolyn Abbate, but this book's usage of it is quite specific. Again a dictionary definition can prove helpful. *The Concise Oxford Dictionary of Literary Terms* defines mimesis's antipode, 'diegesis', as

> an analytic term used in modern narratology to designate the narrated events or story (French, *histoire*) as a 'level' distinct from that of the narration. The *diegetic* level of a narrative is that of the main story . . . In an older sense outlined in Aristotle's *Poetics*, diegesis is the reporting or narration of events, contrasted with mimesis, which is the imitative representation of them: so a character in a play who performs a certain action is engaged in mimesis, but if she recounts some earlier action, she is practising diegesis. The distinction is often cast as that between 'showing' and 'telling'.[29]

Abbate explores the temporal differences between diegesis and mimesis while retaining the Aristotelian differentiation between 'told' diegetic narrative and 'shown' mimetic drama.

---

[28] T. S. Eliot, 'The Dry Salvages', *Collected Poems 1909–1962* (London: Faber and Faber, 1974), p. 213. This is a widely held intuition, not original to this book. It appears in a different formulation in fairly recent phenomenological criticism of music by David B. Greene: 'Music is important to us partly, perhaps even largely, because it offers us aural images of temporality.' See Greene, *Temporal Processes in Beethoven's Music* (New York: Gordon and Breach, 1982), p. vii. Also see his *Mahler, Consciousness and Temporality* (New York: Gordon and Breach, 1984), which also applies phenomenological critical methods to Mahler's music. But see Section 4 below on the differences between my project and phenomenologies of music.

[29] 'diegesis', *The Concise Oxford Dictionary of Literary Terms*, ed. Christopher Baldick. My interest in mimesis is limited to its position in a philosophical ontology of musical works, that is to say as a 'quality' of the nature of a musical artwork, and not as a narratological structure or function of an artwork; I am not so much interested in how mimesis 'works' as how it 'is'. The definition for 'diegesis' is taken from a dictionary of literary terms for the simple reason that no entry for it exists in the *Routledge Encyclopedia of Philosophy* or the *Oxford Companion to Philosophy*. Likewise, the following discussion of

In terms of the classical distinctions, what we call narrative – novels, stories, myths, and the like – is diegetic, epic poetry and not theater. It is a tale told later, by one who escaped to the outside of the tale, for which he builds a frame to control its dangerous energy. Music's distinction is fundamental and terrible; it is not chiefly diegetic but mimetic. Like any form of theater, any temporal art, it traps the listener in present experience and the beat of passing time, from which he or she cannot escape. No art is purely mimetic (that is, no art *is* merely the phenomenal world); rather, the mimetic genres move us by performing, they *mime* or even dance out the world in present time.[30]

It seems on this definition that mimetic arts like music can only deal with 'the time of telling',[31] i.e. the time of actual performance, and that the past is not open to them as a thing that can be brought to bear on the listener or viewer. Although it runs against Ingarden's view of music's 'supratemporality', this definition suits Abbate's purposes. Further, even a musical citation – say, a reference to Wagner in the music of Mahler – 'refers to an artifact from the past, but cannot create a past tense'.[32] Yet she quickly qualifies her position by saying (she is quoting another author's view of 'epic voice', but applies these comments immediately to music) that 'varied repetition *does not, in isolation, invariably* establish two such different registers'.[33] It is unclear whether she thinks that internal (or, through citations, external) repetition in music absolutely 'cannot' or merely 'does not' ('invariably') open up different time frames. What she first states with complete certainty she soon seems to doubt.

Let us consider specific examples. It would probably be too much to attempt to open two almost concurrent time frames in the mind of a listener when a minuet in a piano miniature returns after its thirty-second trio; but conversely, it is a dull listener who does not open up a century and a half of history in his or her mind at the moment when Robin Holloway evokes (among other things) a Chopin barcarolle in his Second

---

Carolyn Abbate's ideas is focused on the ontological, not narratological, aspects of her thoughts on mimesis. Recent Elgar scholarship has begun to shed interesting light on more functional, narratological questions. The most sustained exploration of Elgarian narrative structures and techniques is Charles Edward McGuire, *Elgar's Oratorios: the Creation of an Epic Narrative* (Aldershot: Ashgate, 2002). Readers interested in narratology will want to seek out Gerald Prince, *A Dictionary of Narratology*, rev. edn (Lincoln, NE: University of Nebraska Press, and Chesham: Combined Academic, 2003).

[30] Carolyn Abbate, *Unsung Voices: Opera and Musical Narrative in the Nineteenth Century* (Princeton, NJ: Princeton University Press, 1991), p. 53.

[31] Ibid., p. 54.

[32] Ibid.

[33] Ibid., p. 55, emphases mine.

Concerto for Orchestra. And Abbate is probably being too unyielding when she says that although moments like the recapitulation of the second-act duet at the end of *Tristan* count as temporal signposts to the past, they only 'remind us of the elapsed time of our . . . listening, and belong to the artifice of discourse, not to the story it allegedly represents'.[34] What are the grounds for this assertion? One could take such logic to an implausible extreme by saying that *any* human memory of the past – say an elderly woman's memory of a day at school – does not actually evoke a past tense, but merely reminds her of the elapsed time of her experience of life. Such theory murders history.

Abbate's argument does not make a clear and objective distinction between 'legitimate' and 'illegitimate' opening up of past tenses. In fact it seems that we just have to take this point on trust: rather than using our judgement to assess the difference between the repetition of a short minuet after a short trio (which probably *doesn't* open two temporal registers) and a repetition of something first heard many hours, or even centuries, ago (which almost certainly *does*), we are asked to believe that such distinctions are impossible. Furthermore we are to believe that any sense we might have that *this* piece of music is opening up temporal registers for us is purely illusory, for no other reason than that she tells us so. Of course even if her argument's logic does not absolutely compel us to believe her, Abbate may be right. In any case she attempts to eradicate a sense of proportion which in all likelihood the majority of listeners are capable of controlling, and we may take or leave her assertion. But certainly it is not unreasonable to argue that *some* pieces – and here large pieces have freer rein – can perform this temporal sleight of hand. But if some musical works open up different temporal registers, are they being diegetic or mimetic?

Probably both. Human temporality, on Heidegger's account, is 'ecstatic' by its nature; it stands out from the flow of time as generally understood: it does not simply exist in a succession of instants or 'nows' which terminate only at death. Human temporality is constantly roaming forwards and backwards, seeing possible goals and looking back into its own or the entire human past to find useful possibilities for a construction of that desired future. These past possibilities are reflected on, and laid out in a kind of 'narrative' form for digestion and interpretation.[35] That is to say we each have our moments like Wotan in Act II Scene ii of *Die Walküre*.

---

[34] Ibid.

[35] I use the word 'narrative' here, and in the following pages, very loosely, and only as an analogy. Human temporalizing is *not* the same as telling a story; but Heidegger's thought can be clarified by the analogy as long as it is borne in mind that the concept of narration

So human temporality, experienced in each case as a narrative of a human life shaped and reflected upon from the inside, is in this sense 'diegetic': it 'tells the tale of the past' in such a way that it is made relevant for the present and future. So a Dasein seeing itself as spouse with family will root around among various options for a husband or wife and make a succession of decisions throughout its life which, if worked with 'authentically' (i.e. in the way most appropriate to that individual, most identifiably 'its own way' of proceeding), will lead to the fulfilment of the goal.

It could be any goal at all, or countless hundreds of them, but the essential nature of Dasein is to stand out from 'clock-temporality' and make plans for the future, judgements in the present, and interpretations of the past; so in witnessing (and reporting on), living, and (through reflexion) forming its own existential narrative, each Dasein acts not just as a mimesis of a human Form, but also as a diegesis of a human Form, constantly questioning and reshaping that Form as life goes on – a narrative of human life told by an author which is at once internal and external, like a character in a music drama who recounts the past in order to make sense of his future.

A musical mimesis of human temporality which bears any relation to its object must, therefore, paradoxically, operate 'diegetically' in some sense: but not because it is dealing cavalierly with human temporality, and subjecting it to an unusual fragmentation – although that is always an option, and one which can be seen explored in many works from Schumann or Schubert and through the twentieth century. If musical mimesis is diegetic, it is so only because human temporalizing is in some sense diegetic too: its narrator, the self, is forever reflecting on the past and re-harnessing it for the present and future. And artists can hardly fail to reflect that Janus-faced temporal motion within human Being and the attempt to make time's passage cohere as a kind of narrative. T. S. Eliot wrote that this historical sense of being 'compels a man to write not merely with his own generation in his bones, but with a feeling that the whole of the literature of Europe from Homer and within it the whole of the literature of his own country has a simultaneous existence and composes a simultaneous order'.[36]

That is the meaning of 'mimesis' intended in this book, and from now on the word will be used in this sense. The consequence of this

---

is not evoked for its own sake, but purely to make the otherwise obscure Heideggerian analysis feel more familiar.

[36] T. S. Eliot, 'The perfect critic', in *The Sacred Wood: Essays on Poetry and Criticism*, 2nd edn. (London: Methuen, 1928), p. 11.

combination of diegesis and mimesis will soon be further elaborated, but in brief, the word 'mimesis' is meant to refer to the *nature* of musical mimesis (i.e. of human temporality, which is itself both mimetic and diegetic), rather than to its *structure* (which is, as Abbate does not entirely straightforwardly admit, paradoxical).

This conception of musical mimesis is what Abbate calls 'prosopopœic', pertaining to 'the rhetorical figure that grants human presence to non-human objects or phenomena',[37] but it is not naively so. No attempt is made to force a human form directly onto a musical one, or to suggest that in bringing the past to bear on the present and future (as humans do) the music 'makes choices' in the existential sense that human beings do. But there *is* a plain correspondence between what happens in music (through a human being's choice) and what happens in human lives. So if it is said that a piece of music 'chooses' to go in a certain way towards a certain goal, the rhetorical figure is the same as the one used when suggesting that a river 'winds' or 'turns south'. It implies suitability of linguistic fit, not actual belief in a driving intelligence in (as opposed to behind) the notes.[38]

Even if it has been decided that music is a mimesis of human temporality, the question remains how it is so. It is a question of music's relation to reality; and music (as mimesis) is emphatically 'realistic': it engages with reality. But Heidegger rejects the suggestion that art is a representation of reality, so would he not reject the suggestion here and throughout this book that music is a mimesis of our temporal existence? I think not. His problem is with the Platonic conception of art as a mimesis of a mimesis, a representation of something that is merely a representation of a Form (ἰδέα). But I intend the word 'mimesis' in the stronger sense used by Heidegger's pupil, Hans-Georg Gadamer, and not the weaker Platonic sense, in which the imitation's derivative nature makes art 'inferior' to reality.

On Gadamer's view, upheld here, art is not merely the *reproduction* of the thing that is represented: it is the *appearing of an aspect of reality* in the thing that is represented. Art reveals aspects of things which cannot otherwise be discovered – or, as Heidegger would put it (making a verb out of the noun), art 'allows things to thing'. 'Whatever comes to speak to us through representation [in the artwork] cannot be grasped or even come to be "there" for us in any other way.'[39] And, as Paul Gorner acknowledges, this

---

[37] Abbate, *Unsung Voices*, p. 13.

[38] Greene makes a similar point about a 'deciding agent' in Beethoven's music. See *Temporal Processes in Beethoven's Music*, pp. 24–5.

[39] Hans-Georg Gadamer, 'The relevance of the beautiful: art as play, symbol and festival', trans. Nicholas Walker in *The Relevance of the Beautiful and Other Essays*, ed. Robert Bernasconi (Cambridge: Cambridge University Press, 01986), pp. 3–53 at 36.

understanding of mimesis 'does not contradict Heidegger's rejection of art as imitation'.[40] Mimesis is about disclosure, not reflexion.

But what sort of realistic engagement does music have with human existence? It is the kind of realism which presents one with a study of something which, while satisfying on its own terms, actually heightens one's sensitivity to other examples in the world of the subject of the study. In this case, the object is time: whatever other complex things a piece of music may be about, time is its inescapable focus. So, returning to Heidegger's example of the van Gogh painting, one does not simply learn about the boots in the painting, or even just of the life of the wearer: one learns something about 'bootness' just as obviously as in looking at a portrait of a young man one learns something about physiognomy which heightens one's sensitivity to the expressions in the faces on the train after leaving the gallery. But is it not very odd to suggest that a musical work's scrutinization of time somehow better equips one to understand temporality itself? Just what kind of verisimilitude are we talking about here? I suggest that it is a kind of 'exaggerative realism' which has been defined, through an analogy with the visual arts, by A. D. Nuttall.

> Impressionist paintings are commonly more blurred than the visual field of a normally sighted person, yet the more intelligent contemporary observers felt at once that these paintings were astonishingly true to visual reality. The problem is resolved when we realize that previous *paintings* were *less* blurred than the average visual field. Painting had been unnaturally clear. This generated the sense that sustained clarity of outline is characteristic of painting and that blurring belongs with real vision. With this expectation feeding perception, the paintings of Pissarro could at once be understood as 'exaggerative realism', where the words no longer connote a contradiction but become once more intelligible. Just as a caricature can be 'more like Margaret than Margaret herself', so an Impressionist painter could harness his departures from previous art to the task of conveying a heightened sense of what it is really like to see.[41]

Music, like Impressionist painting, is a form of exaggerative realism in the sense that its preternaturally bright spotlighting of the tripartite unity of time heightens our appreciation of that time; and since on Heidegger's view time itself is the basis and form of our very existence, music is

---

[40] Paul Gorner, *Twentieth Century German Philosophy* (Oxford: Oxford University Press, 2000), p. 137.

[41] A. D. Nuttall, *A New Mimesis: Shakespeare and the Representation of Reality* (London: Methuen & Co., 1983), p. 79.

directly concerned with uncovering aspects of human being that we are simply not otherwise aware of. Music as (existential) temporality laid bare heightens our awareness of us.[42]

But a Heideggerian might raise two objections. First, if art reveals otherwise undiscoverable aspects of things, then human temporality seems an unfitting object for music, since Heidegger has already revealed it, without the aid of music. Surely music's object is sound; nothing could disclose the nature of sound, perhaps, more successfully than music. Second, even if Heidegger hadn't got there first, music wouldn't disclose our temporality very well, since listening to music is not our *typical* temporal existence – the way we experience time in 'everydayness' – but is unusually unpractical.[43]

In response to the first objection one may ask whether 'sound' is really part of music. It is certainly part of performance, and perhaps *in performance* music discloses the nature of sound. But is 'the work' of music really in the performance, or the score, or our mental states? None of these places, according to Ingarden. But even if music discloses the nature of sound (in addition to what I claim it discloses), couldn't the first part of the objection also be directed towards many other things? The leatheriness of shoes, for instance, might not be a good subject for art, since one can discover what that is without van Gogh (or Heidegger). And surely the fact that Kafka often discloses something of our 'thrownness' even to someone who knows no Heidegger – and he did it a few years before Heidegger, too – doesn't make Heidegger's project superfluous?

Would Heidegger claim to be the only human capable of understanding temporality? One can imagine he probably would, but surely others can also grasp it. And some people may grasp it in words other than Heidegger's. In which case it is even possible that their chosen language may be artistic (if all art is in essence, as disclosure, poetry),[44] and could the language not be musical? If it can be Kafkaesque it is not clear why it cannot also be musical. It is hardly more difficult, in some ways, to work out what music is saying than it is to work out what Heidegger is saying. Both require training and a fondness for headaches.

The second objection is more complex. In *Being and Time* Heidegger's approach to an analysis of Dasein's existence is based on close scrutiny of

[42] There will be more to say on the specific mimetic function of sonata form in Chapter 6, during the hermeneutic analysis of the First Symphony. Particular stress is laid there there and in Chapter 5 on sonata form's commensurability with the literary 'quest narrative', and the mimesis of human historical existence.

[43] I am grateful to Michael Inwood for bringing these questions to my attention.

[44] Heidegger argues that it is. See 'Origin of the work of art', p. 168.

Dasein's usual comportment towards the world, its 'everydayness'. Rather than reflecting on the unusual philosophical state of mind that is the usual focus in the Idealist tradition, Heidegger prefers to analyze human beings at their most ordinary, since it is in this way that the world and things in it presence themselves most clearly. So in suggesting that listening to music – by no means an average everyday comportment to the passage of time – can disclose our temporality, am I not arguing against Heidegger, and so destabilizing my argument? Yes and no.

Earlier Heidegger maintains that there is an 'ontological difference' between Being and *a* being. A being is 'ontic', while Being is 'ontological'. It seems to him that Dasein is ontically of the first rank because alone of all beings, its Being is an issue for it: human beings care and wonder about being alive. For the Heidegger of *Being and Time* it follows from this ontic primacy that Dasein must be ontologically primary too. Hence his focus, in a work ostensibly about Being as such, on an analysis of Dasein. But Herman Philipse sees a problem with this.

> One might endorse Heidegger's premise that Dasein is an ontically privileged being because it understands its own being and that of other entities . . . But does it follow from this *ontical* priority of Dasein that the *ontology* of Dasein is more fundamental than the other regional ontologies, as Heidegger claims in the conclusion of his argument? . . . From the fact that astronomy is a human activity it does not follow that the sciences of man are somehow more fundamental than astronomy [i.e. the facts astronomy deals with: stars, planets, etc.]. Similarly, from the fact that Dasein is able to develop ontologies of worldly things, it does not follow without more ado that the ontology of Dasein is the fundamental ontology, 'from which alone all other ontologies can take their rise'. In short, the ontic privileges of Dasein do not imply its ontological primacy, and from the fact that Dasein is the author of ontology and science it does not follow that Dasein should be its privileged topic.
>
> We may conclude that the problem of the primacy of Dasein in relation to the question of being remains a *crux imperitum* of *Sein und Zeit*. In the introduction to that book, Heidegger neither explains clearly why the ontology of Dasein is fundamental ontology, nor does he clarify the sense in which this ontology is 'fundamental' in relation to regional ontologies or in relation to the question of being as such. The problem is all the more crucial because . . . Heidegger gave up the ontological primacy of Dasein in his later works.[45]

---

[45] Herman Philipse, *Heidegger's Philosophy of Being: a Critical Interpretation* (Princeton, NJ: Princeton University Press, 1998), p. 44.

This resolves an apparent contradiction in my argument about music being a mimesis of temporality, the contradiction pointed to by the second objection, above. On the understanding of *Being and Time*, the most suitable way to analyze Dasein's temporality is in its everydayness. But musical listening, the retention and protention of musical moments, is not average-everyday: it is radically unpractical. My argument seems to conjoin opposed positions. Yet as Philipse says, Heidegger does not establish that the analysis of Dasein, let alone in its everydayness, should be the privileged topic of ontology. It is certainly an illuminating way into ontology, as *Being and Time* demonstrates, but is not, or appears not to be, the *fundamental* one.

Later Heidegger considers the move away from phenomenological analysis of everydayness into meditative thinking on art ultimately more profitable, but perhaps there is still a contradiction in my argument, which works on the one hand from *Being and Time*, and on the other from certain claims of the later Heidegger. Yet is this really a contradiction? It may be one of the places where earlier and later Heidegger can meet, however cautiously. The concern in both cases is the same – the question of Being – and even if Heidegger later came to view one way of thinking and one object of scrutiny better than the other, it was the same truth he was searching for.

I agree with earlier Heidegger that an understanding of temporality is essential to an understanding of Being. I also agree with later Heidegger that artworks disclose the nature of things. Early Heidegger gets to the first conclusion by analyzing everydayness. But if we do not need to accept Dasein's primacy in the discussion of ontology, then we may follow later Heidegger's suggestion that one of the best ways to disclose Being is to reflect on artworks, to be 'transport[ed] . . . out of the realm of the ordinary',[46] i.e. *not to be in an average-everyday state at all*. Musical listening isn't average-everyday, but if the analysis of everydayness isn't the best way to truth, that may not matter.

2.4. Heideggerian intentionality and musical phenomenology

As will be demonstrated below, the belief that the best way to analyze musical appreciation is *not* to analyze our average-everyday comportment towards it places this study at some distance from musical phenomenologies, whose focus on everydayness is central. It is the first (and by some way more straightforward) belief which would exclude this book from

[46] Heidegger, 'Origin of the work of art', in the translation in *Poetry, Language, Thought*, p. 64.

that company even if it was an attempt to create a phenomenology from scratch (which it is not). The driving force behind this reformulation of Schenker's phenomenology is not a desire to replace his with another; it is merely to reconstruct it in the light of an analysis of the ontology of artworks which impinges on the phenomenology of musical listening only insofar as music can be seen as a mimesis of human temporality – and in the case of the music discussed here, as only one manipulation of musical time, and through it the artistic dissection of human temporality, by only one composer. It is not an attempt to show how to listen to 'music', what 'its' view of temporality is, or what 'it' means, but rather an attempt to analyze the temporal musical structures and meanings of Elgar's music alone. As a discussion of musical time per se it is impoverished.

A glance through Jonathan D. Kramer's much more wide-ranging *The Time of Music* reveals around thirty different kinds of 'time', among which 'gestural time', 'moment time' (modelled on Stockhausen's 'moment form'), 'multiply-directed time', 'nondirected linear time', and 'vertical time' are probably the most significant.[47] To hear many of them the listener is required to suspend ordinary listening strategies and adopt one or more of Kramer's. One could wonder whether the music actually demands such different listening attitudes, but once one is adopted, different temporalities can be perceived.

Although Kramer very thoroughly codifies the different temporal *presentations*, especially of twentieth-century musics, it seems that in the final analysis, the temporality *understood* by the listener is still traditionally linear. For instance, although a piece written in 'moment time' – like the style of a modern novel or film which switches back and forth through time and establishes a narrative through a series of vignettes which can only gradually be pieced together into a comprehensible and meaningful structure – may require the listener to hold temporally disjunct and non-sequent episodes in mind throughout the listening experience, only to assemble the finished structure right at the end, nevertheless the final structure thus assembled from such great effort is, inevitably, a conceptually *linear* one. That is to say that even in artworks which are constructed along non-traditional temporal lines, the synthetic appreciation of the finished artwork is traditional. Modern artworks (and Schumann and Schubert sometimes play this same temporal game) do not 'create' new temporalities: they merely subject traditional temporality to a new form of analysis.

---

[47] Jonathan D. Kramer, *The Time of Music: New Meanings, New Temporalities, New Listening Strategies* (New York: Schirmer, 1988).

The temporality of Elgar's music, both in presentation and in understanding, is linear – an attribute it shares with most music – and the composer's outlook on the linearity of that time is, perforce, idiosyncratic. The discussion of musical time in this book is almost entirely limited in application to Elgar's musical temporality, and may not be applied directly to music by other composers. What may be carried over into work on other composers is, however, the revised Schenkerian analytical method which provides an alternative crux to the *Ursatz* (a musical *Augenblick*) and thereby opens up the possibility that any linearly organized musical time by any other broadly tonal composer might be analyzed, producing similarly non-universalizable results.

So although some of this book's findings may be applied usefully to other music, either before or after Elgar, there is little guarantee that the purely *temporal* aspect of Elgar's music will be echoed in the work of any other composer (technical details of pitch organization, harmonic structure, and so on, are more likely to have wider resonances). But that is the nature of a particular composer's music's comportment towards time – and if Kant and Heidegger are right, it is the nature of all human beings' comportment towards time: as a thing through which we understand the world, not a thing we live 'inside'.

Heidegger's formulation of this widely shared insight is to say that 'temporality "is" not an *entity* at all. It is not, but it *temporalizes* itself … Temporality temporalizes, and indeed it temporalizes possible ways of itself. These make possible the multiplicity of Dasein's modes of Being, and especially the basic possibility of authentic or inauthentic existence.'[48] It is through the *Augenblick* – and that 'moment' is authentic only to an individual Dasein – that temporality 'temporalizes' ('extemporizes' might be a less opaque translation) a form for this particular instance of human existence. And it is so with music: the temporalization or extemporization of temporality in a single work by a single composer, being the basic possibility of its authentic existence, means that the precise temporal structures of the work (in details if not in broad outline, which of course is always identifiably 'musical' in some sense) and its meaning are unique to it alone, and any critical approach which works precisely for that work is almost guaranteed not to work precisely for any other. Nevertheless in examining, taking apart, and reassembling the critical tools required to access the structures and meanings of the work, we may find reconstructive critical strategies which could be of use in the analysis of works by other composers and in other epochs.

---

[48] Heidegger, *Being and Time*, p. 377.

Kramer's book attempts to produce a theory of musical time(s) which can have broad applicability (although it is difficult to imagine any single study managing it). It argues, as its subtitle makes clear, for a pluralistic approach to temporali*ties*, listening strate*gies*, and perhaps most importantly, meaning*s*. Towards the end of that book he writes that we 'as listeners (and as composers and performers) know, and know how to utilize, many varieties of musical time. Thus the meanings of our music are vast and varied. And, in response, our listening strategies are (or at least should be) flexible and creative.'[49] This statement, taking into account my proviso about the 'presentation' of musical times, is in accord with the Heideggerian view of time limned above; and because any of these temporalities can reflect temporalities in the world while at the same time not being part of the temporalities of specific performances, this statement is also consonant with Roman Ingarden's argument for music's 'supratemporality'.

To recapitulate, the present study is merely one creative response to the work of a single composer which advocates one particular set of listening strategies and argues for one particular set of meanings. The only universalizable aspect of it might be the small light it sheds on how a methodology can be reconstructed in a way which holds the plurality of musical times (decided between in each discrete case in a musical *Augenblick*) in a single analytical system. It is in no wise a phenomenology of musical time.

The third and most complex way this book parts company with several phenomenologists of music predominantly influenced by Husserl, and even those influenced by Heidegger, is my acceptance of Heidegger's reinterpretation of the central phenomenological concept of 'intentionality'.[50]

---

[49] Kramer, *The Time of Music*, p. 397.

[50] Thomas Clifton, *Music as Heard: a Study in Applied Phenomenology* (New Haven, CT: Yale University Press, 1983), attempts to sweep away what, in musical listening, is contingent on academic traditions of sonata form, Schenkerian prolongations, and so on; his objective, pointed to in the title, is to write about music 'as heard' rather than 'as we are taught to hear it'. Like him, Alfred Pike (*A Phenomenological Analysis of Musical Experience and Other Related Essays* (New York: St John's University Press, 1970)) would have listeners 'bracket' learned assumptions about musical forms and structures and attend to 'the sounds themselves'. As already noted, Greene combines the phenomenological with traditional forms of analysis. Lawrence Ferrara insists on 'open listening' ('Phenomenology as a tool for musical analysis', *The Musical Quarterly* 70 (1984), pp. 355–73) which pays no attention to the 'plethora of fruitful methods for musical analysis of tonal music' (p. 358). His object is an analysis of Varèse's *Poème électronique*, but one suspects that in an analysis of Bach he would avoid Schenker or

Phenomenologists aver that experience is, epistemologically, sufficiently strong for it to provide all the evidence required for understanding of structures and meanings in the world. Its purpose is to cut through preconceived modes of understanding, and to return to simple and direct experience of things. This experience, phenomenologists argue, reveals more than the prejudiced understandings of more traditional ways of thinking.

But even Heidegger-as-phenomenologist, in *Being and Time*, seems to argue something radically different from his teacher, Husserl. This is because on Heidegger's view the tradition of philosophical error (the long forgetting of the question of Being) stretches from Ancient Greece right through to Husserl, and therefore contains Brentano's and Husserl's delineations of 'intentionality', which is at the heart of the theory of experience for them and for post-Husserlian phenomenologists of music (including Ingarden and Clifton, among others).

Heidegger does not deny the phenomenologists' epistemological claims for experience, but after cutting through the structures of understanding and returning 'to the things themselves', as Husserl implored, his conclusion is that both human beings and their world (and everything in it) are so inextricably intertwined that to cut through historically and culturally determined understandings to a direct experience of 'the things themselves' (i.e. to 'do phenomenology') is actually to *reaffirm* that the most fundamental part of our human Being is, after all, to exist in a state of always already being in an understanding that is determined by our historical and cultural situation.[51]

Heidegger differs, then, from all other phenomenologists in his view of intentionality. For Husserl, Brentano's original formulation of intentionality is problematic. Brentano holds that intentionality is the defining characteristic of consciousness; it is simply a labelling of the directedness of consciousness towards an object, a thing 'intended'. The problem with

---

other theorists because they would restrict the 'openness' he desires. Smith's writing does not aspire to doing phenomenological analysis, only to defining how it might be done; but his recommendations are, in this respect, Husserlian. See F. Joseph Smith, *The Experiencing of Musical Sound: Prelude to a Phenomenology of Music* (New York: Gordon and Breach, 1979).

[51] The phrase 'always already' (*immer schon*) has a special meaning in Heidegger, which I intend on the handful of occasions it is used in this book. It is formed by analogy with *immer noch*, whose literal meaning would be 'always still', and indicates the emphatic form of 'still' in sentences like 'you *still* haven't tidied your bedroom'. So to say that such and such an aspect of Dasein is 'always already' thus and thus is to bind it up with the state of 'thrownness' in which all Dasein finds itself throughout its life.

this formulation is that mental objects which have no reference in the real world – like hallucinations of pink polka-dotted elephants – cannot be explained by the theory. Husserl therefore revised it and added a third part to the model. Where Brentano insisted that every act has an object in the real world, Husserl argued that every act had a *noema*, or 'intensional structure' (with an 's') in consciousness, which gives it meaning. It is now perfectly acceptable for me to imagine a pink polka-dotted elephant; the lack of supporting evidence in the world is not a problem for Husserl's modified model.

But that model is still not good enough for Heidegger, because in common with the tradition he wishes to criticize, it is contingent on the subject–object model he deems misleading. Although he says very little explicitly about intentionality in *Being and Time*, nevertheless his critique of the Husserlian view can be clearly read in its pages. The foundation for this critique is Heidegger's radical insistence on the indivisibility of intentionality and world.

> There are at least three crucially important and crucially different notions of intentionality and world for Heidegger. There is (1) the intentionality and world of the theoretical subject (the passive observer or traditional knower and the objects observed or known), (2) the intentionality and world of the practical subject (the active, involved participant and the objects utilized), and (3) a more primordial intentionality and world (Heidegger would prefer 'worldhood'), which precludes any use of the subject–object model and without which the understanding of the other two sorts of intentionality and world are necessarily misunderstandings. The most common misinterpretation of Heidegger's thinking here is to stop short of this more radical understanding of intentionality and world and to see him as simply drawing special attention to and asserting the special importance of the world of practical activity with its skillful subjects and useful objects. It is important to avoid this misunderstanding if we are to grasp Heidegger's departure from Husserl and the tradition.[52]

And this radical reinterpretation of intentionality comes about because Heidegger insists that our ordinary relationship to objects in the world is not one of observing perceptual properties (as on the traditional view of intentionality) but one of *use* in-the-world (hyphens indicate the indivisibility of things and the world). We don't *observe* the gear-stick in our car as we drive to work; we *use* it, and as an object it slips out of perception,

---

[52] Harrison Hall, 'Intentionality and world: Division I of *Being and Time*', in *The Cambridge Companion to Heidegger*, ed. Charles Guignon (Cambridge: Cambridge University Press, 1993), pp. 122–40 at p. 124.

becomes invisible, as our focus is on where we are going and what we are going to do when we get there. The gear-stick only becomes perceptible when something goes wrong with the smooth running of our driving, for instance when we can't push the stick into the reverse gear. Objects are thus, for Heidegger, primarily instrumental ('equipmental'), not perceptual. Intentionality is therefore not directed at objects, not even as 'useful' objects, but at goals towards which we are working. And there are no *noemata*, no mental contents which mediate that understanding of our world.

This radical realignment of intentionality has repercussions for Husserl's famous 'phenomenological reduction'. If we assume the correct phenomenological attitude, we 'bracket' the understood structures of meaning in the world and reflect solely on 'the things themselves'. But because Heidegger gives intentionality this different focus, the assumption of the phenomenological attitude will have a different effect for him. Although he does not set out his case explicitly, he nevertheless provides examples of his form of the phenomenological reduction in terms of things in the world and human beings in the world.

Consider first Heidegger's favourite object, the hammer. My conditioned understanding of it is, first, that I can use it to knock in nails. I do so with it until the head falls off. At that point I 'bracket' my conditioned understanding of it (as a thing to hammer with in order to build my aunt a table), but I do not retreat into my own mental contents, as Husserl advocates. I throw myself back into the world and start to think about what to do next to achieve the ends I aimed to achieve with the hammer – I could use that heavy block of wood over there to hammer with instead, and my aunt's table will still be made.

Phenomenological reduction, for Heidegger, means showing up the links between practical involvements with objects on the one hand and the world on the other, or as he puts it, it means switching the emphasis from looking at beings to looking at the *being* of beings. Phenomenological reduction is not a movement back into our mental contents; it is a movement right into the world, but a world that we see suddenly with all the lights switched on.

Heidegger believes that to look at the relation between human beings and objects in the traditional way – i.e. to build up from specifics to contexts – is actually impossible. No matter in what detail one lists the physical and other properties of a thing, say a hammer, one can never construct simply from perception (of the scientific or traditional phenomenological sort) a context in which the thing will be used. One may know precisely the weight and strength of a hammer, but until a Dasein who wishes to build a house establishes a world of meaningful equipmental contexts, that hammer will never become more than 'a thing that is heavy and strong' – will never be heavy or strong *for a given purpose.* Yet from Heidegger's viewpoint, where useful interrelationship with the world is the most basic and essential form of existence (he calls it Dasein's 'primordial' comportment towards the world), it is perfectly possible to 'strip away' equipmental meanings until we are left with 'a thing that is heavy and strong'. So starting in the midst of a world and stripping meaning away from things in their context is the basis for the 'objective' scientific or phenomenological attitude which observes 'the things themselves' outside of context. The traffic is all one-way.

It is difficult to deny Heidegger's insight here, and it is crucial to a view of musical phenomenology. Few people would deny the existence of things like 'sonata form' and 'tonality', but it seems in the light of Heidegger's argument that they cannot be built up from scratch by 'bracketing' all our cultural assumptions and learned responses to music. We can strip away forms, pitch hierarchies, rhythms, genres, topoi, and the rest until we are left with 'a violin string being bowed' or just 'pure sound', but it is, on Heidegger's view, logically impossible to build *up* to sonata form from the cool phenomenological attitude; and given that sonata form *does* exist, this poses a serious problem for traditional phenomenologies of music.[53]

If it does not draw on the resources provided by contexts like music theory or the tradition of cultivated listening, musical phenomenology makes the job of listening more difficult than it ought to be. A phenomenologist who brackets out (for example) forms or topoi or voice-leading from his analysis of musical listening is approaching a work rather like the Neanderthal Lok approaches Cro-Magnon man in William Golding's novel *The Inheritors* – i.e. from a position of distinct epistemological disadvantage.

The novel is narrated from Lok's perspective. Events are framed only as Lok understands them, and the reader is forbidden access to analyses of

---

[53] Some phenomenologists strongly influenced by Heidegger, for example David Greene, do not turn their backs on traditional musicological constructs, like 'sonata form', and their writing is stronger for this reason. But Lawrence Ferrara, who claims that his method is more Heideggerian than Husserlian, baldly states that 'Before one hears music intellectually as sound in form, one can hear sound as such. To do so requires a bracketing out of one's formal training' ('Phenomenology as a tool for musical analysis', p. 359). This is un-Heideggerian both because, as we have seen, Heidegger insists that we cannot hear 'pure noise', and also because Ferrara's understanding of intentionality has recourse to the Husserlian 'bracketing' process which is so different from Heidegger's.

contexts which Lok is incapable of grasping. Very often, Lok describes in a few hundred words events which we would explain by a single specific verb. He does not have the understanding of context to condense the description into specific verbs; to him the Cro-Magnons' behaviour is often inexplicable. Lok can perceive the Cro-Magnons – can perceive them in acute and brilliant detail – but cannot understand what he perceives, because he does not have a prior understanding of Cro-Magnon man and cannot therefore fit his observations of their behaviour into a context of behaviours which would allow him to label and taxonomize them.

A toddler who sees his parents making love and producing sounds which to him sound like expressions of pain could only imagine that mummy and daddy are hurting one another. Lok makes a similar mistake when observing the sexual behaviour of Cro-Magnons (which, in Golding's treatment, evidently differs markedly from Neanderthal sex). But the impossibility of constructing a contextual edifice without already knowing that one is observing bricks with which to build that edifice is brought out in more complex form by Golding. Remember that Lok, as Neanderthal, has more in common with the Being of the Cro-Magnons than modern musicologists have in common with the Being of musical works. Yet merely as an observer, he cannot hope to build up an understanding of the actions he witnesses if he does not *first* have a basic understanding of how Cro-Magnons exist. The result is passages of opaque or elliptical description.

> The bushes twitched again. Lok steadied by the tree and gazed. A head and a chest faced him, half-hidden. There were white bone things behind the leaves and hair. The man had white bone things above his eyes and under the mouth so that his face was longer than a face should be. The man turned sideways in the bushes and looked at Lok along his shoulder. A stick rose upright and there was a lump of bone in the middle. Lok peered at the stick and the lump of bone and the small eyes in the bone things over the face. Suddenly Lok understood that the man was holding the stick out to him but neither he nor Lok could reach across the river. He would have laughed if it were not for the echo of the screaming in his head. The stick began to grow shorter at both ends. Then it shot out to full length again.
>
> The dead tree by Lok's ear acquired a voice.
>
> 'Clop!'
>
> His ears twitched and he turned to the tree. By his face there had grown a twig: a twig that smelt of other, and of goose, and of the bitter berries that Lok's stomach told him he must not eat. This twig had a white bone at the end . . . He was lost in a generalized astonishment and excitement.[54]

---

[54] William Golding, *The Inheritors* (London: Faber and Faber, 1955), p. 106.

That is all that Lok can get out of the situation. And if we as readers had no notion of what the Cro-Magnon might actually be doing, that is all we could get out of the situation too. (In other parts of the novel there are aspects of Lok's behaviour, probably transparent to him, which remain wholly mysterious to us for the same reason.) Bushes, trees, sticks: Lok understands these things, and his understanding of the situation makes them the active subjects in his sentences. We have the upper hand on Lok. He doesn't understand the other man, but we know that the Cro-Magnon is shooting a poisoned arrow.[55] And once that context is established, the significance of the observations Lok makes from his own direct experience suddenly becomes clear. His acute perceptions are worked together into a meaningful whole. But without the pre-understanding of archery which we share with Cro-Magnon man, we would, like Lok, be trapped in a dangerously nescient world.

Heidegger spends much time arguing that prior understanding (of the sort we have but Lok does not) is the basis of all understanding: that Dasein is thrown into a world of which it already has a basic under-standing. Without that prior understanding, nothing much about Dasein's life could ever be made manifest by pointing or observing what is pointed at. (Wittgenstein makes a similar point in his *Philosophical Investigations*.) And it seems to be the same for phenomenologies of music. Once a prior understanding of a musical work is allowed – it may be a Schenkerian view of tonal structure, or it might be a *Formenlehre* view of form – the ob-servations of the phenomenologists can be relocated in a proper context. But one cannot work up to the context from the analysis of experience alone.

Therefore Heidegger's view of intentionality confirms the need for a musical phenomenology to begin with context, a focus on encultured experience, and not on an idealized 'cultureless' experience of music. It seems to demand engagement with theory and analysis, musical history, the culture of 'informed listening', and the other bailiwicks of traditional musicology; to regard musical works not as individual objects which a subject can perceive dispassionately, but as part of our world with which we are actively involved in a manner determined fundamentally by our historical and cultural situation. It calls for a phenomenology of music which fits with Heidegger's view of Dasein's place in the world, as well as one which assimilates later Heidegger's view that artworks are just

---

[55] We further learn from this passage that the Cro-Magnon has a high forehead, prognathous chin, lighter skin, and less facial hair than Lok.

as disclosive as is Dasein's ordinary everyday attitude – the one that traditional phenomenologists place at the centre of their method.

In this connexion, an analysis of the 'inauthentic' and 'authentic' forms of human being provides the opportunity, in Division II of *Being and Time*, for a formulation of the phenomenological reduction in existential terms.[56] The trigger from ordinary life into the phenomenological attitude in the case of human being is 'anxiety'. In a state of anxiety, Dasein wakes up to its problems and responsibilities: it wakes up to its place in the world, to its groundlessness. In the normal progress of our lives we deny our groundlessness by allowing ourselves to become absorbed in our busy day-to-day affairs. But the experience of anxiety stops us short and makes us realize that it is all going to end in death, our own death, not a death by proxy: the invigorating 'I will die', not the evasive 'everyone dies'. The experience lays bare the responsibility we have for shaping our lives, in the way that the breaking of a hammer lays bare its place in the proper functioning of the workshop. To make things work again, we must choose and act in certain worldly ways. Heidegger explicitly states that although this phenomenological reduction in the anxious state appears to be solipsistic, it is not. He writes, with my gloss in brackets, that

> Anxiety individualizes Dasein and thus discloses it as '*solus ipse*'. But this existential 'solipsism' is so far from the displacement of putting an isolated subject-Thing [myself] into the innocuous emptiness of a worldless occurring [by this he means a perceptual object; a self-sufficient mental content attended to in the phenomenological reduction], that in an extreme sense what it does is precisely to bring Dasein face to face with its world as world, and thus bring it face to face with itself as Being-in-the-world.[57]

We may summarize this by saying that anxiety reveals to us our worldliness, and that worldliness – for me as for Elgar, a Western, and specifically English, musical world with all its cultural and theoretical accretions

---

[56] Greene deliberately confuses the notions of 'authentic' and 'inauthentic', and the reader is left incapable of understanding how he views either. His gloss is that each human being is 'an undifferentiated blend of authenticity and inauthenticity' (*Temporal Processes in Beethoven's Music*, p. 175). It is difficult, without detailed explanation (which he does not provide), to see how such radically different states of being could be 'undifferentiated' in every human being. In the present study, the total difference between authentic and inauthentic states of being is critical.

[57] Heidegger, *Being and Time*, p. 233. Thus while I agree with Ingarden that music is an intentional object with a supratemporal form, my view of intentionality is different from his in a significant way.

– is an essential part of the listening experience. It is a worldliness that contains cultural understandings like 'tonality' and 'form', 'the Beethovenian symphonic tradition', and for me (and the realization makes me anxious), Schenkerian analysis. There is no 'me' and 'it' when it comes to listening to music. Situated in my world, I listen to music, and by spotlighting and analyzing my mode of being, it makes me radically aware, as if in the anxious state, of both myself and my world.

This rejection of the subject–object dualism still present in Husserl and resurrected by the French existentialists marks Heidegger out as a phenomenologist of a unique kind. My assent to this interpretation of intentionality and the phenomenological reduction is the third factor which excludes me from the company of musical phenomenologists who, in their rich and various ways, are more concerned than I am to 'bracket' preconceived understandings of musical structure such as that proposed by Schenker and who describe the experience of music 'as heard'[58] rather than music 'as already understood', which would, it seems for the reasons outlined above, be the Heideggerian way.[59]

There is nothing more primordial than the place in space and time into which we are thrown, and the presuppositions that come with it. We cannot get beyond it or them, and in a strong sense therefore Husserl's

---

[58] These words appear in Clifton's title.

[59] A recent doctoral dissertation offering a Heideggerian phenomenology of music analysis has a diametrically opposed view to the one put forward in this chapter – namely that 'Schenkerian analysis is not so concerned with temporal aspects as it is with a special view of voice-leading' (see Andrew Anderson, 'A phenomenology of music analysis', Ph.D. thesis, University of North Texas (1996), p. 125). He has a peculiarly low opinion of listening, which he considers unfit to be classed alongside the 'primary' musical acts of composing and performing. (Listening requires performance and composition, true; but almost no composer or performer could compose or perform without first having listened to music.) This leads to a jaundiced view that musical analysis *must only* be related to composing and performing, not listening. His justification for this is Heidegger's analysis of the nature of assertion: an assertion is not the primary locus of truth, because an assertion is a proposition or an idea: but no such entity can exist without a prior understanding, based on experience in-the-world, on the part of Dasein – so Dasein is therefore the primary locus of truth. Because (specifically Schenkerian) analysis – which is based on listening, a 'secondary' musical activity – is not, in his view, an active involvement with music but 'primarily assertive (apophantic) in nature, [it] is a derivative approach to the music that it analyzes' (p. 117). He therefore advocates a performing–composing form of analysis as the only one advisable for a Heideggerian: namely, Hans Keller's 'functional analysis'. But once allow listening its proper position among 'primary' musical activities and this particular objection to Schenker (and the recommendation of functional analysis) disappears.

phenomenological reduction, the act of stepping outside preconceptions and into a privileged and direct experiential communion with 'the things themselves' is on the Heideggerian view impossible – and in any case an impoverished way of understanding things or ourselves.

2.5. The musical *Augenblick*

An analysis of musical mimesis need not, therefore, run in the opposite direction from formal analysis. On the contrary, an insistence that music's temporal unfolding is a mimesis of our own, whose meanings can be drawn out by thought and reflexion, depends fundamentally on an analytical method which can lay that mimesis out in a way that is clear to the mind, i.e. that part of us which constructs narratives. Even if the tale comes from the telling, not the teller, we still need to invest imaginative effort in order to understand how the telling hangs together. If we refuse to make that effort, we cannot hope to achieve success. Taruskin makes this point explicitly in his review of *Unsung Voices*, when he points out the phenomenological root of Abbate's 'voice':

> Roman Ingarden's concept of the 'nonsounding', covering everything from expression to form to rhythmic or harmonic structure – everything which, while indisputably a part of the experience of music as music rather than noise, nevertheless is not given in the sounds but has to be constructed by a competent listener. Just so, Abbate's novel formulation names something that informs everyone's musical experience to the point where (I will declare) it has to be regarded as a measure or a test of listening competence. Unless you hear Abbate's unsung voices (I will assert), you aren't hearing music.[60]

Taruskin is actually understating the case. These nonsounding elements in music, or unsung voices, are not merely 'constructed by a competent listener'. We no more 'construct' these elements than we 'construct' a human face by following the curves of nose and lips till we have decided they *are* a nose and lips, then assembling from our garnered data the 'abstraction' that we are looking at a girl: we simply see the girl, and that is the end of the matter. And hearing music is like that, too: we don't have to construct musical objects out of an imbroglio of toots, twangs, and scrapes: we simply hear music. Abbate's unsung voices are always already in our head when we are listening to music, and neither 'old' nor 'new' musicological ears are deaf to them.

---

[60] Ibid., p. 189.

But a major obstacle to understanding those voices is that they are speaking a language we have to struggle to understand. And if the burden of their 'words' is the adumbration of a mimesis of human temporality through a singular musical concretization (one biased towards the composer's particular view of human life), then technical analysis of the nonsounding elements of music – insofar as existing methods can be adapted to allow them to speak in their own terms – is essential.

Unless we subject music to rigorous technical analysis it is difficult to see how, except by sublime and never-to-be-relied-upon good luck, we can identify and evaluate the disruptions and excrescences in the musical texture which Abbate interprets as muffled narrative cries, or Lawrence Kramer discerns as light peering through 'hermeneutic windows'.[61] It is only through use of formal analytical tools that we can see when they break – only by hammering, Heidegger would say, that we can see when the hammer becomes useless. And it is precisely when things break down that the meaning of the breakdown *and* the proper functioning (the importance of which it is eccentric to disregard) can become clear. Only a cynic, who believes that everything on earth is always on the verge of disaster, can get away without progressing pragmatically through life and understanding until disaster strikes; and I do not wish to advocate cynical musicology.

Abbate and Kramer have focused critical attention on the significance of breakdown, failure, one might almost say narratological irascibility, in musical works. In this they follow Adorno. Their work is and should be central to musicological discourse, and while I do not wish to shift the position of the microscope, I do nevertheless think that it is just as dangerous to focus solely on fractures as solely on the solid mass. Either approach distorts the evidence. Sometimes – and this happens frequently in the common-practice period – musical difficulties are overcome; but sometimes – and this happens frequently at the end of or beyond the common-practice period – they are not. A critical method should be able to show the different ways that different music has of relating to the same 'ideal'; and it may be that by subjecting the Schenkerian analytical method (a phenomenology which basically works for tonal music) to *Destruktion*[62] one can lay open to scrutiny the mimetic nature of musical works that amounts to a

---

[61] See Lawrence Kramer, *Music as Cultural Practice, 1800–1900* (Berkeley: University of California Press, 1990), and discussion in Chapter 5 of this book.

[62] This concept will be explained in Chapter 5; but put simply for the present purposes, *Destruktion* is the process of taking apart pre-formed understandings of things, understandings which Heidegger shows are considerably more complex than one might imagine.

realistic picture of complex musical works, and their interpretation of human possibilities – warts and all.

The next two chapters attempt to explain the telling of that narrative – the unfolding of that mimesis – in two works by Elgar. It is a narrative told through a series of 'breakages' (Abbate), of 'temporal intercuts' (Clifton), of *Augenblicke*. It will be seen that this focus takes this study far away from phenomenology of music, and towards hermeneutics per se. The two phenomenologies with which it works, Schenker's and Heidegger's, are taken as the starting point (once collided) for a hermeneutics, not a new phenomenology. And in order that the basis for that hermeneutics may be understood, let us go over again the definition of the *Augenblick*, this time in the particular case of music. It will reveal the small but significant modification to Schenker's phenomenology which allows the method to be applied to early modernist music in such a way that the work's 'authentic' nature is mapped out for scrutiny.

We can say that the acknowledgement of the past of the tonal tradition (the 'having been' that is held onto resolutely) as determinative of its present 'Situation' allows a piece of music to exist authentically as itself. If the revelatory focusing of the past that constitutes this 'moment' is held onto into the future, then the piece's authentic individuality can be attained. In other words, in the *Augenblick* all the conventions of the tonal system (the *Ursatz*) as well as all the possible resources of the particular work (its 'Situation') are focused with regard to the particular end of the particular work.

In an inauthentic present the piece 'waits' for the composing-out of the *Ursatz*, but in an authentic Present (an *Augenblick*) the piece – always depending for its identity on its position in musical history and in the composer's oeuvre – will see its 'ownmost' possibilities and work towards its own particular ends. And these ends are revealed in terms of all past possibilities understood in terms of their future applicability in the individual piece. That is, in the *Augenblick* it becomes clear why *this* piece 'is' *as it is*, bearing in mind its dependence on the tonal tradition but not levelling-off its curiosities to regard it (inauthentically) as 'just another Beethovenian symphony'. In the *Augenblick* we encounter the piece, as it is, for the first time.[63]

---

[63] I stress again that I do not mean to equate music directly with Dasein: they are utterly different things. But in the same way that a painting of boots can reveal the nature of the boots it makes a viewer 'see' by presenting certain obvious things about them (e.g. 'boots look like this'), a piece of music can reveal the nature of Dasein by presenting certain obvious things about it (e.g. 'Dasein exists on the retentive–protentive temporal model').

It may begin to sound as if the *Augenblick* is a moment in musical history, rather than a moment in a musical work, but that is not so. The past of the musical tradition is focused in a single work's *Augenblick* just as England's and Europe's past is focused in an *Augenblick* in a Prime Minister's existence. The tradition constitutes an individual work's 'thrownness', its contingency, just as it does with an individual Dasein. But there is also a music-historical component to the situatedness of the musical work: taken as a whole a single musical work may (and, in the case of the two Elgar pieces under consideration here, does) force the tradition to undergo *Destruktion*.

As has already been noted, Scott Burnham argues convincingly that the *Ursatz* is a richly endowed theoretical abstraction of the temporal unfolding characteristic of Beethoven's heroic style. Furthermore, its application to other pieces – either non-heroic pieces by Beethoven, or works by other composers – is indicative of the lasting influence of Beethoven Hero on musicology, and may circumscribe our interpretation of that music. If we hear all tonal music through Beethoven Hero (i.e. the *Ursatz*), we are straitjacketing individual pieces hermeneutically: we make them 'inauthentic', or at least appreciate them inauthentically. To release music from the straitjacket we must first admit that the *Ursatz* has become a 'One-self' (*Man-selbst*) for music, then look for ways the 'authentic' individual piece can project its 'ownmost' possibilities to create an 'authentic Self'.[64] It is my contention that the musical work does the work of *Destruktion* on the tradition; and because I wish to carry this over into our understanding of that tradition, my modification of Schenker's system takes the work of *Destruktion* on into musicology.

But no Dasein exists in a vacuum, and neither does a piece of music. Each individual piece exhibits characteristics common to all pieces (among them, the *Ursatz*), just as even authentic Dasein exhibits traits of every Dasein (among them, acknowledging that 'Dasein tends to die').

My concern here is simply with the influence of a single revelatory moment on the temporal unfolding of an individual piece of music, and comparison with Dasein's *Augenblick* has the potential to illuminate.

[64] Burnham's argument is driven in large part by his persuasive view of the way Beethoven's heroic style relates directly to our sense of self. Of particular interest in the present context are his closing remarks. 'The heroic style engages the listener on this level (that of the inherent self moving through temporal existence) and then allows him or her to experience this subject as having a definitive beginning and end, as self-sufficient completion . . . It can be no surprise that music – and this music in particular – became both the exemplary aesthetic experience and the exemplary expression of the unmediated self' (*Beethoven Hero*, pp. 150–1).

In the *Augenblick* an individual piece as it were *claims the Ursatz as its own*: the *Augenblick* clarifies music's 'Being-towards' its *own* end. The focusing of the musical possibilities of the whole piece, and of all pieces before it,[65] comes in a moment which might otherwise seem unremarkable in an orthodox analysis. This change of focus allows it to speak on its own terms.

The musical *Augenblick* is, then, a singularly important moment of focus in a work, in which past possibilities – from this musical work or from the entire tradition – are considered for their possible uses in moulding an individual shape for the rest of the piece. The *Augenblick* might coincide with the conventional closure of the *Ursatz*: it does so with most of the music written during the common-practice period, where the reaffirmation of the tonic after a period away from it is essential to the style. But although a common-practice *Augenblick* will almost inevitably be one which focuses and begins to act upon the possibilities for a conventional tonal closure, it may not be so simple as to be predictable.

One famous musical *Augenblick* is that in Beethoven's *Fidelio*, and it would be wise to acknowledge the inevitable association in musicians' minds with the *Augenblicke* liberally distributed around that opera. (By happy chance the final 'welch' ein Augenblick' corresponds with the work's own *Augenblick*.) The trumpet-call, the work's moment of eucatastrophe, might be heard as an anticipation of Mahler's brass *Durchbruch* in the First Symphony's first movement and elsewhere. Before the trumpet sounds it is conceivable that Pizarro could stab Leonore and Florestan – he has just threatened to do so – and we might then end in D minor. But with that trumpet-call the end of the opera is decided: conjugal bliss; helpless husband saved by devoted wife; *namenlose Freude*; an ending in C major. The *Augenblick* focuses the work's authentic materials in a uniquely striking way.

The *Augenblick* in *Fidelio* is obvious to everyone, both within the opera and within the opera's audience. But consider, by way of contrast, an example of a human *Augenblick* which might go unnoticed (an example

---

[65] Ordinary Dasein has a good idea of the tradition it belongs to. And so does a piece of music written by an informed composer, listened to by a knowledgeable listener.

A musicologist may these days need to apologize for relying on the ear of such a listener, but it seems to me no more unreasonable or snobbish than relying, when writing in French, on the ability of one's audience to understand that language (or, when writing about popular or ethnic music, to rely on the reader-listener's knowledge of it: changing the object does not eradicate the 'problem'). I suspect that very few people listening to Elgar's First Symphony or *Falstaff* know no great symphonic works from the tradition.

more like the *Augenblick* in Elgar's First Symphony). The example is an eleven-year-old boy walking home from school. He is alone, but in a crowd. Earlier that day he had caught sight of one of his (male) friends topless in a changing room. The vision had stuck with him all day and on his lonely walk home had forced him to wonder whether his response to it was sexual. His internal debate on that walk could be explosively revelatory, but nobody around him need be aware of what passes through his mind, or indeed witness how over the years he continues to mould his life based on that arresting momentary vision of his ownmost adult nature.

It is the function of the biographer, not the fellow walker, to discover the boy's *Augenblick* once a broad view of the course of his entire life is known, and it is the role of the analyst to discover the *Augenblick* in a work of music after a similarly holistic analysis of that work. The point is that the *Augenblick* might not be as glaringly obvious as the trumpet-call in *Fidelio*. Not every life has a heroic soundtrack or a happy ending. And whether the *Augenblick* comes with a peal of trumpets or in some more subtle way, there is still no guarantee that it will point to a happy or 'fulfilling' outcome, however 'authentic' it might be.[66] In Elgar the *Augenblick* is rarely a moment to rejoice in with unqualified optimism. Without acknowledging it, an analyst cannot properly account for the 'purely musical' parts of the work (its grammar and structural logic); but after acknowledging it, the analyst is able to open it out into a hermeneutics which reveals what the music's meaning might be – and how that might be significant for us.

---

[66] See, for instance, the discussion of *Peter Grimes* in Chapter 6.

3 Immuring and immured tonalities: tonal malaise in the First Symphony, Op. 55

3.1. Hepokoski's analysis and a Hepokoskian analysis

We have already begun to develop an approach fitted to a particular work, and when the object of study is Elgar's First Symphony there are additional complications. How are we to analyze a piece in four movements, whose middle movements are joined, and which makes such a point of beginning and ending with a 'motto' theme in A♭, but spends most of its time with other material and in or on unrelated keys (A minor, D major, and D minor being especially notable)?[1] This question is not limited to analysis of early modernist music. Despite its grounding on Beethoven's Fifth Symphony, the archetypal four-movement narrative,[2] Schenker's *Ursatz* does not explain how musical arguments are carried over the gaps between movements, or even why there are usually four movements in a symphony instead of, say, seven or two. Both Jonathan Dunsby and Nicholas Marston have tried to answer these questions in analyses of smaller pieces,[3] but I know of no comparable attempt to stretch the *Ursatz* over a whole symphony.[4] The present study, with its deliberately sceptical view of

---

[1] I shall preserve Tovey's careful distinction between passages *in* or *on* keys throughout this book.

[2] See Scott Burnham, *Beethoven Hero* (Priceton, NJ: Princeton University Press, 1995) Chapter 3, especially pp. 99–101.

[3] Jonathan Dunsby, 'The multi-piece in Brahms: *Fantasien*, op. 116', in *Brahms: Biographical, Documentary, and Analytical Studies*, ed. Robert Pascall (Cambridge: Cambridge University Press, 1983), pp. 167–89; Nicholas Marston, *Beethoven's Piano Sonata in E, Op. 109* (Oxford: Clarendon Press, 1995) and 'Trifles or a multitrifle? Beethoven's Bagatelles, Op. 119, Nos. 7–11', *Music Analysis* 5 (1986), pp. 192–206.

[4] Robert Bailey might have a multi-movement *Ursatz* in mind for Brahms's Third Symphony (see 'Musical language and structure in the Third Symphony', in *Brahms Studies: Analytical and Historical Perspectives*, ed. George S. Bozarth (Oxford: Clarendon Press, 1990), pp. 405–22). He suggests that the work may be considered a single sonata-form plan, with the middle movements forming a single unit (the manuscript was in any case organized in three parcels, with the middle movements joined as one). Thus the whole symphony 'in some ways can be likened to that of a traditional first-movement design: presentation of the tonic in the first movement (a movement in which the dominant is conspicuous by its absence), exploration of the dominant at the beginning of Part 2 and its prolongation with change of mode in the latter portion, and then the finale which brings F & C [tonic and dominant] into direct confrontation and provides the

single-movement, Beethovenian–Schenkerian goal-orientation, offers an analysis of Elgar's First Symphony that argues for a four-movement *Ursatz*. As we shall see, the music itself compels and therefore supports such an interpretation.

Elgar's principal structural tool in the First Symphony is the opposition of two powerful tonal centres, the one 'immuring' (A♭), the other 'immured' (D).[5] (The suggestion of imprisonment and the desire to break free, implicit in the strict meaning of those terms, is intended.) The *Ursatz* cannot resolve the tritonal tension between these tonalities, since Elgar's opposition is duotonal but Schenkerian theory's ambit is monotonal. Some other but related way of viewing music's temporal unfolding is required, which is why in the preceding chapter I borrowed the concept of authentic temporality, and especially the *Augenblick*, from Heidegger. By incorporating the *Augenblick* into Schenker's phenomenology, the analytical method can be made to accommodate duotonal (and other unorthodox) structures.

Elgar's use of duotonality is quite unlike that found in (for instance) Wagner, Bruckner, and Mahler. With those composers pairs of tonics often form 'double-tonic complexes'[6] which, put simply, function as a single tonal focus. In Elgar, however, use of such double-tonic complexes is only an incidental strategy, and his principal focus is on opening rifts in the structure of his music by the direct opposition of two tonal areas. The immuring tonic, which opens and closes the work, is challenged by an immured tonic offering a stable alternative that a composer like Mahler

necessary tonal and modal resolutions for them' (p. 410). In at least four important respects, Brahms's Third Symphony might have been a model for Elgar's First: the strongest alternative to the tonic in Elgar's first movement is not the dominant; the middle movements form a single structural unit; the finale contains the first clear presentation, and eventual resolution, of the tonal tensions of the work; Elgar's second subject in the finale is a near-quotation of Brahms's; and both symphonies end with the theme they opened with. Between Brahms's Third and Elgar's First sits Scriabin's Second Symphony in C minor, Op. 29, which is a monothematic, five-movement sonata form. The first two movements form an expositional pair, moving i–III in C minor. The third movement is a slower episode in place of development, in the distant key of B major. The fourth and fifth movements (in F minor and C major respectively) provide a return to the tonic, and the traditional resolution of it into the major (iv–V–I through the movements).

[5] Elgar's duotonal structure was, according to Sir Adrian Boult, the result of a bet that he could not compose a symphony in two keys at once (Michael Kennedy, *Elgar Orchestral Music* (London: BBC, 1970), p. 54).

[6] This formulation is Robert Bailey's, in 'An analytical study of the sketches and drafts', in *Richard Wagner, Prelude and Transfiguration from 'Tristan and Isole'* (New York and London: Norton, 1985).

might have stayed with; but Elgar eschews such 'directional tonality',[7] preferring to resolve the duotonal tension and return to the key of the beginning. His conception of the symphony is therefore Classical at heart insofar as a single tonic must appear to prevail, but I shall argue here and in the closing chapter that the forces welling up inside his music lead to ultimate failure, and a distinctively twentieth-century failure at that. The immured tonic is eventually dismissed, but two remaining problems make the 'victory' seem Pyrrhic. First, various incidents in the work have made the immuring tonic inherently problematic; second, since the triumph of the immuring A♭ comes from processes tangential to the *Ursatz*, the conventional close in the immuring tonic does not carry the Beethovenian stamp of inevitability usually associated with such closure. Put crudely: Beethoven's heroic style dramatizes the arrival on the dominant, empowering the *Ursatz* to compose-out the tonal reconciliation; Elgar dramatizes the arrival of the immured tonic, ♯IV/A♭, so the *Ursatz* can be of only limited use. The principal defining moment of the work might, therefore, be a musical *Augenblick*. The second section of this chapter presents such an analysis. The first section prepares that analysis by identifying the 'problematic' aspects of the symphony's form by using James Hepokoski's theory of sonata deformations and rotations.

The basic characteristics of rotational structures were summarized in the opening chapter. One of the theory's most useful characteristics is its ability to bring almost instant clarification to complex structures, as a preliminary to hermeneutic inquiry, and that is especially desirable in the case of the First Symphony. In this section, a critique of Hepokoski's own thought-provoking analysis of the symphony will offer a way into my own Hepokoskian analysis.

Hepokoski's essay on the two completed symphonies is perhaps the most important study of Elgar's music, a fact all the more remarkable given that an early misinterpretation which has powerful knock-on effects still does not undermine the sweep of his argument.[8] Calling on two of his by now familiar sonata-deformation categories, he suggests that the 'first movement may be described as a "failed" D minor sonata set into an A♭ introduction-coda frame'.[9] Yet, as Robert Meikle observes a little tartly in another essay on the symphonies, apart from the single-flat key

[7] See Robert Bailey, 'The structure of the *Ring* and its evolution', *Nineteenth-Century Music* 1 (1977), pp. 48–61.

[8] James A. Hepokoski, 'Elgar'., in *The Nineteenth-Century Symphony*, ed. D. Kern Holoman (New York and London: Schirmer, 1997).

[9] Ibid., p. 330.

signature, 'every other piece of evidence we can adduce, beginning with our ears, tells us that the key is in fact A minor'.[10] It is more difficult to disagree with him than with Hepokoski, but one should add that the flavour of this A minor is redolent of that in the Prelude to *Tristan und Isolde*: at best, we can regard that key as 'the tonic', but it is never stated (see p. 9). It is a tonic to be yearned for rather than heard, although Elgar's yearning is by intention heroic, not erotic. (See further discussion in Section 2 and Chapter 6.) Most of Hepokoski's argument hangs on this misreading of the first Allegro theme in D minor, yet his analysis still has much to give.

The term 'sonata failure', which Hepokoski uses of this movement, is 'not intended as a criticism; rather it is a way of describing a crucial element of what appears to be the expressive or narrative intentions of the composer – of the musical "story" that is unfolded in, around, and through the sonata'.[11] But if there is a failure in this movement, it is either a failure to resolve into A minor (the first Allegro key) or – to take a different approach to Hepokoski's published interpretation, albeit one which is informed by his writing on rotational structures in other music (see below) – a failure to resolve the recapitulation satisfactorily into A♭, the key of the 'Ideal Call' which opens the symphony. (I shall explain later why the second-theme recapitulation in A♭ is unsatisfactory.)

On Hepokoski's D minor interpretation, the 'second theme' (his scare quotes) at 12:1ff.[12] is 'in the orthodox III, F major',[13] but this cannot be sustained: F major is functionally either VI/A♭ or VI/a, or, as I shall argue in Section 2, both. The sonata failure, which is certainly the overriding structural principle of the movement, comes for Hepokoski at 38:1 in the recapitulation, where this 'second theme' is recapitulated in the 'framing' A♭ rather than 'the expected D major'.[14] But I believe the sonata failure is

[10] Robert Meikle, '"The true foundation": the symphonies', in *Edward Elgar: Music and Literature*, ed. Raymond Monk (Aldershot: Scolar, 1993), p. 49.

[11] Hepokoski, 'Elgar', p. 342, n. 11.

[12] I shall indicate bars in the full score with references of the form 'a:b', where 'a' is a rehearsal figure and 'b' is the *b*th bar after it.

[13] Hepokoski, 'Elgar' p. 331.

[14] Ibid. Elgar appears at first to be on Hepokoski's side against me; he referred to this theme as the '2nd. theme [which] on its 2nd presentation [is] in A♭' (Elgar, *Elgar and his Publishers: Letters of a Creative Life*, 2 vols., ed. Jerrold Northrop Moore (Oxford: Clarendon Press, 1987), p. 710). Yet Elgar also said the movement is 'in [orthodox sonata] "form"' (ibid.), and seemingly viewed the return of A♭ as an orthodox resolution into the tonic. It is possible that his comments are tendentious, his motivation to defend himself from pre-Hepokoskian accusations of formlessness. Hepokoski

evidenced more (and in any case with more obvious and potent gestural emphasis) at 44:1ff., where the A minor tune from 17:1ff. returns on F minor, failing to provide the 'expected' resolution into either A minor or Ab.

I agree with Hepokoski that the arrival of D major in the slow movement is a consummation devoutly to be wished, in the richest possible allusive sense of that now-hackneyed phrase (see Chapter 6 Section 1), and that it is in some important way connected to the interior key of the first movement, but disagree with his claim that it is linked to D minor in the first movement, since that key plays no part there. Similarly, I acknowledge with Hepokoski that the slow movement's recall of first-movement material (he notes the similarity between the Ideal Call and two slow-movement themes)[15] may have hermeneutic significance, but think that the recall of the A minor tune as a counterpoint – the quotation is almost verbatim – to the slow movement's second subject at 96:1ff. is perhaps even more remarkable.

One of Hepokoski's most fleeting but interesting points comes in a footnote. 'We may also note in passing that the default slow movement within a four-movement symphony or sonata – when it, too, is in some sort of sonata structure – may be regarded, in a larger sense, as an off-tonic sonata, but one that in the tradition does not seek resolution within the movement itself.'[16] This really is an important point to consider about the First Symphony, whose D major slow movement stands at a far remove from the Ab in which the work begins and ends. The possibility that such an off-tonic structure might traditionally call for resolution in subsequent movements might be the single most significant grammatical fact about this symphony, in which the challenge of D – if it is right to speak of a 'challenge' – is *not* finally overcome. The opposition of powerful forces in this symphony is every bit as essential to the design as in (to take some modernist examples) Nielsen's Fourth and Fifth Symphonies, but more subtle and pervasive, and ultimately less susceptible to resolution.[17]

emphatically disagrees with the composer that the recapitulation-space return of the 'second theme' in Ab is an orthodox resolution, and his interpretation of the movement therefore departs just as significantly from Elgar's as does mine. And does it even matter? Elgar wrote: 'All this is beside the point because I *feel* & don't invent – I can't even invent an explanation' (ibid.).

[15] Hepokoski, 'Elgar', p. 332.

[16] Ibid., p. 342, n. 9.

[17] On the subject of modernist closure, see Daniel M. Grimley, 'Modernism and closure: Nielsen's Fifth Symphony', *The Musical Quarterly* 86 (2002) pp. 149–73, and Arnold

In addition to his analysis of these basically immanent features in the work, Hepokoski suggests possibilities for an intertextual approach by drawing attention to two *Parsifal* allusions in the symphony, one obvious (the Spear motive in bb. 3–6 of the Ideal Call), one less so (the 'Amfortas-like brass cries' of the A minor tune at 17:1ff.).[18] I shall reserve my own intertextual observations till the hermeneutics in Chapter 6, but suffice it to say here that this symphony and that music drama possess one striking symbolic tonal feature in common: the pairing of A♭ and D. Allusions to Amfortas's cries and the redemptive potential of Good Friday D major might have much light to throw on this First Symphony, and so too may the *Hamlet* quotation Elgar wrote over the last bars of the slow movement's closing theme, which Hepokoski also notices in passing.[19]

In preparation for the close, modified Schenkerian reading of Section 2, I shall now propose a Hepokoskian overview of the form of the symphony which goes against much of Hepokoski's own analysis; but where we agree on important details I shall make acknowledgement.

The first movement is a quadruple rotational structure, each rotation beginning with the 'Ideal Call' (see Fig. 3.1).[20] Classical early models for this aspect of the movement (there are other models for other aspects, as we have seen)[21] are probably Beethoven's Piano Sonatas in C minor, Op. 13, and in D minor, Op. 31 No. 2, which both use slow-introduction material in a similar way. The first, expository rotation (R1) opens with a grand

Whittall's cautioning against unambiguous readings of Sibelius in 'The later symphonies', in *The Cambridge Companion to Sibelius*, ed. Daniel M. Grimley (Cambridge: Cambridge University Press, 2004), pp. 49–65. Strauss's *Also sprach Zarathustra*, with its famous opposition of B and C, was probably also an inspiration for Elgar's tonal design, although it is extremely unlikely that any philosophical or intertextual significance may be attached to this.

[18] Hepokoski, 'Elgar', pp. 330–1.

[19] See Robert Anderson, *Elgar in Manuscript* (portland, OR: Amadeus Press, 1990), p. 97, Hepokoski, 'Elgar', p. 332, and Chapter 5 below.

[20] Hepokoski notes the suggestion of rotations in the finale ('Elgar', p. 342, n. 17), but otherwise says no more on the matter. The label 'Ideal Call', preferred by Hepokoski to the more common 'motto theme', comes from Elgar: 'the opening theme is intended to be simple &, in intention, noble & elevating . . . the sort of *ideal* call – in the sense of persuasion, not coercion or command – & something above everyday & sordid things' (Elgar, *Edward Elgar: Letters of a Lifetime*, ed. Jerrold Northrop Moore (Oxford: Clarendon Press, 1990), p. 200). (In Moore, *Edward Elgar: a Creative Life* (Oxford: Oxford University Press, 1984), p. 520, the same is quoted with brackets substituted for dashes, and with the italicization of '*ideal* call' reversed.)

[21] See p. 66, n. 4.

Figure 3.1. First movement, rotational structure

Exposition	R1	Intro. ('Ideal Call')	−5:1	A♭	
		P ('Sub-Acid Theme')	5:2–8:18	?a	
		TR¹	9:1–11:10		
		S¹	12:1–13:19	F	
		TR²	14:1–16:9	?a	
		S² ('Amfortas Tune')	17:1–8	a	EEC: 17:5
		C	17:9–16		
Development	R2	Intro. ('Ideal Call')	18:1–12	C	
		P	19:1–20:8	?a	
		TR¹	21:1–23:12	E	
		E1	24:1–25:10	?b	
		TR²	26:1–27:12		
		S¹	28:1–18	b	
		E2	29:1–30:6	D	
		TR¹	30:7–14		
	R3	Intro. ('Ideal Call')	30:15–25	D→A	
		P	31:1–12	?e	
Recapitulation		P ('Sub-Acid Theme')	32:1–35:12	?a	
		TR¹	36:1–37:15	→e♭→E♭	
		S¹	38:1–40:7	A♭	
		TR²	40:8–43:9		
		S² ('Amfortas Tune')	44:1–8	F	ESC (rhetorical): 44:8
		C	44:9–47:8		
Coda	R4	Intro. ('Ideal Call')	48:1–51:8	A♭	ESC (tonal) 49:5
		P	51:9–13	?f	
		E1	52:1–12	a♭	
		E2	53:1–14		
		E2/intro. ('Ideal Call')	54:1–14	A♭	
		S² ('Sub-Acid Theme', 'soft & gentle')	55:1–4	a	
		C	55:5–7	A♭	

introductory paragraph of A♭ and the Ideal Call's referential statement.[22]
The harmony is purely, atavistically diatonic (only one accidental, a D♮ at
3:6 lasting two beats), and rather static: there is no departure from the
proposed tonic, and therefore – since the allusive language of this paragraph initiates a conversation with the musical style of a century before
1908, and must be examined in that light – it does not quite establish itself
as the first key in a monotonal hegemony. No other key has yet been
proposed, but since there is no constellation of different tonal spaces by
which the historically aware listener may find his or her bearings, A♭
cannot yet be affirmed definitely as 'the tonic' of the symphony, and its use
to close the slow introduction is thoroughly unusual. The listener remains
to be convinced.

With the arrival of the primary thematic group (P) at 5:3, the opening
of the Allegro exposition proper, A♭'s role is seriously questioned. The key

---

[22] Throughout this analysis and the one of *Falstaff* which follows, I shall designate
rotations, thematic blocks, and so on in accordance with the conventions established by
James Hepokoski and Warren Darcy in their works listed in the bibliography. So,
rotations are 'R1', 'R2', etc., primary themes are 'P', secondary 'S', transitional 'TR',
closing 'C', and so on. I shall introduce further abbreviations in the course of the
discussion.

of this new theme is ultimately indefinable, but leans strongly towards A minor (see below, p. 76); at any rate, it is nowhere within the ambit of A♭, and the immediate and irrevocable impression is of the manifestation of a new tonal universe in powerful contradistinction to the first. Not only has the tonal focus changed, but the language too is utterly different, with the new theme, which Elgar said has 'a nice sub-acid feeling',[23] charting a chromatic, modernist course.

The energy created by the Sub-Acid Theme's rising octave displacements is discharged into transitional material (TR^1) beginning on C minor at 9:1. There are four distinct elements here: $TR^{1.1}$ (9:1–4); $TR^{1.2}$ (10:1–8); $TR^{1.3}$ (11:1–4); and – most importantly, for it will return later, transmogrified, as the goal of the exposition – $TR^{1.4}$ (11:5–10).[24] Gradually they convert C minor into V/F (the A minor of the 'sad & delicate'[25] tune at 11:5–10 provides a desiderated E♮), and there is a perfect cadence into F major for the first of the secondary materials (S^1) at 12:1.

Hepokoski identifies this as the 'second theme', but I believe it is only the first, and not the more consequential, of *two* secondary themes. Its tonal feel brings us closer to that of the opening, but is not in the same time warp; the diatonicism here is identifiably post-Wagnerian (NB 13:11ff.), whereas the Ideal Call is purely Beethovenian. If F major is the secondary key, as Hepokoski suggests, then it is probably VI/A♭; apart from A♭ there has been no other clear key (save the C-leaning material that prepares and is subsumed under this F) thus far in the work. It is difficult to support the D minor tonic argument which would make this F functionally III.

This new theme may indeed be the first of the secondary materials, but it is a mistake to regard it as telling the whole tale of the secondary area in the sonata space. A central part of Hepokoski's recent critique of Rosen[26] concerns the latter's conception of the second group, or S-space,

---

[23] Elgar, *Lifetime*, p. 203. The exact sense in which Elgar intended 'sub-acid' is unclear. The *OED* offers, as sense 2: 'Of character, temper, speech, etc.: Somewhat acid or tart; verging on acidity or tartness'. But since Elgar was an amateur chemist (and even more amateur linguistic comedian), the precise scientific sense 1.b. might also be (jocularly) applicable: '*Chem.* Containing less than the normal proportion of acid'.

[24] Superscript ordinals – TR^1, TR^2, etc. – indicate identifable structural sections, in this case a first or second transition; numbers after a point – as in $TR^{1.1}$, etc. – indicate subsections, perhaps of only a few bars, within the broader paragraph.

[25] Elgar's description of the theme in a letter to Ernest Newman, 23. xi. 08, cited in Moore, *Creative Life*, p. 529.

[26] See James A. Hepokoski, 'Beyond the sonata principle', *Journal of the American Musicological Society* 55 (2002), pp. 118–30.

which Hepokoski considers too rigid and prescriptive. Put very simply, Hepokoski wishes to draw our attention to where S-materials are going, rather than where they begin, viz. to their structural function as provider of essential expositional and structural closure. It is the function of S-materials, considered as a whole, to establish the secondary tonal space of a sonata movement, but that may often mean that the gestures and tonal intimations of the opening of the S-space are later repudiated by stronger S-materials. His comment on Haydn's String Quartet in B♭, Op. 64 No. 3, applies well, *mutatis mutandis*, to the first movement of Elgar's First Symphony (and to numerous other pieces):

> The S^1 basic idea ... and its varied, distorted repetition ... represent not so much a 'regular-sounding melody' as a basic idea destabilized by [tonal] decay. Far from serving 'to reaffirm [III]' ... what it actually illustrates is the opposite, namely, the difficulty that *this* S^1 is having in its task of reaffirming F major in the expected way, that is by proceeding to a major-mode perfect authentic cadence. S^1 may well begin as blissful security, but the composer has it soon run into problems of insecurity. One might interpret the music as suggesting that the decay [of 13:11ff.] ... represents a refusal to continue the perhaps overly serene S^1 – a dissatisfied jettisoning of that idea and the beginning of a search for another.[27]

In the late-eighteenth-century sonata exposition, such a search may be reinvigorated by an 'apparent double medial caesura' leading into a more successful (because more stable) S^2, which properly establishes the secondary key by means of a perfect authentic cadence (PAC).[28] By 1908, however, the use of explicit medial caesura rhetoric would be disconcertingly anachronistic, and Elgar manoeuvres to the more solid S^2 by different means.

A second passage of transition, TR^2 (14:1–15:10), first recalls the C minor third-descents of TR^1, then resurrects the Sub-Acid material from the opening of the Allegro (14:9ff.): the original theme is now reduced to rising fifths and falling seconds, a bare skeleton of its former identity. The effect is to construct a conceptual temporal continuity between the end of the introduction and the beginning of the next section, S^2. The emphasis on the new theme – the 'sad & delicate' theme in a

---

[27] Ibid., p. 123.

[28] For a succinct explanation of the essential expositional (and structural) closure, and a number of other terms in 'Sonata Theory', see James A. Hepokoski, 'Back and forth from *Egmont*: Beethoven, Mozant and the nonresolving recapitulation' *Nineteenth-Century Music* 25 (2001-2), pp. 127-54, and especially his diagram on p. 129.

radically different guise (the two forms seem to operate as a Jungian persona and shadow of the same personality) – is therefore very great: even without the *fff* dynamic and the 'Amfortas-like brass cries' (17:1ff.) the rhetoric would suggest a focusing of energies, a thrust towards a principal goal; with the extra emphasis, the structural significance of what we may call the Amfortas Tune is unmistakable. With a strong perfect cadence (17:5), A minor has now arrived unequivocally as the secondary key of the movement – a realization of the tonal function nebulously proposed by the Sub-Acid Theme near the beginning of the structural rotation, and the Amfortas Tune's first appearance (sad and delicate) at 11:5–10. What Hepokoski calls the 'essential expositional closure', the EEC, is in this moment provided by the first satisfactory PAC in the new key (17:5). The 'structure of promise'[29] is complete, and the remainder of the movement must act to confirm or deny that promise.

The development space and R2 begin timidly (*pp*) on C major, with an unassertive twelve-bar remembrance of the Ideal Call (18:1–12). The Sub-Acid Theme (19:1–20:8) is represented synecdochically by a counterpoint derived from its original bass line.[30] The outline of this counterpoint was first given at 8:9–13, but not until now has it achieved a distinct, quasi-thematic form. As in R1, the Sub-Acid Theme (P) gives way to TR^1 (21:1–23:12), but this time the transitional modules are slightly rearranged and modified, as follows:

Exposition	Development
$TR^{1.1}$ 9:1–4	$TR^{1.2}$ 21:1–7
$TR^{1.2}$ 10:1–8	$TR^{1.1}$ 21:8–22:11 (extended and edulcorated)
$TR^{1.3}$ 11:1–4	$TR^{1.3}$ 23:1–8 (extended and intensified)
$TR^{1.4}$ 11:5–10	$TR^{1.4}$ 23:9–12 (abbreviated)

[29] See ibid.

[30] On the 'synecdochic strategy', 'whereby a part of the original S is used to stand for the recovery and resolution of S-space', see Hepokoski, 'Beyond the sonata principle', p. 130. Hepokoski does not use the phrase in quite the same sense that I mean it here; the 'synecdochic strategy' is a recapitulation-space phenomenon, and 'not an idea to be invoked lightly'. He does not refer to counterpoints standing for whole themes, but rather individual modules of secondary materials standing for the secondary area as a whole. Yet in a broader rhetorical sense, Elgar's adumbration here of the Sub-Acid Theme in the development *is* synecdochic, insofar as a part (an as-yet-unexplained contrapuntal relation) is made to represent the whole. But there is no structural significance to this moment – cf. the entirely different synecdochic recall of the 'immured tonic' in the coda-space (Section 2) – beyond the fact that it gives the developmental R2 a more recognizably rotational feel.

The 'sad & delicate' theme, in its anticipatory guise (i.e. as persona to the Amfortas Tune's shadow), is now on E major – perhaps the dominant of the movement, if it is to prove an 'off-tonic sonata'?[31] – and at a higher dynamic level: f over against pp. It is the only appearance of this theme in the development space, and it is perhaps appropriate that it finds a rhetorical half-way house between the two extremes of its presentation in the exposition space.

The insertion of episodes into the developmental space was a common practice in the late nineteenth century,[32] and prior to 1908 Elgar had followed the practice in the overtures *Cockaigne*, Op. 40, and *In the South*, Op. 50. He does so again in the first movement of the First Symphony, with the insertion of two such episodes.

The first (24:1–25:10) introduces a 'restless, enquiring & *exploring*' idea, a B-minor-centred, angular theme, with an accompanying 'wail', e♭–f–e♭ (d♯–e♯–d♯), on horns, trumpets, and woodwind.[33] Its immediate function is to preface a return of the TR^2 version of the Sub-Acid music (cf. 15:1ff. and 26:1–27:12), which now leads into a development of S^1 (28:1–18). This is garish and blaring, and introduced by the same transitional materials that S^2 had been introduced by in the exposition space. In massiveness of orchestration it takes on some of the powerful insistence of that earlier moment; but this is not S^2, and it does not have the same crushing weight. Imitative string counterpoint over a gradual diminuendo and ritardando (28:13ff.) dissipates the rhetorical energy built up in the preceding paragraph, and the second episode begins, this time on D major. It is the first appearance of what Hepokoski regards as the tonic of the movement.

The second episode is, like the second episode of *In the South*, the 'canto popolare', more tranquil than the first, although here it is based partially

---

[31] 'The "sonata" or "inner" portion [of the first movement] is in dialogue with the rare sonata-deformation family of the off-tonic sonata, those that are unfolded entirely, or nearly so, in a sonata-governing key that is not the overriding tonic of the movement' (Hepokoski, 'Elgar', p. 330). 'Two of its most prominent predecessors are (possibly) the first movement of Schumann's Piano Fantasy in C major and (more certainly) the finale of Mahler's First Symphony' (ibid., p. 341, n. 9). My own view, which I shall explain fully in Section 4, is that the off-tonic sonata of this first movement has a profounder structural function than Hepokoski intimates. It stretches across movements, and is reinterpreted by events in those later movements so that its own tonal function, which poses problems for A♭, is scrutinized and redefined.

[32] See Hepokoski, 'Beethoven reception: the symphonic tradition', in *The Cambridge History of Nineteenth -Century Music*, ed. Jim Samson (Cambridge: Cambridge University Press, 2001), p. 451.

[33] Both quotations Elgar, *Lifetime*, p. 200.

on the same material. Three four- or five-bar units (29:1–4; 29:5–9; 29:10–13) wander around D major, before being repeated at half their original length (30:1–2; 30:3–4; 30:5–6). The falling third-progressions from $TR^{1.2}$ return briefly to close the rotation.

Immediately prior to the onset of the recapitulation, R3 begins with the first of two tonally ambiguous statements of the Ideal Call in the symphony. Beginning clearly on D major (30:15), within the space of three bars it has sidled into A major, the major mode of the secondary key established by the marmoreal Amfortas Tune in the exposition. It is a subtlety easily passed by, but I shall say more on it in Section 2. As at the start of R2, the Sub-Acid material follows immediately in its synecdochic, bass-counterpoint guise, on D major, but now the connexion between this counterpoint and the theme it stands for is made explicit. After a side-step to put the bass counterpoint into G, the recapitulation begins with the 'nice sub-acid [i.e. mildly bitonal] feeling' Elgar drew attention to: G, implicit now in the bass, and the strong suggestion of A minor rub against each other (32:1ff.). Compare the outline of the cello part in 32:1–8 and 5:3–8. Every note of the earlier form is present, in roughly the same position, in the later; the later form is merely an intricate decoration, not a new counterpoint. Is G therefore implicit in the start of the exposition too? We may be permitted to think so; in which case, the bass A♭ of the Ideal Call is quitted immediately in two directions: it has chromatic neighbours on G (actually) and A♮ (conceptually).

The recapitulation follows the rotational format of the exposition (P–TR^1–S^1–TR^2–S^2–C) and S^1 returns, as Elgar notes, on A♭.[34] But recall that the essential function of S-materials is to establish the grounds first for the essential expositional closure (EEC) in the exposition space, then the essential structural closure (ESC) in the recapitulation space. It was Elgar's tactic in the exposition space to subject S^1 to tonal decay, and leave the search for the EEC still open; and in the recapitulation space, his stratagem is the same (cf. 40:1ff. and 13:11ff.). TR^2 again leads on to the structurally decisive S^2, and the result is sonata failure. S^2 returns emphatically not on A♭ minor, nor even on A minor, but on F minor (44:1–8). The rhetorical ESC is thus in an unsatisfactory key, whether we regard A♭, A minor, or even D minor as the tonic, and if the non-resolving recapitulation is to be resolved in the coda, there must be a strong feeling of closure in one of those three keys.

Famously, the abortive R4 in the coda brings back the Ideal Call in A♭ major at 48:1–49:4, and especially 49:5–51:8, which presents the real

---

[34] See n. 14, above.

ESC – here not a conclusion but merely an abandonment of the present attempt at concluding, a recess rather than a verdict. Yet that is by no means the end of the narrative. R4 follows the format of R2: the Sub-Acid Theme is presented synecdochically by its bass-counterpoint theme (51:9–13), and that is followed by the development-space episodic material, beginning on A♭ major (52:1–53:14).

The 'framing tonic' is now subjected to a process of liquidation. When, finally, the Ideal Call returns *poco tranquillo* to close the movement, the *Urlinie* fails to descend. It remains stranded on $\hat{3}$/A♭: note the repeated emphasis on c^2 on clarinet I, 54:7–14, and see further below. Instead of descending, the *Kopfton* is held over into the A minor remembrance of the Amfortas Tune (sad and delicate persona) which had produced both the EEC and the failed rhetorical ESC. This generates an instability in A♭ qua tonic, and therefore much work for the remainder of the symphony to do if any key is to gain a strong foothold in the shifting tonal quagmire. Surely no such ostensibly confident diatonic theme had ever before had its facile optimism exposed and – for the final bars are pitch-blackly comic – ridiculed.

The structure of the middle movements of the symphony is, by comparison with that of the outer movements, very simple. Almost every writer has commented on the fact that they share a tune, although to my knowledge only John Caldwell is wise enough to note that 'their common thematic basis [is] noticeable only to someone previously primed'.[35] In fact to point to the thematic similarity (but not identity: cf. the fourth bar of the Allegro molto theme with its counterpart, the seventh bar of the Adagio theme) is merely to offer a pseudo-explanation for the structure and function of the movements. Certainly the two movements together make a case for D major as the goal tonality of the symphony; but there is a danger of being blind to a broader chain of events through the first *three* movements if we accept too readily that in the shared theme we have a sufficient summary of what is going on at its heart. Even were we only to consider the issue of thematic recall in the middle movements, the returns of the Amfortas Tune and the Ideal Call in the Adagio are at least as significant as, and perhaps more significant than, the common theme of the second and third movements. But we should look even more deeply than that.

The Allegro molto alternates 'scherzo' and 'trio' materials a third (spelt as a diminished fourth) apart, in F♯ minor and B♭ major respectively; a

[35] John Caldwell, *The Oxford History of English Music – Volume II: From c.1715 to the Present Day* (Oxford: Clarendon Press, 1999), p. 294.

Figure 3.2. Second movement, rotational structure

A	R₁	P^{gen}	–65:12	f♯
B		S^1	66:1–67:14	B♭
		S^2	68:1–70:18	→d
A/B	R₂	P^{gen}	71:1–76:9	f♯
B		S^1	77:1–78:10	B♭
		S^2	78:11–81:10	d
A/B	R₃	P^{gen}	82:1–84:13	f♯
B	(abbreviated)	S^1	85:1–8	B♭
A	Coda	P^{gen}	86:1–92:8	d♭/c♯→f♯

Figure 3.3. Third movement, rotational structure

Exposition	R₁	P^{tel}	–93:7	D	
		TR	93:8–95:9		
		S	96:1–97:4	A	EEC: 97:1
		C	97:5–99:9		
Recapitulation	R₂	P^{tel}	100:1–101:5	D→A	
		S	102:1–7	C♯	
		TR	103:1–7		
Coda		*Telos*: 'Heaven Tune'	104:1–107:7	D	ESC: 107:7

summary of its structure is given in Fig. 3.2.[36] It will be noted that both keys are a third distant from D, and in fact D minor seems (68:5–70:18 *passim*, and 78:11–81:10 *passim*) to bridge the gap between B♭ and F♯ for the first and second return to the 'scherzo' material, thereby creating an equal division of the octave into major thirds: F♯–B♭–D–F♯.

This sense of tonal flux, with no concretely established centre, is terminated with the beginning of the Adagio, where D major emerges as the first key in the work to receive both a bold thematic emphasis (as had the Ideal Call) and orthodox harmonic–structural support, with an S-theme on the dominant, A major (96:1–97:5). The structure of the movement is summarized in Fig. 3.3. The P-theme it shares with the preceding movement is bound to give the listener who has been tipped-off a sense of the attainment of a goal or *telos* (Greek, lit. 'end', meant here as the goal of the piece), especially after the careful preparation at the end of the Allegro

[36] Elgar does not use the term 'scherzo' in his symphonies (and avoided the genre altogether in the incomplete Third), but the designation is not inappropriate. There is, to someone of my generation, an imperial feeling to the movement's main theme, although it is an intergalactic, rather than a British, imperialism which its passing resemblance to Darth Vader's identifying theme in John Williams's soundtrack to *The Empire Strikes Back* calls to mind.

molto (87:1ff.).[37] Yet if it is an arrival, it is only at a new beginning, a new chance to 'compose-out' the fulfilment of the hopes built into and up from the slow introduction to the first movement. A successful D major sonata here could do much to heal the wounds of the failed sonata of the first movement.

And this sonata explicitly draws the first movement into itself, just as the shared theme draws in the second movement. The Ideal Call is clearly alluded to in the slow-movement form of the shared theme (P): the 'spear motive' from *Parsifal*, prominent in the Ideal Call, is given special emphasis in its fifth and sixth bars – NB the d^2–$g\sharp^2$/ab^2 ascent in the latter, which pauses for a moment having opened up the tritone that provides much of the structural material of the symphony[38] – while the climax (93:4–6) mirrors and apotheosizes the Ideal Call's $\hat{3}$–$\hat{2}$–$\hat{1}$–$\hat{7}$ descent. The Adagio theme is shown in Ex. 3.1. It is a striking teleological arrival. With the arrival of the S-material (96:1), even more of the first movement is resurrected. The Amfortas Tune appears – in the major mode, but almost verbatim – as a tenor-voice counterpoint to S, whose rising fifth-progression recalls the same progression in S^1 of the first movement at 12:1ff. so closely that even the chromatic passing motion between the fourth and fifth steps is retained (Ex. 3.2).

Not only themes but also key schemes seem to be sucked into this new vortex. We have already seen the slow movement's D take a decision on the second movement's tonal flux, giving it a sense of direction and purpose. Furthermore Elgar himself considered the second movement's F$\sharp$ to be plagally related to the first movement's A$\flat$ (as the enharmonic equivalent of IV/IV/A$\flat$),[39] and so by extension the first key of the work is also drawn in. But much more importantly, the direct appropriation of the A minor secondary tonality of the first movement as the D-tonicizing A *major* of this movement clinches the argument, and the Amfortas Tune's appearance at both points underlines their structural significance. D major is the teleological goal of this symphony. Although I believe he is wrong to

---

[37] I label the second-movement form of the theme 'P^{gen}' (the middle movements' primary theme in a generative form) and the slow-movement form 'P^{tel}' (the same at its point of teleological arrival) in Figs. 3.2 and 3.3, following the system used in discussion of teleological genesis (a Sonata Theory concept) in, for example, Warren Darcy, 'Bruckner's sonata deformations', in *Bruckner Studies*, ed. Timothy L. Jackson and Paul Hawkshaw (Cambridge: Cambridge University Press, 1997), pp. 256–77.

[38] Less obvious are the references to the rising fourth motive in the tune's second to fifth notes, in the alto register of the third bar, and in the bar before figure 93, or its inversion in the tenor part of the fifth and sixth bars.

[39] Elgar, *Publishers*, p. 710.

Example 3.1. Symphony I/iii, opening

Example 3.2. Symphony I/iii, fig. 96:1ff. (with Amfortas Tune)

identify its first arrival in the first movement's Allegro, Hepokoski is absolutely right to note its importance in the Adagio and in the symphony as a whole.

But the goal is not attained at the beginning of the movement, with the first solid arrival of the key; at that point, the astonishing self-referential focusing of all the symphony's potentialities has not yet been laid before the listener. It is only after the end of the exposition (the EEC is at 97:1) that the structure can begin to confirm or deny its promise. In a conceptual sense, the whole of the symphony up to this point has been a single sonata exposition, beginning radically off-tonic and passing through immense structural difficulties and insecurities, but now finally clear about its identity and goal. Even if it were not typical for sonata-form slow movements to have no development section – this, like most others, is a Type 1 sonata[40] – a heightening of tension at this point would be almost unbearable. The weight of the symphony rests on this sonata's shoulders, and the recapitulation therefore enters with all speed.

P is recapitulated, *pp* as before, on D major (100:1–101:5), but the displacement of the TR-material from the exposition means that S, the theme whose goal is to confirm or deny the promise of a D major sonata completion, is recapitulated on C♯ (102:1–7). Therefore, although it comes much closer to a successful sonata form than the first movement, still the third movement's sonata is non-resolving. After a repeat of TR (103:1–7), D major is finally confirmed in a magical second-*telos* paragraph based on a new theme which Elgar's publisher and friend August Jaeger said brings us 'near Heaven' (104:1ff.).[41] At last a key has unequivocally been put forward as a tonic for the symphony (the ESC is at 107:7), and has been blessed with one of Elgar's most beautiful thematic creations. But it is the *secondary* tonic, and it still remains to be seen whether the primary tonic can be similarly strongly affirmed.

The finale begins the task of quitting D for A♭ by repudiating the major-mode conclusion of the Adagio (Fig. 3.4). Material from the developmental episodes of the first movement returns mysteriously on muted strings and low woodwind. Then, six bars into the Lento introduction, comes the entry of what will later turn out to be S^2, the most important theme of the movement; it has motivic links with the Ideal Call, although Elgar apparently did not intend them.[42] Other TR and S-materials follow, and the Ideal Call itself makes two appearances, the second time on an A♭ which is quickly forced into E major (II/d: 110:6) in preparation for a perfect cadence into the movement's first tonic, D minor.

The Allegro which follows is another rotational sonata structure. It sticks to the $P–TR^1–S^1–TR^2$ plan of the first movement and, like the first and third movements, has a non-resolving recapitulation. But more remarkable than the failure of the recapitulation space to provide a

---

[40] On Hepokoski's view there are five 'numbered' sonata forms: 'the Type 1 sonata is what has been called by others the "sonatina" or "sonata without development"; Type 2 refers to "binary" sonatas without full recapitulations; Type 3 is the standard "textbook" sonata form; Type 4 encompasses sonata-rondo hybrids; and Type 5 comprises adaptations of sonata form within concertos' (Hepokoski, 'Beyond the sonata principle', p. 137, n. 69).

[41] Elgar, *Publishers*, p. 715.

[42] See Moore, *Creative Life*, pp. 538–9. The fact that it immediately follows the 'exploring' theme may be important, since this new theme is in a sense the most exploratory idea of the symphony; its structural function, especially in relation to the *Augenblick*, will become clear in Section 4: see esp. p. 83.

Figure 3.4. Fourth movement, rotational structure (italics in the second column indicate music taken from outside this movement)

Introduction	*E_1*	(5 bars)	d	
	S^2 ('March Tune')	(4 bars)		
	TR	108:2		
	Ideal Call	108:3–7		
	E_1	109:1–3		
	S^2 ('March Tune')	109:4–7	f	
	El	110:1–2	a♭	
	Ideal Call	110:3–5	A♭→E	
	TR/*Ideal Call*	110:6–111:4	A	
Exposition	P	111:5–112:12	d	
	TR	113:1–11		
	S^1	114:1–115:8	B♭	
	TR	116:1–117:4		MC: 117:4
	S^2 ('March Tune')	118:1–119:8	d	EEC: 119:8
Development	P/S^2 alternation	120:1–126:7	d→b	
	S^1	127:1–128:5		
	S^1/*Ideal Call*	128:5–129:10	a♭	
	S^2 ('March Tune')	130:1–133:12	e♭/G♭	*Telos 1*
Recapitulation	P	134:1–135:14	e♭	
	TR	136:1–11		
	S^1	137:1–138:8	G♭	
	TR	139:1–140:8		MC: 140:8
	S^2 ('March Tune')	141:1–142:7	f	ESC (rhetorical): 142:7
Coda	TR	143:1–144:7		
	TR^2	145:1–9		
	Ideal Call	146:1–148:15	A♭	*Telos 2*
	TR^2	149:1–10		
	S^1	150:1–151:4		
	Ideal Call	150:5–13		ESC (tonal): 150:13

satisfactory ESC is Elgar's curious handling of the tonic in the exposition. The P theme (111:5–112:12), with a mercilessly repetitive ♩ ♪ rhythm which can sound very awkward in performance if not driven on quickly and energetically, establishes D minor as tonic, and the side-step to B♭ for S^1 (114:1–115:8) shores it up with the familiar neo-Romantic/early modernist double-tonic pairing of keys a third apart. But with the move to S^2, for the secondary theme one might expect to establish the secondary key of the movement, something peculiar happens. After six bars of old-fashioned medial-caesura material, incorporating a palpable 'breath' in the final bar (116:8–117:4), the 'secondary' key duly arrives, with an EEC at 119:8. But it is D minor, *the opening tonic of the movement*.

This may seem an insignificant point, but Elgar is actually doing something remarkable here, and setting up the *Augenblick*, of which much more will be said below (p. 101). Suffice it to say for the moment that by prefacing the return to D minor with such a classic sign of formal rupture as the medial-caesura material of the six immediately preceding bars, and presenting a secondary-key-affirming new theme to go with it, Elgar establishes the grounds for a negation of the D minor tonic which will allow him to move ultimately towards A♭. It is one of the basic elements of Elgar's style to use the rhetoric and gesture of the Classical tradition – and even the symphony itself – to *comment on* that tradition in a radically modernist way (radical in the sense of returning to its roots). By resurrecting here the Classical preference for a clearly defined medial caesura, Elgar brings back too the feeling in the listener that the new key really *is* new; because he or she is familiar with Classical rhetoric, the listener hears it not as the tonic, but as the secondary key of the sonata.[43] As yet the full implications of this ploy are not known to the first-time listener, but since D minor will increasingly from this point be treated as the secondary key, I shall go on referring to it as such.[44]

The development and R2 begin immediately after S^2, at 120:1, on the 'secondary' key, D minor. Robert Meikle is ready with a jibe: 'it soon appears that we are possibly into a development section, though if that is the case, it is an odd exposition to have ended, just before [figure] 120, in the tonic'.[45] I would argue that the listener is aware immediately, not just 'soon', that the development space has been entered, and that the fact it sticks with the 'secondary' key of S^2 increases his or her already strong sense that D minor is no longer the tonic in the broad scheme of the movement. Far from handling the sonata form clumsily, as Meikle wishes to suggest, Elgar is on the way to achieving a masterstroke. The development space moves frantically through several fleeting key areas, but has important moments of arrival on B minor (125:7) and A♭ minor (129:1),[46] thus moving downwards through a chain of minor thirds. Then

---

[43] See Nicholas Marston, 'Schubert's homecoming', *Journal of the Royal Musical Association* 125 (2000), pp. 248–70, for an important precedent in Schubert.

[44] Hepokoski considers the D minor exposition close as a 'tonic expositional close' deformation, as seen in Mahler 4/i and 8/i (see Hepokoski, 'Elgar', p. 342, n. 17). For once, I think Hepokoski's aquiline distance vision fails him, for the effect and intention of this D minor close seems to me emphatically individual, purposefully unique; even Sonata Theory's more realistic (because generously open-minded) formulation is in danger of unjustly constricting the semantic content of this moment. To put it another way, there are other examples of tonic expositional closes in modernist symphonies, but those examples are not parallels: as so often, Elgar goes his own way and plays his own 'language game' (*pace* Wittgenstein), giving his 'grammar' a distinct Elgarian twang.

[45] Meikle, 'The true foundation', p. 51.

[46] Melodically, at least: the bass sticks recalcitrantly to G♭, preparing the next section. Here there is 'a nice sub-acid feeling' in the Ideal Call.

follows the achievement of the movement's first *telos*, i.e. the first clear renunciation of the D tonic.

At 130:1–133:12 the march-like S^2 theme, whose debut had proposed a secondary status for D minor, enters in a luxuriantly scored E♭ minor, touching sometimes on G♭ major. It is the movement's 'breakthrough' (*Durchbruch*), and necessitates a reinterpretation of the entire sweep of what has gone before it.[47] Elgar was clear on the significance of this moment, which comes in accordance with his intention that the 'coarser themes are well quashed'.[48] If the march tune had suggested in the exposition that the opening tonic was really secondary, then its lyrical apotheosis here proposes an answer to the difficult question which springs from the initial hijacking of D minor: what is to be the movement's tonic? By leaving D minor in preference for E♭ minor, Elgar turns the tonality of the movement flatwards, towards an eventual A♭.

Yet the recapitulation and R3 do not begin on A♭ minor; instead, E♭ minor is carried over the structural boundary, just as D minor had been at the join between R1 and R2. By itself, this recapitulation on ♭ii might be counted as a 'crisis', were it not for the sense of teleological genesis so obviously reinforced by the attainment of the first *telos* in the preceding pages. The recapitulation 'must' begin on E♭, because that is where the argument has led us. Text book notions of sonata form, or even of Sonata Theory, are of limited use here. R3 follows R1's structure closely, retaining the P–TR^1–S^1–TR^2–S^2 form; but the rhetorical ESC, which as in the exposition comes at the end of S^2 (142:7), is in the unsatisfactory key of F minor. I shall have more to say about the significance of this key and this moment, but it is enough to note here that F minor very quickly becomes vi/A♭, and the work closes, with what effect we have still to decide, with the Ideal Call in A♭, the second and final *telos*. The tonal ESC, the final satisfactory close

---

[47] On the 'breakthrough' in Hepokoski's sonata deformation categories (like the very concept of 'deformation', it is adapted from Adorno), see his 'Fiery-pulsed libertine or domestic hero? Strauss's *don Juan* reinvestigated', in *Richard Strauss: New Perspectives on the composer and His Work*, ed. Bryan Gilliam (durham, NC: Duke Univeristy Press, 1992), pp. 135-75, esp. pp. 148ff. 'The concept of breakthrough, closely related to the category of peripeteia, or sudden reversal of fortune, involves abandoning or profoundly correcting the originally proposed sonata (the one proposed in the exposition) through the inbreaking of an emphatic, unforeseen idea at some post-expositional point, usually during the space customarily given over to development' (ibid., p. 149). On the Jungian implications of 'peripeteia', see my discussion of *Falstaff*'s Dream Interlude in Chapter 4, n. 106.

[48] Letter to Neville Cardus, quoted in Moore, *Creative Life*, p. 539.

Example 3.3. Symphony I/i, middleground

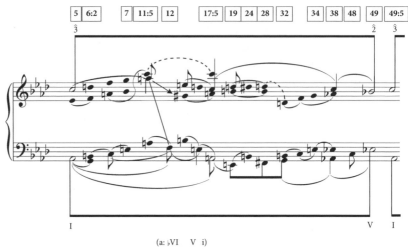

(a: ♭VI   V   i)

into the tonic that has taken an entire symphony to cement itself, comes with the consummation of the *Ursatz* in the last bar of the work.

3.2. A Heideggerian–Schenkerian analysis

Now that the general shape and some of the principal characteristics of the symphony have been adumbrated, a more detailed analysis may be undertaken.[49] This symphony is radical – more so, not less so, for retaining a tonal language – and a radical methodology is required to understand it. Its peculiarities have been brought to the surface, and can now be examined. I shall concentrate most on the duotonal tension that shapes the whole work across its four movements, and thereby provide a basis for the discussion in Chapter 6 of the hermeneutic significance of this conflict and its fallout. The first movement, which generates most of the tensions and most of the possibilities for resolution that will be explored in the rest of the work, is discussed under seven subheadings, which will act as signposts into the remainder of the symphony. A middleground graph of the movement is given as Ex. 3.3.

---

[49] A very different, and much more orthodoxly Schenkerian reading of this symphony was given by Timothy L. Jackson in a session at the 2002 international Elgar Conference at the University of Surrey, in the second half of a two-paper session in which a very condensed form of my own analysis had just been given. Jackson strongly supports the D minor reading of the first-movement exposition, and diverges from my own analysis in many other details. The paper, 'Design and structure in Elgar's First Symphony', remains unpublished at present.

Example 3.4. Symphony I/i, Sub-Acid Theme

(a) The frailty of the immuring tonality is exposed

I have already noted that as a theme, the Ideal Call's diatonicism is back-ward-looking, especially unusual in 1908. And with such a very old-fashioned symphonic opening (in terms of language, if not of gesture: no other symphony opens quite like this)[50] come certain expectations: principally, a strong presentation of the tonic. But although it is not challenged by any other key in the introduction, A♭ is not yet, although it could prove to be, 'strong' or 'sure': it has still to show its mettle. The Ideal Call's first appearance, then, is bland: splendid, perhaps, but untested, unproved, and even uninspiring.[51]

[50] I am grateful to Arnold Whittall for pointing out that earlier orchestral near-parallels might be the first movement of Schubert's Ninth Symphony or Wagner's *Tannhäuser* Overture. But the 'closed' feeling of Elgar's opening is still unique, even if the soft-then-loud statement of the theme is not.

[51] This may be one of the great ironic moments of 'imperialism' in Elgar. The theme, whose dignified martial character calls to mind glittering coronations of monarchs in Westminster Abbey, is, despite its great nobility, actually quite 'weak' in terms of tonal asseverativeness. One can easily imagine that if the boy who carries the king's train were to give it a seditious yank, the coronand would not have the gravitas to prevent his noisy clattering to the floor. However pompous and circumstantial, this cadentially (and therefore tonally) weak theme signifies a relatively emasculate imperialism.

But there are no cadences at all in the Sub-Acid Theme (P) that barges into the work at 5:3, hastily reinterpreting the Ideal Call's final bass A♭ as an upper neighbour to the root of a seventh sonority (Ex. 3.4). It translates insipid diatonicism into trenchant chromaticism, and is awash with dominant and secondary sevenths:

a. a weak V^7/f♯ on the upbeats to the first and third bars, and a strong V^9/f♯ in the fourth;
b. a strong V^7/C, or perhaps II^7/F, on the downbeats to the first and third bars;
c. V^4_3 on the first beat of the second bar, and II^4_3/A in the eighth bar;
d. II^7/A♭ in the fifth bar of the theme, which denies the expected resolution of the powerfully accented V^4_2/f♯, spelt B♮–f¹–ab¹–c♯² on the last beat of the previous bar.

The theme is, in tonal terms, very unorthodox. As such, it is difficult to agree with those (Maine, Moore, Hepokoski, Kennedy, McVeagh)[52] who hold that the key is D minor, since the closest it comes to that key is V/V, and the key signature probably has more to do with the F major second subject at 12:1. But neither can we agree wholeheartedly with Anderson's and Meikle's more persuasive suggestion that the key is A minor[53] without making the claim that some unresolved sevenths are more equal than others. The purpose of this theme, which is a maze of false signals and abruptly locking doors, is to rattle the tonal cage, not yet to provide a stable focal point for a new key area. The seventh chords point outwards, not inwards: to the A♭ of the opening, which will frame the movement; to the F♯ of the second movement (or, more locally, to the G♭ presentiment of it at 6:5); to the long passage on C from 7:1 (and the F that results at 12:1); and to the A minor that is immured in this movement. Any listener familiar with the symphonic tradition of the *Eroica* will recognize at once the dynamic, Beethovenian imprint of a theme that defines itself not by where it *is now* but by where it *is going to*, and a good analysis should reflect this, rather than attempting to impose an order the music does not possess.

---

[52] Hepokoski, 'Elgar', pp. 330–1; Michael Kennedy, *Portrait of Elgar*, 3rd edn (Oxford: Clarendon Press, 1987), p. 244; Basil Maine, *Elgar: His Life and Works*, 2 vols. (London: G. Bell & Sons, 1933), vol. II, p. 126; Moore, *Creative Life*, p. 528; Diana M. McVeagh, *Edward Elgar: His Life and Music* (London: Dent, 1955), p. 164.

[53] Robert Anderson, *Elgar* (London: Dent, 1993), p. 322; Meikle, 'The true foundation', p. 48.

For these reasons, suffice it to say that the first music to move away from A♭ simply launches the first and most critical form-generating progression of the movement – a sixth-unfolding from the *Kopfton*, c^2, whose scattered reflexions and refractions dapple the entire symphony (see Ex. 3.5).

(b) Sixth-unfolding, c^2–a^2

A neighbouring c♯^{1} and a descending third-progression adequately establish the melodic identity of d^1. On the Sub-Acid Theme's repeat in the work's original register, the line begins to rise. The egregious intrusion of a dynamically spotlighted, registrally isolated a^3 at 6:4 dams up the flow of the theme. The dissonant prolongation of the chord on G ends, and the melodic line rises to g^2; note that the bass A♭ at 6:6 supports F minor: A♭ major is slipping away. An unusually long and stable plateau on C now persists from 8:1, and switches modes at 9:1, where the spotlighted melodic a^3 becomes an *ff* appoggiatura. By its insistent puncturing of the line, a^2 asserts itself as a goal in the middleground, a goal that is attained when the sixth-unfolding reaches this pitch at 11:1, albeit without bass support till 12:1. This slight disjunction of the point of arrival will allow Elgar to arrive at his immured tonality twice, and so put it two steps ahead of the immuring A♭: recall that that was never 'in' any other place that it may 'arrive' back from.

(c) Kopfton *as cover note*

The *pp* A minor entry of the 'sad & delicate' tune at 11:5 is prepared only by II$_3^4$/a; when it returns, *fff*, at 17:1 the movement's immured tonality will be tonicized strongly by its dominant. Since it is the goal of the exposition, A minor makes its first tentative entrance precisely when the sixth-unfolding is completed at 11:1. But such a notable tonal realignment (I–♯i in A♭) would be more effectively established with solid harmonic support, so the target of the unfolding, a^2, is treated as 3̂/F and the 'real' resolution into A minor, the perfect authentic cadence into the essential expositional closure, does not come till 17:5.[54] Hence, the 'sad & delicate' theme's primary melodic pitch, c^2, appears in this still-unstable context as a cover note, recalling the A♭-*Kopfton*. The middle movements of the work will go on to make interesting and structurally meaningful use of the *Kopfton* as cover note.

---

[54] Cf. the understated return of A♭ in the recapitulation.

Example 3.5. Symphony I/i, sixth-unfolding

(d) Pivot from immuring to immured tonalities

Elgar gives F major strong support with the arrival of S[1] at 12:1: an expansive new theme; slow-moving diatonic harmonies; and a clear, rising fifth-progression moving in tenths with the bass.[55] The movement away from A♭, which seems for now to have reached its goal, is therefore transacted by the unfolded sixth in melody and bass; but there is a piquant ambiguity here, because the melody unfolds c^1–a^2, i.e. in F major, while the bass unfolds A♭–f, i.e. in F minor. F will prove an important pivot in this symphony, with its mode, in context, throwing weight either towards or away from A♭. So, at 12:1 F *major* functions as VI/a, into which it eventually closes at 17:1–5,[56] constituting a great lurch towards the work's immured D major, while in the finale, at 142:5, F *minor* functions as vi/A♭, thus pushing the music back to the immuring tonality at the end of the finale. In both cases tonally stable thematic material shores up the pivot.

---

[55] See the analysis of the third movement for another use of this progression.

[56] The main theme arrives at 17:1 (the point given in the formal summary of Fig. 3.1), but A minor is not solidified until the cadence into 17:5 (marked 'EEC', 'essential expositional closure', in Fig. 3.1 and given as the reference point in Ex. 3.3).

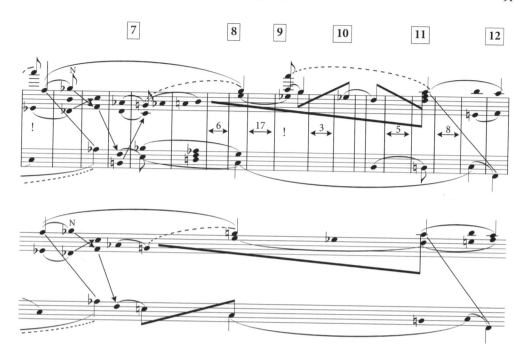

Elgar does not allow the F major of 12:1 to congeal into an immured tonic, despite its being the first solidly projected key of the work, more solid even than the Ideal Call, because of its strong, grandly drawn out dominant preparation.[57] By 13:11 the direction changes again, leading to a return of the Sub-Acid Theme at 14:9. So, the arrival at 17:1 on the first movement's immured tonic, A minor ('sad & delicate' no more), is given harmonic support by the F major (VI) that resulted from a resolute contrapuntal move away from the immuring A♭; but Elgar supplies an even more telling structural emphasis by the direct connexion he makes with the Sub-Acid Theme immediately before A minor's arrival.

(e) Pun on the Kopfton

Beginning at 16:7, three climactic statements of the first Sub-Acid bar propel the register from d¹, the first pitch of the Allegro, to the stratospheric c⁴ of 17:1, and the *Kopfton* is regained in spectacular fashion – *but as a pun*: it is now 3̂ within A minor, instead of A♭ (see Ex. 3.6).[58] Elgar's

---

[57] Recall Hepokoski's words on S-materials, quoted and discussed on page 75.

[58] Elgar puns on the *Kopfton* in *Falstaff* too, with G functioning variously as 5̂/c, 3̂/E♭, and 3̂/e. In both works the 'capture' of the identifying melodic mark of the immuring tonic by the immured tonic gives the advantage to the usurper. See further, Chapter 6.

Example 3.6. Symphony I/i, pun on the *Kopfton*, and the Amfortas Tune

juxtaposition of the Sub-Acid and Amfortas tunes at this point makes clear the role of the first Allegro theme. Although the arrival of A minor is associated with the Amfortas Tune, it is the Sub-Acid Theme that initiates the bridging motion from A♭ to A minor. It takes an entire exposition to open this chasm between the keys, with a hinge on the pivotal F, itself receiving generous dominant support, reached by the A♭-negating sixth-unfolding. But Elgar's resuscitation of the Sub-Acid Theme at 14:9 conjoins the disruptive cage-rattling of 5:3 and the orchestral clamour of the Amfortas Tune at 17:1: now we hear that this is the goal the movement has been seeking, and we finally understand the sphinxian intimations of the Sub-Acid Theme. It is a goal that commandeers the *Kopfton*, and has the potential to subvert the hegemony of the symphony. The repercussions of this pun, and of the drastic weakening of the immuring tonality, are central to the argument of the rest of the work; for this is not a bonhomous, Haydnesque pun, which is charming and to the point, but a cynical, blackly comic pun, which reveals its significance only much later.

(f) Prolongation of the immured tonic

The keys through which the development passes – among them E minor, B (minor and major), D, F♯ minor, and A minor – are all closer to the immured than to the immuring tonic. In voice-leading terms, this section is an intricate and nuanced prolongation of V^7/a, with a melodic d^1, neighbour to the battered and registrally demoted *Kopfton*, tonicized in the second episode. A turn back towards A♭ is made early in the recapitulatory rotation when an abbreviated repeat of the Sub-Acid Theme at 35:1, accompanied by a change of key signature (from one to four flats), begins a swift retransition to the immuring tonic. The Amfortas Tune returns (in its quiet form) on v/A♭ at 37:7, and S^1, originally on F, returns on A♭ at 38:1 (see Ex. 3.3, full-movement graph). The immuring tonic arrives, therefore, with minimum fuss, and one is bound to say with minimal structural effect. The cadence onto A♭ is almost unnoticeable (only a single crotchet of the major-mode dominant in the bar before the second subject), and the point of arrival is rhetorically unemphatic. But Elgar is doing the same in the recapitulation as he did in the exposition: there the immured tonic's first appearance at 11:5 was understated; here the *immuring* tonic's return is understated, although it is more expansive than the equivalent point in the exposition. Twice Elgar reveals his objective in a (structural) whisper, but he cannot open the door without a good pivot: in the exposition the F major second subject has that function at 12:1; in the recapitulation the loud Amfortas Tune has it on its return at 44:1 on F minor. This is the 'sonata failure' mentioned above.

(g) *Static* Kopfton

When the Ideal Call returns at 48:1 A♭ is approached by $vii^{♭7}$, which resolves on to a first inversion A♭. The theme is obscured by a remembrance of the elaborated bass line of the Sub-Acid Theme, which has been a prominent melodic feature since 19:1. A V–I close back into the immuring tonic comes at 49:5, accompanied by the regaining of the *Kopfton*, once again $\hat{3}$/A♭, and the Ideal Call is given a brief glimpse of victory. But the struggle is Sisyphean. By 51:9 the Ideal Call gives way to thematic snatches from the development, and when it returns in the closing bars of the movement at 54:1, the *Kopfton* fails to descend (see Ex. 3.7). Twice an upper neighbour on clarinet emphasizes c^2 and ties it over the bar-line to 55:1, where the Amfortas Tune, in its sad and delicate persona, quietly makes clear the pun on the *Kopfton* that reinforced the crisis of this movement: the vitiation of the immuring A♭ by the immured A minor, here telescoped into twenty-one closing bars. Since A♭'s tenuous hold on the movement has been broken by this reminder of A minor, it is impossible for the *Urlinie* to descend. Elgar has raised a temple to Schenker's fundamental contrapuntal tension between I and $\hat{3}$, by punning

Example 3.7. Symphony I/i, static *Kopfton*

on the *Kopfton*; his temporary solution (an appeasement rather than a resolution) is to transfer the *Kopfton* down an octave and end quietly, unambitiously, and only provisionally, on the immuring tonic. This closing page is a structural scream belying its ostensible quietness. If the movement ended with a satisfactory $\overset{3}{I}-\overset{2}{V}-\overset{1}{I}$ close in either Ab or A minor the piece would come to a rest between movements, but the recurrence of the chief problem of the work in these last bars means that the tension carries over the pause between movements.

I know of no definite source for Elgar's static *Kopfton*.[59] Although Julian Rushton has found *Urlinien* which do not descend scattered about in the works of Berlioz, they are fairly localized and certainly do not constitute unified gestures of the spectacular proportions seen in Elgar's First Symphony.[60] As such the static *Kopfton*, as distinct from the locally stubborn *Kopfton*, may justifiably be called an Elgarian fingerprint. As used by Elgar it has the long-range structural effect of prolonging contrapuntal closure so extensively that its eventual attainment is seriously called into question.[61]

---

[59] Schenker finds one in Beethoven Op. 106/iii, in an unpublished analysis. I am grateful to Nicholas Marston for bringing this to my attention.

[60] See Julian Rushton, *The Musical Language of Berlioz* (Cambridge: Cambridge University Press, 1982), esp. pp. 178–9 and 253.

[61] A note should be given now on a possible confusion of my 'immuring–immured tonal structure' with James Hepokoski's 'introduction–coda frame/off-tonic sonata' interpretation, with which it seems to have some similarities (see Hepokoski, 'Elgar'). We

Example 3.8. Symphony I/ii, opening tune

Having established the means by which the first movement sets up and conducts its argument, we can see how these salient details – viz. the fragile immuring tonality, the rising sixth-unfolding, the *Kopfton* as cover note, the pivot, the pun, the prolongation of the immured tonic, and the static *Kopfton* – are worked out in the three remaining movements.

Elgar originally sketched the middle movements together in the last quarter of 1907 as part of a string quartet.[62] For that reason, and also because they share thematic material (the opening themes of each movement), are in related keys (F♯ minor and D), prolong common melodic pitches (f♯^{1} and a^1), and are joined without a break, they form a single unit. The two-movement unit gradually establishes D major as an immured tonality, which by the end of the slow movement can claim to control the structure of the symphony.

The first nine bars of the Allegro molto establish a^1, the chief melodic pitch of the middle movements (see Ex. 3.8). If we hear the second

differ in at least one important respect: Hepokoski's analysis of the symphony offers no explanation for *why* keys change when they do, or how they interrelate or interpenetrate. This is not a flaw in his analysis; it is simply not his intention to answer that question: but it is at the heart of my own, because I believe that for a convincing hermeneutics we must have a means of answering questions about compositional choices which start with the word 'why'. My Heideggerian adjustments to Schenkerian theory provide one route to some answers.

[62] See Anderson, *Elgar*, p. 80.

movement as a continuation of the first, then a sixth-unfolding from c^1 to a^1 again leaves the first movement's *Kopfton* behind and establishes a new melodic focus. And there are good reasons to believe that we *do* hear the second movement as a continuation of the first. The *Urlinie's* failure to descend, intensified by the nettling reminder of the pun on the *Kopfton* (at 55:1), is one good reason; another is that Elgar himself suggested in a letter to his publisher and close friend, August Jaeger, that A♭ functions as II/f♯,[63] and the drooping bass pizzicatos, enharmonically G♯–F♯, seem to relegate the immuring tonic *ex post facto* to the status of a neighbour. So, a^1 dismisses c^1 and becomes the new focus, and there is another pun: at 12:1 a^2 had been $\hat{3}$/F; here a^1 is $\hat{3}$/f♯. The pivotal F from the first movement thus becomes F♯ minor; the music is moving closer to an immured D major goal.

A rising sixth-unfolding, then, continues to disrupt and complicate, but rising and falling fifth-progressions have the opposite effect. In the first movement the sixth-unfolding discharges immediately into the second subject on F (12:1). That theme gains stability from a pair of fifth-progressions rising in tenths (a^2–e^3, F–c) over eighteen bars, composing-out a I–V progression on F major; its stability beguiles us into considering F as a goal, but its later reinterpretation as VI plays us false. In the slow movement the second subject at 96:1 also composes-out a I–V progression, this time on V/D, by a pair of fifth-progressions rising in tenths (c♯^{2}–g♯^{2}, A–e) over eight bars. This A major second subject is especially remarkable because of its counterpoint, a major-mode version of the Amfortas Tune, which was bound up with the problems at the centre of the first movement. The theme and its motivic connexions are presented in Ex. 3.2.

At 96:1, then, the first movement's immured A minor is reinterpreted as a dominant and the first movement's immured tonic is sucked into D major. In a sense, D major's role as global immured tonic had been 'available' since the beginning of R3 in the first movement, where the Ideal Call returns on D major at 30:15. As we saw in the preceding section, that D major crumbles into A major, the major mode of the first movement's immured tonic; but in that juxtaposition, which is unremarkable except insofar as it is one of only two two-key presentations of the Ideal Call in the symphony, we might, 'listening back', hear early hints of a deeper structural purpose.

There was no substantial dominant prolongation during the F♯ minor of the Allegro molto (which cycled through a chain of thirds, F♯–B♭–D–F♯), so this dominant prolongation of and close into D is momentous.

---

[63] See n. 39, above.

Example 3.9. Symphony I/ii, middleground

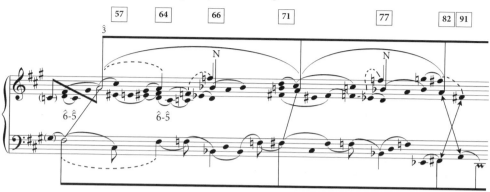

(Although it is tenaciously prolonged through the development, V/a in the first movement fails to provide the expected cadence.) By integrating two themes from previous movements – the F♯ minor theme from the fifth bar of the Allegro molto in D major at the beginning of the Adagio, and the Amfortas Tune counterpoint on A major at 96:1 – Elgar reveals that the immured tonality of the whole work, D, was presaged as long ago as the opening movement. But this thematic theft leaves an unresolved problem for D: it has no theme of its own to stand for the immured tonic in the way the other themes had stood for A minor and F♯ minor before they were stolen. Elgar solves that particular problem at the beginning of the coda (104:1), by introducing the new theme and second *telos* which brings us 'near Heaven'. Thus, by the end of the movement we feel closer to the achievement of a goal than at any other point in the work. Little wonder that the first audience made the composer rise to the stage at the end of this movement, to receive its grateful applause.[64] However, even given that Elgar grants D major its 'own' theme, his presentation of the immured tonic still raises questions.

The middle movements concoct an enigmatic relationship between a^1 and $f\sharp^1$. The *Kopfton* of the second movement is definitely a^1, but the B♭ sections that alternate with the main F♯ minor music (at 66:1–71:1 and 77:1–82:1) prolong a covering inner voice $f\natural^2$, which is transferred up an octave from the $f\sharp^1$ that lies beneath the *Kopfton* in the opening F♯ minor (see Ex. 3.9). This spotlighted inner-voice neighbour note prompts a

---

[64] Lady Elgar reported in her diary that 'after 3rd movement E. had to go up on platform & whole Orch. & nos. of audience stood up – Wonderful scene. also [initial sic] at end' (Moore, *Creative Life*, p. 545).

Example 3.10. Symphony I/iii, middleground

cover note f♯² at 82:1, which establishes a precedent for the following movement. The Adagio's *Kopfton*, f♯¹, is reached by means of a voice exchange at the end of the Allegro molto; and since that pitch can be parsed as either î/f♯ or 3̂/D Elgar can seize on its potential dual agency.

The Adagio opens on f♯¹, but as in the theme's original incarnation on F♯ minor in the Allegro molto it unfolds to a¹ by two bars before figure 93 (see Ex. 3.10). This covering a¹ is prolonged by neighbouring motion till 96:1, when another inner voice reaches over to begin the long, falling fifth-progression that culminates in the reaffirmation of f♯¹ at 100:1, the recapitulation and resumption of the immured D-structure. But again, a¹ is unfolded in only four bars and prolonged throughout the rest of the recapitulation. The new coda theme at 104:1, which promises D major the surety that its borrowed themes could not quite offer, reproduces the D-structure *in nuce*. Its opening f♯¹ unfolds to a¹, and that pitch is prolonged throughout a long dominant pedal starting at 96:1, which underpins ten brief a–g♯–f♯ figures. Only at 107:1, in the final statement of the theme, does a¹ yield fully to f♯¹, with a conclusive descent in the last three bars (Ex. 3.11).

Example 3.11. Symphony I/iii, Heaven Tune

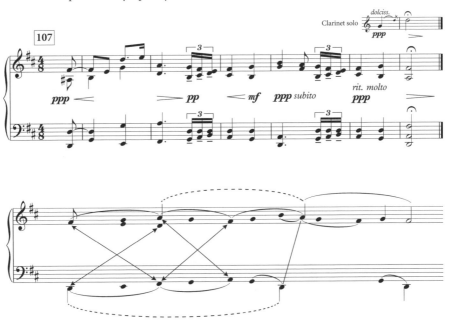

The pairing of f♯^{1} and a^1 in these middle movements not only joins them as a single unit, but also allows Elgar to pull off the impressive sleight of producing an overwhelming sense of closure, all the more powerful because we have to strain to hear its *ppp* susurrations, without actually closing at all. By making f♯^{1} the *Kopfton* of the Adagio – and the evidence of the opening and the falling fifth-progression suggest that interpretation – Elgar sets up a reference point; the a^1 that is prolonged for much of the movement can then become part of a satisfying contrapuntal descent. But it is a descent *to* the *Kopfton*, not *from* it: the end is suggestive, not conclusive. The final bar of the movement achieves a return to the $\frac{3}{I}$ of the opening, but no more: as Elgar wrote above a sketch for this theme, 'the rest is silence'.[65]

The delicate structural ambiguity of this movement, which might conceivably have either a $\hat{3}$- or a $\hat{5}$-line, means that a conclusive descent is impossible, because Elgar only decides on the starting point for such a descent in the last bar of the movement. Therefore, the middle movements establish a pair of interchangeable 'immured *Kopftöne*', neither of which

---

[65] BL Add. MS 47907A, fol. 87. The sketch is dated '21 Augt 1904', but the quotation is signed and dated 1908, the year of the symphony's completion. For a discussion of the Shakespearean overtones of some aspects of this symphony, see Chapter 6.

produces a closing descent. Yet again Elgar leaves hanging at the end of a movement challenges that have gradually revealed themselves in the course of it.

Somehow the fourth movement must solve all the accumulated problems of the symphony, by rescuing the frail immuring A♭, which the title-page proclaims the symphony's tonic; by restoring and enlivening the torpid immuring *Kopfton*, which stands in ambiguous relation to both A♭ and A minor; and by banishing the powerful immured D major tonality, which received strong dominant support, a kind of qualified 'closure', and drew in the Amfortas Tune (the very theme that usurped the *Kopfton* and devalorized A♭).

The finale's D minor Lento introduction offers a direct rebuttal of the immured tonic's major mode. At 110:3 the Ideal Call appears on the immuring tonic, after a two-movement absence; but a conclusive return to A♭ cannot, of course, be accomplished so easily, and a striking enharmonic change (a♭^{1}–g♯^{1}) in the fourth bar of the Ideal Call jolts the music onto II of D minor, the key of the exposition. The finale's parameters are set.

The Allegro exposition is the most immediately comprehensible thematic presentation of the work: a first subject in D minor (111:5); a second in B♭ (113:1); and a third, march-like, back in D minor (118:1). Such unabashed early revelling in the tonic, albeit without a dominant, flatters our desire for a panacean finale; but the development section is just as acidic as the first movement's exposition had been, and it harries D minor in precisely the same way, by unfolding a sixth, and amplifying the rhetorical thrust with a pun.

The immured *Kopfton*/cover note a^1 is carried on into the finale as $\hat{5}$/d; the first and third themes, both in D minor, stress the pitch with insistent $\hat{6}$–$\hat{5}$ neighbouring figurations. At the start of the development (120:1) the first subject returns, *still* in D minor (see discussion of this beginning above), but by 122:3 a quicksilvery flight away from the immured tonic and *Kopfton* is underway (as shown in Ex. 3.12). The first half of the development (to 127:3) navigates to E♭ (V/A♭), thus making a decisive move away from the immured tonic; the second half, which is mostly on E♭ *minor* (or G♭ major, which results from a tonicization of the third in the bass), forestalls the longed-for resolution. Progress in the first half is rapid, passing over E♭ minor, F♯ minor, and A minor, and the orchestration is prickly – *ff* throughout, with accents or staccato markings on almost every beat. The result is a melodic line unfolding the sixth a^1–f♯^{2}, coupled with a bass unfolding equivalently, D–b. D minor is quitted, then, for B minor, and the two immured *Kopftöne* are linked again. But the

Example 3.12. Symphony I/iv, middleground

bass puns on D, changing it from the root of D minor into the first inversion of B minor.[66] The ascent of the first half of the development, which creates a destabilizing effect similar to the first movement exposition, thus leads the structure away from the immured tonic, if not yet decisively towards the immuring tonic.

When the second subject returns on E♭ at 127:1 Elgar seems to be preparing for a recapitulation on A♭, but the progress stalls with an A♭ *minor* false recapitulation of the Ideal Call at 129:1.[67] The remainder of the development, from 130:1 to 134:1, is taken up with a serene G♭ rendering of the theme originally heard in march-like form at 118:1; its D-tonicizing sting is 'quashed' (Elgar's word). This is the finale's first *telos*. It leads directly to the recapitulation at 134:1, and the 'crisis' of the movement: a reprise of the first subject on E♭ minor instead of D minor. Still the effect is to weaken D minor, and not to strengthen A♭. With so much stress placed on A♭'s putative dominant, any structural cadence resulting directly from this point would probably be unsatisfactory, because dominant-heavy.

As in the first movement, the two opposed tonalities hinge on a pivot that has the strength to throw weight one way or the other. In this movement it comes at 141:1, when the march-like theme returns on F minor, vi/A♭: this is the crux of the whole work, and the arrival of the *Augenblick*. The theme, which is transposed up a minor third from its first

---

[66] Cf. the pun on the immured *Kopfton* f♯[1] across the join between the second and third movements.

[67] Recall, however, the sub-acid G♭-ness of the bass: the false recapitulation has no firm contrapuntal support.

Example 3.13. Symphony I/iv, the *Augenblick*

(a) F minor

(b) D minor

appearance, rises sequentially till it reaches a diminished seventh on B♮ at 142:4, a chord that could easily resolve onto either F minor or D minor (see Ex. 3.13). At the equivalent point in the exposition (119:4), the same chord resolves to D minor, the minor-mode immured tonic, but here the chance is seized to cling to the pivotal F minor that can propel the work towards its 'authentic' conclusion in A♭. In this resolution to F minor, D minor's last lambent hope is smothered.

The moment might seem unremarkable, given that Elgar simply repeats the theme note for note, up a minor third from its original manifestation; but it is crucial, because it focuses the work's central 'possibilities' in a singular way. Note that nothing actually *happens* here, or at least nothing 'new', but that if the possibilities that shine out in this moment are all projected resolutely to the end of the work, its significance in the entire structure will be revealed. First and most obviously, this moment recalls the pivotal F from the first movement, substituting the minor mode, which leans more markedly towards A♭ than the earlier A minor: the pivot, it suddenly becomes clear, can potentially swing both ways. Second, the theme's melodic sequences lift the line from c^2 to $a♭^1$, a sixth-unfolding that suggests that the first troublesome progression of the work, which led to an almost total disregard for A♭ through to the coda of the finale, can also be taken over into the immuring tonic. Third, the melodic $\hat{5}$/f in this theme can, if punned on, also become $\hat{3}$/A♭. Fourth, the curious stasis

of all the *Kopftöne* in this work can be used to A♭'s advantage: if c² is punned on again the immuring *Urlinie* can be picked up where it was left in the first movement, since there has been no conclusive descending motion in the vast tracts between to mark a full stop. Fifth, and most startling, the quasi-cadential fall from B♮ to F in the bass at 142:4 suggests that implying a dominant is as good as giving one: ♯4 can 'be' 5 in the grammar of this symphony; and if that is so then perhaps ♯IV, i.e. D major, can 'be' V, too – and the immured tonic will be subordinated within an A♭ hegemony.

None of these five crucial possibilities is unique to this passage (141:1–143:1), but that is precisely why it is so remarkable. These possibilities, with the exception of the tritonal cadence-figure, which belongs to the march-like theme, have all been tantalizingly available since the Adagio failed to compose-out a conclusive descent in D major. But loose threads, no matter how noticeable, still need pulling together. This *Augenblick* lays bare in striking fashion both what the symphony has been and done so far, and what the rest of it can and must do if it is to achieve its ends, and the rest of the movement acts resolutely on these possibilities. The F-pivot descends by fourths to ♯IV⁷/A♭ at 145:9, and the tritonal cadential fall of the march-like theme, first heard at 119:4, is used to close D♮–A♭ for a resurrection of the immuring A♭-*Ursatz* at 146:1. Simultaneously, a pun on c² restores that pitch to its original function as 3̂/A♭, and picks up the static *Kopfton* from the end of the first movement (as shown in Ex. 3.14: breaks between movements are indicated by vertical lines). The *Urlinie* descends at last ($\hat{2}_{\text{V}}$ at 151:6, $\hat{1}_{\text{I}}$ at 151:11, the final chord), but covering Cs on woodwind and brass serve as a reminder of the long-sustained immutability of the *Kopfton*. From the moment the symphony's ownmost possibilities come into focus there is little doubt that it will end in A♭, and the rhetoric of victory in the closing pages is unmistakable. But are those syncopated orchestral eruptions from 146:1 joyous or dyspeptic? Is the coda's posturing ingenuous?

Whether one considers the ending happy probably depends on whether one deems a single bar of $\hat{1}_{\text{I}}$ in A♭ sufficient to stabilize the immuring tonic after an hour of turbulence. Another deciding factor will be whether the means of A♭'s 'victory', i.e. its use of the very tools that were used to destroy its hold in the first movement exposition, are thought conclusive. One might argue that if the symphony continued those same tools could be used to leave A♭ again, and perhaps close convincingly in another key. But isn't the simple fact that the work *doesn't* continue, and that it *does* end in A♭, enough corroboration for the immuring tonic's ultimate claim to have won a secure place in control of the symphony? Herein lies the powerful ambiguity of this symphony's close.

Consider another 'conservative' twentieth-century 'there and back again' quest narrative to which we shall return in Chapters 5 and 6; its relevance to Elgar's musical meaning might be as surprising as its sudden appearance here. Suppose that J. R. R. Tolkien had ended *The Lord of the Rings* soon after the Ring had been destroyed – had provided an untarnished happy ending, that is. Tolkien would have spared his readers the Hobbits' heartbreaking return home, to a scourged Shire (a heartbreak too adult for the recent cinematic adaptation), and Frodo's final realization that he has sacrificed his world to save it for others, and that the best he can do is leave it behind. If Tolkien ended with rejoicing, would we imagine that the Hobbits' return home would also be happy, or just that Tolkien had not written about it? For anyone who thought deeply about the way things had gone in the book, hopes for a traditional happy ending would be impossible.[68]

It may not be obvious why I am discussing Tolkien's *Ring* rather than Wagner's. The answer is that in Wagner's case the parallel with Elgar's First

---

[68] For a start, it is unthinkable that Frodo should enjoy a hero's victory: he *fails* in the quest, and only luck destroys the Ring – which is precisely the point. Difficulties (evil) cannot be overcome by anyone in this world: there are no heroes. See Chapter 5 of this book on musical parallels to the quest narrative in literature.

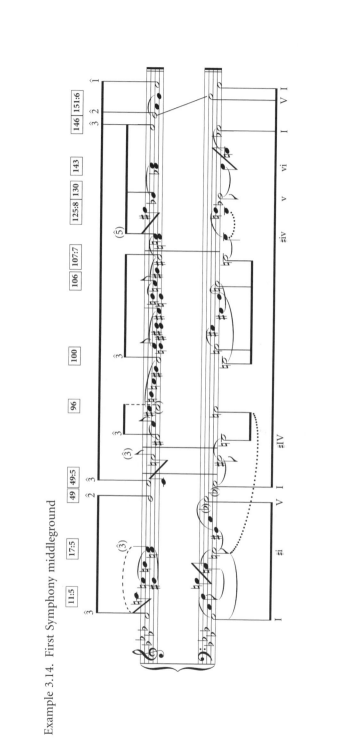

Example 3.14. First Symphony middleground

Symphony is much less exact in at least one important respect. Even before the final bonfire, Wagner's drama contains the human catastrophe of Siegfried's death. The disaster of *Götterdämmerung* is therefore sealed long before the final curtain, as Wagner moves from tragedy to cataclysm. Maybe the twilight of the gods is good for humanity, but at the end of the cycle this is by no means certain. A listener could be forgiven for believing that the pulse-quickening final pages of Elgar's First Symphony stand for pure, unadulterated joy; but a listener taking the same impression away from the end of the *Ring* would have less justification. Wagner is much more honest and direct in expressing his ambiguous conclusion than Elgar is, and at the end of the *Ring* we know there is a riddle to be answered.[69] In this sense, then, Tolkien's story is a better analogue, because in his case, as in Elgar's (and indeed as in the nobility of the final pages of *Beowulf*, if we disregard the Geat woman's brief but critical lament), a definitely 'happy' ending is reached. Parallels with Beethovenian heroism may even be drawn. Yet as I have noted, Tolkien moves on from that happy ending to a sadder and (to the twentieth-century mind) more realistic one; and although Elgar does not move on from his happy ending, the question remains whether a sadder ending is implied in the material.

And so we are confronted again with the possibility that Elgar has stopped in the middle of his narrative, and must ask whether the evidence so far supports the happy-ending hypothesis. I think there is sufficient to worry us when Elgar's First Symphony ends, especially regarding the security of that final chord, that we cannot honestly claim the work's message is assuredly optimistic, *even though* the *Ursatz* closes. Elgar may end by hiding the difficulties beneath a blazing *Grandioso* apogee of the Ideal Call on A♭, but that does not mean we should believe all is well. The immuring tonic has the last word, but can we be certain that it does not ring hollow?

---

[69] The symphony has certain intriguing links with *Parsifal*, however, and these will be discussed in Chapter 6.

4 'Fracted and corroborate':[1] narrative implications of form and tonality in *Falstaff*, Op. 68

4.1. The nature, subject, and intent of a symphonic study

Falstaff is curious: an amalgam of literature and music, it is not necessarily limited by either the narrative structures of the one or the syntactic structures of the other. Elgar does not call *Falstaff* a symphonic- or tone poem, but its similarities to the Lisztian/Straussian genre are obvious and central. James Hepokoski defines the musicologist's task in analyzing such a piece in an article on *Don Juan*:

> The essence of a *symphonische Dichtung* is situated in the listener's act (anticipated by the composer's) of connecting text and paratext, music and non-musical image, and grappling with the implications of the connection. The genre exists, *qua* genre, solely within the receiver, who agrees to create it reciprocally by indicating his or her willingness to play the game proposed by the composer; it does not exist abstractly in the acoustical surface of the music. Consequently, by the rules of the symphonic-poem game, we are not permitted to ask whether we could deduce the proper images had we not been supplied with them in advance, or had we not at least been given some broad hints in their direction. If we wish to play, we must abide by the rules; otherwise we are playing a different game or redefining the original one to suit our own purposes.[2]

It is interesting that Tovey's 1932 analysis of *Falstaff* was written before he had read Elgar's own 1913 article.[3] Tovey writes that his 'delinquency has its advantages; for it gives rise to a unique opportunity for demonstrating how far a great piece of "programme music" can be intelligible as pure music and at the same time convey the subject of the composer's illustration to other minds without the use of words'.[4] Notwithstanding

---

[1] *Henry V*, II. i. 124. See Chapter 6 Section 2 for discussion.

[2] James A. Hepokoski, 'Fiery-pulsed libertine or domestic hero? Strauss's *Don Juan* reinvestigated', in *Richard Strauss: New Perspectives on the Composer and His Work*, ed. Bryan Gillan (Durham, NC: Duke Univeristy Press, 1992) pp. 136–7.

[3] Donald Francis Tovey, ' "Falstaff", symphonic study, Op. 68', in *Essays in Musical Analysis Vol. IV, Illustrative Music* (London: Oxford University Press, 1936), pp. 3–16; Edward Elgar, 'Falstaff' (hereafter, 'analytical note'), *Musical Times* 54 (1913), pp. 575–9.

[4] Tovey, ' "Falstaff" ', p. 3.

this eloquent self-defence, we should note that few are blessed with Tovey's level and brand of perceptiveness. Hepokoskian caution is a safer model for the analyst.

Yet we are still not on sure ground, because in playing the symphonic-poem or, in the case of *Falstaff*, 'symphonic-study' game we are at risk of allowing our imaginations to run away with us in certain respects. For instance, Elgar's note explicitly affirms that the inbreaking of Hal's tune at 108:1[5] 'represents' Pistol's announcement that 'Harry the Fifth's the man',[6] but that moment is also an E^6_4 chord that also has a critical musical/ structural function at that particular point in the piece. We must be aware of a real danger of restricting the music with such specific associations, and reducing musical moments or processes to mere narrative signposts; we must be careful to remain dissatisfied with the reductionism of accounting for transitory musical effects only by what has been established as the 'general narrative purport' of a given passage. So, for instance, the paragraph from figures 114 to 127 might comfortably be viewed as the new king's processional, but that is only one interpretation of it. It is also an incremental unfolding of a progression from C minor to E♭: a specifically musical event which in turn projects semantically onto the narrative, as I shall demonstrate in Section 4.

Listening to *Falstaff* 'as music' does not mean listening 'away' from a programme: it simply means understanding how the programme is expressed by the music in musical terms. We follow the practice without worry in other artistic disciplines. For instance, we know that Shakespeare drew upon various familiar sources for *Troilus and Cressida*, and when examining the play it is important to be aware of these sources, and Shakespeare's indebtedness to them, especially where he makes explicit, deliberate acknowledgement; but we must and usually do approach Shakespeare – and this is crucial – from the perspective of his own style and idiolect: we do not expect Latin word order or Middle English vocabulary, nor do we even expect the source to shape the later work. A simple search for signposts in Chaucer or Homer is unlikely to produce satisfactory or interesting results, just as reading footnote references will not necessarily aid comprehension of an academic's argument. And so in

---

[5] As in the previous chapter, I shall indicate bars in the full score with references of the form 'a:b', where 'a' is a rehearsal figure and 'b' is the *b*th bar after it.

[6] *2 Henry IV*, V. iii. 113–14. All Shakespearean references are to the latest Arden editions of the plays: second series (1960 and 1966) for the *Henry IV* plays; third series (1995) for *Henry V*. I shall also adopt Arden's practice in *1 Henry IV* of using 'Gad's Hill' for the place, to distinguish it from the character 'Gadshill'. (Elgar's note does not differentiate.)

analyzing Elgar's 'symphonic study', we must not shy away from making purely musical observations and conclusions, independently of the paratext. Elgar's style, which is in a different language and springs from a different age and society than Shakespeare's, may hide as much of the paratext as it illuminates or reveals: and Elgar will certainly have things to add which Shakespeare did not intend. There would be no need to produce a new piece of art unless bringing something genuinely new into being was a basic intention. I therefore depart from Hepokoski's position insofar as I assert that in extreme cases where text and paratext appear irreconcilable, the text must have the pre-eminence: if the two seem not to fit, the integrity of the music should guide the interpretation.

We must therefore take Elgar at his word about *Falstaff*, as far as he felt the need to comment, and ground our hermeneutic observations on the information he gave, but never lose sight of the discretely musical semantic content.

Falstaff had been brewing in Elgar's mind since at least 1901, but he did not set to work with any seriousness until Easter 1913.[7] It is interesting and perhaps significant that one of the critical essays Elgar cites in his analytical note had been included in a collection of critical essays on Shakespeare in 1903, and was published in a new edition in 1912: Maurice Morgann's 1777 *Essay on the Dramatic Character of Sir John Falstaff*.[8] I think that Elgar's reading of this essay brought into focus his interpretation of the fat knight, and even provided a theoretical basis for his most personal addition to the characterization, the Dream Interlude. And since he proudly draws attention to his reading of this essay in his analytical note (which, as we shall shortly see, he insisted we read), we have to add a third consideration to our analytical preliminaries: Elgar's use of criticism, and Elgar's self-declared critical role – what we might call *Falstaff*'s 'meta-paratextual content'.[9]

Before coming to Morgann, I shall first consider the part played by Edward Dowden's *Shakspere: a Critical Study of His Mind and Art*[10] in

---

[7] Jerrold Northrop Moore, *Edward Elgar: a Creative Life* (Oxford: Oxford University Press, 1984), pp. 374 and 644.

[8] Maurice Morgann, *An Essay on the Dramatic Character of Sir John Falstaff* (London: T. Davies, 1777).

[9] The coinage is clumsy and unattractive, but has the benefit of being pithy, so I shall stick to it.

[10] Edward Dowden, *Shakspere: A Critical Study of His Mind and Art* (London: Henry S. King, 1875; 20th edn London: Kegan Paul, Trench, Trubner & Co., n.d.).

Elgar's understanding of the character of Falstaff; in any case, I believe Elgar came to Morgann only through this later book.

Dowden's project is to reveal the character of Shakespeare through a study of his works. He was part of the 'rambling, gentlemanly conversation'[11] of Victorian literary criticism, and in such a positivistic age of 'facts' it is unsurprising to find that he was obsessed with them. In Shakespeare he found the very embodiment of literary factuality. He considered that 'no other body of literature has amassed in equal fulness and equal variety a store of concrete facts concerning human character and human life'.[12] In Shakespeare's historical plays, 'facts . . . group themselves around his strongest feelings and most cherished convictions regarding human life'.[13] Yet his concerns, Dowden points out, are not the same as in the comedies and tragedies. In the histories Shakespeare's focus is on practicalities and expediencies rather than on profound spiritual issues. It is from this position that Hal/Henry V appears as 'Shakspere's ideal of manhood in the sphere of practical achievement'.[14] Yet in the history plays such willingness to deal in 'facts' has an 'unyielding justice'[15] as its corollary. Practical he may be, but Hal/Henry V's justice is harmful to those characters who do not deal in 'facts' – or, in the case of Falstaff, positively loathe them. We are bound to sense in Hal's actions a chilling premeditatedness. Starting with a quotation from Morgann, Dowden goes on:

> 'There is no such thing as totally demolishing Falstaff; he has so much of the invulnerable in his frame that no ridicule can destroy him; he is safe even in defeat, and seems to rise, like another Antæus, with recruited vigour from every fall.' It is not ridicule, but some stern invasion of *fact* – not to be escaped from – which can subdue Falstaff.[16]

And the 'fact' in this instance is that Hal never loves Falstaff in the plays; it is Dowden's chief insight and resurfaces in much later critical writing, as we shall soon see. Dowden holds that the apparent change in Hal's character 'was no miraculous conversion, but merely the transition

---

[11] A. D. Nuttall, 'The argument about Shakespeare's characters', in *Shakespeare's Wide and Universal Stage*, ed. C. B. Cox and D. J. Palmer (Manchester: Manchester University Press, 1984), pp. 18–31 at p. 18.

[12] Dowden, *Shakspere*, p. 23.

[13] Ibid., p. 164.

[14] Ibid., p. 210.

[15] Ibid., p. 165.

[16] Ibid., p. 366, emphasis mine.

from boyhood to adulthood years, and from unchartered freedom to the solemn responsibilities of a great ruler'.[17] The young prince threw himself willingly into the life of the tavern, but he was always 'other' than the people there and 'kept himself from subjugation to what was really base'.[18] In fact, Dowden argues, the Hal we find in *1 Henry IV*, Act I Scene ii is the same Henry V who returns victorious from Agincourt – just a little younger. The young prince is always already against Falstaff in the history plays; they might have been great friends once, but on Dowden's view they never are in the plays, except in Falstaff's mind. This observation is crucial to an understanding of Elgar's symphonic study, as will become especially apparent in Section 4.

Dowden does not try to guess at the sources of their friendship, since he deals with 'facts', not inference; but Maurice Morgann made inference the cornerstone of his work, and from him Elgar took the description of Falstaff's general character:

> He is a character made up by *Shakespeare* wholly of incongruities; – a man at once young and old, enterprizing and fat, a dupe and a wit, harmless and wicked, weak in principle and resolute by constitution, cowardly in appearance and brave in reality; a knave without malice, a lyar without deceit; and a knight, a gentleman and a soldier, without either dignity, decency, or honour.[19]

He also takes his description of the first theme in the work from Morgann; there we find Falstaff 'in a green old age, mellow, frank, gay, easy, corpulent, loose, unprincipled, and luxurious'.[20] The context of the first quotation is Morgann's support of Falstaff against the accusation

---

[17] Ibid., p. 211.

[18] Ibid.

[19] Elgar, quoting Morgann, *Essay*, p. 575. This quotation comes in Elgar at precisely the same point it does in Dowden, i.e. after the Dowden words Elgar quotes just before this. I do not doubt that Elgar read Dowden first, and was inspired by that writer's warm recommendation to read Morgann: 'No piece of 18th century criticism of Shakspere is more intelligently and warmly appreciative than is this delightful essay' (p. 365, note). But Dowden's quotation is from a later edition of Morgann; he has 'liar', where Elgar has 'lyar'. In the original 1777 edition, the quotation, with Elgar's spelling, comes on p. 146. And since the other Morgann quotation in Elgar's essay does not appear in Dowden, it is clear that Elgar actually did read the original. He was proud of his reading, but occasionally disingenuous about its thoroughness. See Brian Trowell's comments on the likely sources of some of Elgar's more abstruse literary allusions – which he often gets at second- or third hand – in 'Elgar's use of literature', p. 189.

[20] Elgar, analytical note, p. 576: Morgann, *Essay*, p. 116.

(from Hal and most subsequent critics) of cowardice. He seizes percep-
tively on a simple stage direction as sufficient grounds for doubting the
accusation. During the second Gad's Hill robbery, when Hal steals from
Falstaff, the direction is: 'They all run away, and Falstaff *after a blow or two*
runs away too, leaving the booty behind them.'[21] With those words Falstaff
is elevated from the status of a stage buffoon. The thieves run, in typical
comic style, but Falstaff exchanges blows. It is not his fault, save that he
drinks, that he is not built for battle; but he does not flee until he has
ascertained that this *particular* battle is beyond his abilities. He cannot
reasonably be called a coward. Having established this, Morgann goes on
to say that, since Shakespeare conceals the cause of some of his characters'
actions, it is appropriate to *guess* at the cause. To aid in this, Morgann
developed the idea that a critic could 'infer' aspects of character by reading
them off the real world. He perhaps ran too far with the idea, and has been
almost universally derided because of it; yet in the last twenty years he has
gained reasoned support from A. D. Nuttall and Harold Bloom.[22] Nuttall
explains Morgann's technique thus:

> It is clear that he would not have been at all surprised by the observation that
> he, Morgann, on occasion said things about Falstaff which had not been said
> first by Shakespeare. This point, so far from being a brilliant undercutting of
> his enterprise, is in fact anticipated by him. He suggests – and indeed,
> properly considered, the suggestion is hard to resist – that the meaning of
> Shakespeare's plays cannot be confined to that which is explicitly and
> formally stated in them. If this is granted, one cannot censure Morgann
> *merely* for indulging in inference. I myself believe that certain of Morgann's
> inferences are extravagant, but my ground for saying this is not 'Shakespeare
> does not mention this', but (because I accept the method of inference)
> 'Shakespeare does not imply or hint this'. . . Morgann is in fact proposing
> that where literature proposes probable human beings it is wholly natural
> and proper to apply one's sense of what is likely in real life, in making sense
> of an evidently incomplete (*deliberately* incomplete) presentation.[23]

He goes on to trace Morgann's ideas of 'latency' through Freud:

> The latent area which Morgann found in Shakespeare is frequently
> psychological. It is a matter of 'motives not acknowledged'. We might have

---

[21] *1 Henry IV*, II. ii. after l. 98; emphasis mine. Margann's argument is offered in pp. 124–7.
[22] A. D. Nuttall, *A New Mimesis: Shakespeare and Representation of Reality* (London:
Methuen & Co., 1983), and Harold Bloom, *Shakespeare: the Invention of the Human*
(London: Fourth Estate, 1999).
[23] Nuttall, *A New Mimesis*, pp. 174–5.

thought, therefore, that in Freud, rather than in the history of literary allegory, we should find a true analogue of Shakespeare. But it is not so. Freud's latent area proves more purely fictive (more 'literary'!) and less mimetic than Shakespeare's. Some may say that Freud's 'images', viewed as such, are richly informative. I would not agree. They seem seldom to function in a genuinely heuristic manner. In truth, Freud is the allegorist, Shakespeare the psychologist.[24]

I want to suggest that these 'motives not acknowledged', which are present latently in Shakespeare, are of particular importance to Elgar. His addition of the Dream Interlude – as psychological a musical commentary as he could devise, with the audience given the privilege of analyzing Falstaff – is his most concentrated act of 'inference' in the work, but the use he makes of tonality throughout constitutes a profound exploration of 'motives not acknowledged'.

Yet it is still not entirely clear what in the plays might lead us to infer other things, or how we might go about such inference. Taking his lead from Morgann and Nuttall, Bloom has recently given this exploration of latency in Shakespeare a new definition, and uses it as the central thesis of his book. I shall go into his interpretation of Falstaff in a little detail, since it springs from the same critical source as Elgar's, and comes fairly close to the interpretation Elgar's symphonic study presents. It would clearly be wrong to say that Bloom's interpretation represents the *source* of Elgar's 'meta-paratext', but I think it is the sort of critical engagement with the text, based on Morgann, that seems closest to the interpretation Elgar presents in notes, and has the potential to illuminate the present discussion.

Bloom quotes Ralph Waldo Emerson's words to the aspiring young poet Walt Whitman, 'I greet you at the beginning of a great career, which yet must have had a long foreground somewhere, for such a start',[25] and goes on to say:

> The 'foreground' Emerson sees in Whitman's career is not, as he makes clear by his strange and original use of the word, a background. That latter term has been employed by literary historians during the twentieth century to mean a context, whether of intellectual, social, or political history, within which works of literature are framed. But Emerson means a temporal foreground of another sort, a precursory field of poetic, not institutional,

---

[24] Ibid., p. 177. Inference and Freud in this Elgarian context come into focus in my discussion of the Dream Interlude in Chapter 6.

[25] 21. vi. 1855; the letter is often reprinted in editions of *Leaves of Grass*.

history; perhaps one might say that its historiography is written in the poetry itself. *Foregrounding*, the verb, means to make prominent, or to draw attention to, particular features of a literary work.[26]

This 'foregrounding' is necessary because 'Shakespeare's literary art, the highest we ever will know, is as much an art of omission as it is of surpassing richness'[27] – and that is Morgann's insight too. In his analysis of Falstaff Bloom isolates what he sees as the knight's central character trait, his affirmation of life, and explores this in relation to Hal/Henry V. It seems to Bloom that Falstaff's philosophy (he dubs him 'the Socrates of Eastcheap')[28] places him totally at odds with the young royal. 'Falstaff, who is free, instructs us in freedom – not a freedom *in* society, but *from* society.'[29] Hal, meanwhile, stands for 'power, usurpation, rule, grand extortion, treachery, violence, hypocrisy, fake piety, the murder of prisoners and of those who surrender under truce'.[30] All these, he notes, come under the banner of 'honour', which Falstaff discredits and denounces.[31] The two are set fundamentally apart, yet they clearly love one another. Bloom wonders why, and asks, 'How did Hal and Falstaff enter upon their original friendship?'[32] The question might seem strange (or unacademic), but it is natural enough, and finding the answer by 'foregrounding' the play will explain much about their relationship during the stage action. Bloom's conviction is that 'Shakespeare does not allow us to unravel the psychological perplexities of the Falstaff– Hal relationship, but while a puzzling matter, it is not beyond all conjecture. Hal has fallen out of love.'[33] It is by understanding that Hal's love for Falstaff is already dead before 'the Falstaffiad'[34] begins that we come to a clearer appreciation of his actions: he is always already planning to reject Falstaff, because he has always already fallen out of love. This

---

[26] Bloom, *Invention of the Human*, p. 737. It is unfortunate that Bloom has chosen a word – 'foreground' – so close to a familiar Schenkerian term, yet I see no way around the potential confusion of using it, other than to dress Bloom's term in scare quotes each time I use it, and treat the Schenkerian form as understood vocabulary.

[27] Ibid., p. 738.

[28] Ibid., p. 275.

[29] Ibid., p. 276.

[30] Ibid., p. 285.

[31] *1 Henry IV*, V. i. 127–41. Verdi transplants this soliloquy on honour into his opera, but his source is of course principally *The Merry Wives of Windsor*.

[32] Bloom, *Invention of the Human*, p. 290.

[33] Ibid., p. 302.

[34] This is Bloom's preferred description of the *Henry IV* plays: ibid. p. 276 and *passim*.

disarmingly simple observation has wide-ranging significance for an understanding of Elgar's symphonic study, in which the ongoing disintegration of their relationship is played out from a beginning that already suggests the end.[35]

Returning to the narrative paratext, we see that Elgar's adumbration of the 'story' is simplicity itself. Elgar charts the doomed friendship between Hal and Falstaff through robberies on Gad's Hill and their soporific discussion in Eastcheap, which lead into a journey through Gloucestershire, after a battle Falstaff manages to avoid, during which Hal's accession is announced. Falstaff rides to meet the new king, who rejects him, and finally dies. Elgar's note points to much in Shakespeare and enough in Dowden and Morgann that bears closer scrutiny, and the simplicity of his narrative design allows Elgar to 'compose-out' the psychological effects of the change in their friendship, rather than being limited to mere scene-painting. That Elgar published his analysis a month before *Falstaff*'s premiere suggests strongly that he wanted the informed members of his audience to be clear about the general nature and symbolism of the work before they heard it; and that he was deeply irritated by Tovey's failure to read the *Musical Times* article just about confirms it.[36] It is, moreover, clear that Elgar intended the work as a piece of literary criticism; he makes the point explicitly. 'If we take the word "study" in its literary use and meaning, the composer's intention will be sufficiently indicated.'[37]

Elgar's reading of Falstaff, as hinted at in his critically aware analytical note and, to my mind, confirmed by the music, probably comes close to the instinctive response of most unprejudiced viewers of the history plays. Sir John Falstaff is presented as a lovable and utterly hilarious character who is rejected by a 'young wanton, and effeminate boy'[38] with a lesser wit: it all seems rather a shame. The text supports even if it does not prescribe an interpretation of Hal which makes him in certain respects Falstaff's inferior, and not only because of their surrogate father–son relationship. Through all their bonhomous exchanges in the

---

[35] See especially my discussion of tonal association in Section 4.

[36] In a letter to his daughter Carice on 1. xii. 1932 he writes: 'That tiresome & tireless Tovey has written a long acct of Falstaff, & wanted me to read it. I glanced at it & it seems all wrong: so I "quit". I sent him my own notes & he now drearily wants to print *his* with my notes to shew where he is wrong – a most misguided idea. I have said to do what you like. I wish people wd. drown themselves in ink & let me alone' (Elgar, *Edward Elgar: Letters of a Lifetime*, ed. Jerrold Northrop Moore (Oxford: Clarendon Press, 1990), p. 458).

[37] Elgar, 'analytical note', p. 575.

[38] *Richard II*, V. iii. 10.

Henry IV plays, the fat old knight leads the way in verbal display. Hal's contribution, witty enough, pales beside Falstaff's, and often merely apes it; Falstaff, not only witty in himself, is the cause of Hal's wit too. In their first scene together Falstaff accuses Hal of 'damnable iteration' for using verses of scripture tendentiously,[39] and it is bitterly ironic that the percipience of his donnish cavil should be confirmed so quickly and (ultimately) so tragically. His gentle raillery in this first scene correctly predicts Hal's eventual intentions. Falstaff's pilfering lunar imagery establishes a frame of reference against which Hal's royal solar imagery will oppose itself:

FALSTAFF: Marry, then, sweet wag, when thou art
king, let not us that are squires of the night's body be
called thieves of the day's beauty: let us be Diana's foresters,
gentlemen of the shade, minions of the moon; and
let men say we be men of good government, being
governed as the sea is, by our noble and chaste mistress
the moon, under whose countenance we steal.
                              (*1 Henry IV*, I. ii. 23–9)

Elgar directly associates Falstaff's words here with the E minor tune at figure 7:1;[40] and throughout the work E minor will carry with it the flavour of this initial presentation, with its connotations of Kingship. It may be that its mildly bitonal flavour (e/e♭) is significant, since Hal's tune is in E♭.[41] Certainly, these words echo chill in Hal's famously uncompromising soliloquy at the end of the scene (ll. 190–212).

It is possible and perhaps usual to evaluate Hal's motivations and actions generously,[42] but difficult to block out the astonishingly discourteous volley of words he unleashes in the direction of his myrmidons: in

[39] *1 Henry IV*, I. ii. 88.
[40] Elgar, 'analytical note', p. 575.
[41] I shall enter into detailed discussion of these themes and the interrelation of keys and their associations in *Falstaff* in Section 4.
[42] A. R. Humphries views this soliloquy as 'a morality-manifesto rather than heartless policy' (*2 Henry IV*, ed. A. R. Humphries (London: Arden Shakespeare, 1966), p. lix). Tovey too seems to have found the soliloquy unobjectionable, and thought Hal's E♭ theme at figure 4 captured the prince 'when he declares his intention of imitating the sun by allowing himself to be hidden in base contagious clouds in order to be more wondered at when he breaks through them' (Tovey, 'Falstaff', p. 6); a note confesses he missed Elgar's stated intention, but I shall show in Section 4 below that his instinctive interpretation can still be sustained.

his metaphor they are 'idle', 'base', 'contagious', 'foul', 'ugly' men, who while themselves 'unyok'd' in their 'idleness' 'smother' and 'strangle' his 'beauty'.[43] These are hard words, fighting words – and disingenuous, since Hal himself is the proposer of the Gad's Hill robbery.[44] In his promise to be very good after first being quite bad, there are even shades of St Augustine's prayer: 'da mihi castitatem et continentiam, sed noli modo' ('give me chastity and continency – but not yet').[45] I think it is beyond question that Elgar's interpretation of the prince's character is as uncharitable as I have presented it here, and we shall see that it forms the basis for his symphonic study. On Elgar's view, Hal's rejection of Falstaff is brutal, selfish, and premeditated from the start.

This essentially martyrological interpretation might seem extreme, but Elgar has Bloom on his side, and Johnson, Hazlitt, Swinburne, Bradley, Goddard, and Auden would find much to agree with. On Bloom's slightly hyperbolic view, Falstaff is, with Hamlet, nothing less than 'the invention of the human, the inauguration of personality as we have come to recognize it'.[46] Falstaff's mistake and the 'origin of his destruction' is simply to love Hal too dearly. 'Critics have insisted that this love is grotesque, but they are grotesque. The greatest of all fictive wits dies the death of a rejected father-substitute, and also of a dishonoured mentor.'[47] None of this insight is absent from Elgar, who sympathetically presents Falstaff's love, limning it guilelessly. Yet Hal's rejection is inevitable, and already in his mind the time we first meet the pair: he ultimately kills a character who, Bloom maintains, created us. Falstaff's universality, expressed in these terms, led Elgar to give the title 'Falstaff' to a work as broadly about human nature and possibilities as it is about 'the mortal god of [Bloom's] imaginings'.[48]

The following analysis of *Falstaff* will describe several hermeneutic circles. I shall give an overview of the form of the entire work in Section 3, using the opportunity to tease out specific connexions between text and paratext. Then in Section 4 I shall survey the whole work again from the point of view of tonal associations and their narrative significance in a Falstaffian context, and in Chapter 6 I shall examine the work from an

---

[43] Hal's pettifogging distancing of himself from Falstaff's whole character is completed by his polarized expression of his relationship to time: cf. ll. 1–12 and l. 212.

[44] *1 Henry IV*, I. ii. 96.

[45] St Augustine, *Confessions*, 8. 7. 17.

[46] Bloom, *Invention of the Human*, p. 4.

[47] Ibid., p. 272.

[48] Ibid., p. xix.

intertextual point of view, to suggest ways we might interpret the work as bearer of meanings that extend far beyond its Shakespearean roots. I hope that by going round in hermeneutic circles in this manner the delicious richness of this score will be cumulatively grasped and revealed. But before my overview of the form, certain important analytical problems must first be addressed.

4.2. Preliminary analytical questions

Deciding upon an analytical approach that will keep in balance the different, but not conflicting, goals of this chapter is not easy. No single method will serve text and paratext – and 'meta-paratext' – equally well, so I propose to use several together. While examining the musical side of the dialectic, my comments will again be informed by the contrapuntal voice-leading analysis of Heinrich Schenker; but except at points in the argument where such analysis is indispensable, I shall largely avoid explicit reference to Schenker's theory. It is not immediately clear how the demonstration of an organic unity in *Falstaff* will inform the present discussion. I shall focus instead on more recent ideas that are to a greater or lesser degree indebted to Schenker's work. Those most apposite in the present context are (a) the slightly different understandings of tonal 'parenthesis' put forward by William Kinderman and Christopher Lewis; (b) the idea of the 'double-tonic complex' in the work of Robert Bailey and Christopher Lewis; (c) the use of 'associative', 'directional', and 'extended' tonality, as explored variously by Warren Darcy, Patrick McCreless, and Kofi Agawu; and (d) a number of structural features which James Hepokoski has found to be typical of early modernist music.[49] As will gradually be seen, *Falstaff* is a tragic and diamantine work, one of the crowning achievements of early modernism; and we cannot grasp Elgar's subtle interweaving of text and paratext without harnessing all these analytical approaches.

---

[49] On 'parenthesis' see William Kinderman, *Beethoven* (Oxford: Oxford University Press, 1995), esp. pp. 240–3 and 300–2; and for a late-nineteenth-century enhancement see Christopher Lewis, 'The mind's chronology: narrative times and harmonic disruption in post-Romantic music', in *The Second Practice of Nineteenth-Century Tonality*, ed. William Kinderman and Harald Krebs (Lincoln, NE: University of Nebraska Press, 1996), pp. 114–49. On the 'double-tonic complex' and 'associative' and 'directional tonality' see the bibliography in Chapter 1, n. 32; Kofi Agawu discusses 'extended tonality' in 'Extended tonality in Mahler and Strauss', in *Richard Strauss: New Perspectives on the Composer and His Work*, ed. Bryan Gilliam (Durham, NC: Duke University Press, 1992), pp. 55–75.

Despite my protean analytical approach to this work, the examination of 'associative tonality' in Section 4 will bind the rest together; for that musical device above all others makes direct, deliberate, and easily comprehensible links between text and paratext: it is, in short, Elgar's principal extramusical–semantic tool. In a recent article, Daniel Harrison suggests that the fruitfulness of the union between Hepokoski's structural deformations and Bailey-inspired duotonal readings of Romantic and early modernist music, which this chapter explores, might be explained by their shared and implicitly Heraclitean emphasis on 'impressions of emergence, organic growth, endless Becoming, and goal-directed movement'.[50] As the *Ereignis*, this same 'becoming' was also a central concern of the later philosophy of Martin Heidegger. Hepokoski seems to be aware of this, and as an epigraph to *Sibelius: Symphony No. 5* he has a quotation from the essay that is usually considered the start of Heidegger's philosophical 'turn', 'The Origin of the Work of Art'; he goes on to make passing reference to Heidegger's reflexions on art's way of 'bringing beings forth'.[51] In Chapter 6 I shall examine the relationships between sonata deformation theory, duotonalism, and Schenkerian analysis on the one hand and Heidegger's philosophy of being on the other; for the moment it is not my concern.

In the next section I shall provide a general overview of the form of this work, for which it will be useful to appropriate some of James Hepokoski's classifications. I do this partly because they provide useful tools for understanding the shape of *Falstaff*, and partly because they provide sure support for weighty interpretative conclusions.[52]

I have already introduced Hepokoski's concept of the sonata deformation in Chapter 1, and we can be sure that Elgar intended the sonata/multi-movement deformation in *Falstaff*, because he presents us explicitly with both interpretations. The score does not mark separate movements, and so we are presented ostensibly with a single movement; but Elgar's analytical note unequivocally breaks the work into four distinct sections, each of them audible in performance, and so outlines for us a multi-movement form.[53] This is called having one's cake and eating it.

---

[50] Daniel Harrison, 'Nonconformist notions of nineteenth-century enharmonicism', *Music Analysis* 21 (2002), p. 130.

[51] James A. Hepokoski, *Sibelius: Symphony No. 5* (Cambridge: Cambridge Univeristy Press, 1993), p. 27.

[52] Hepokoski's work on *Don Juan* shows especially well the interpretative potential of his structural observations.

[53] Elgar, 'analytical note', pp. 576ff.

Elgar's analytical note acts rather like *Henry V*'s Chorus, cajoling the informed audience to 'work, work your thoughts', and therein see a play between generic conventions and implications. We might not read his note, of course, but then Elgar would carp.[54] This is no game, nor even an intellectual conceit on Elgar's part. Without examining his play with conventions it is difficult to probe very deep into the 'meaning' of *Falstaff*; and since we may safely assume that if Elgar wrote a piece of high-art music 'about Falstaff' it was because he had something to say about it (or something else), and was not merely producing a kind of musical crib note for those who don't know the sub-plot of the history plays, we should be keen to uncover what his 'meaning' might be.

One last preparatory point before the analysis can begin is that as well as being a sonata deformation in dialogue with single- and multi-movement forms, *Falstaff* is also organized more locally on Hepokoski's 'rotational' model, also introduced in Chapter 1. How Elgar works with these complex forms will gradually become clear.

4.3. An overview of the form: deformation and rotation

I give a summary of the motivic associations in the work in Ex. 4.1: all are Elgar's, except the last (in square brackets), and I identify them with numbers for ease of reference. The list is not meant to be comprehensive, and there are some other thematic snippets at various points, but these are the principal motives to appear in more than one location; more localized ideas are given descriptive titles in quotation marks at the relevant points of Fig. 4.1. The reader may wish to read the following formal summary alongside the tabulated versions in Figs. 4.1 and 4.2, with reference to the associations summarized in the table of motives of Ex. 4.1.

Elgar's analytical note divides the work into four parts or 'movements', which I shall discuss under separate sub-headings.[55] The following analysis is intended only to clarify *Falstaff*'s basic structural procedures; the principal hermeneutic analysis comes in Chapter 6, but this survey of the form will reveal detailed connexions between text and specific paratextual references than Elgar had space for in his note. It is not enough merely to have a general idea of *Falstaff*'s Shakespearean resonances, and although

---

[54] Recall his comments on Tovey, above.

[55] Since my frequent references to specific associations and quotations in Elgar's analytical note are all contained within five pages of his short article, and can be found easily, individual references will not appear in this section.

Example 4.1. *Falstaff*, table of motives

Figure 4.1. *Falstaff,* outline of form

Structure	Motives	Notes	Shakespearean references
Exposition			
R1 (start–20:16)	1–2–1–3–1–4 ⎱	Pᵃ: *Falstaff complex*	*1 Henry IV*, I. ii.
(introductory rotation)	2–1–3/1–4–1 ⎰		
Development	5–6–7–8–9 (x2)	Pᵇ: *Eastcheap complex*	
	10	Sᵃ: 'Arthur song'	*2 Henry IV*, II. iv.
R2 (21:1–29:4)	5–6/1/4	Pᵃ/ᵇ	
(tavern rotation)	5–6–7–9′–8		
	11–10/11–10/6	Sᵇ: 'colossal mendacity'	
R3 (29:5–49:1)	5–6–7–8	Pᵇ	
(robbery rotation)	12	⎫	*1 Henry IV*, II. ii.
	'calls'–4–3′–'struggle'– ⎬	Sᶜ: Gad's Hill	
	11–11–10 ⎭		
R4 (49:2–75:8)	5–6–5′–5–6	Pᵇ	*1 Henry IV*, II. iv.
(revelry rotation)	12–10–12	Sᶜ: Gad's Hill (mendacious)	ll. 110–279
	scherzo: 9/4–'lyrical 9') ⎫		ll. 371–498
	trio: 11–8–'sleep 1' ⎬	Sᵈ: 'Falstaff is Monarch'	
	scherzo: 9		
	coda: 11–1–'sleep 2'–1 ⎭		
Dream interlude (76:1–80:7)		Iᵃ	*1 Henry IV*, III. iii.
Recapitulation			
R5 (81:1–113:8)	*sub1:* 2–1′–13–4/9–1′	Pᵃ/ᵇ	*1 Henry IV*, IV. ii.
(battle rotation)	*A:* (13–)14–15 ⎫	Sᵉ: Gaultree	*1 Henry IV*, V. iii.–iv.
	B: 1–'battle'–5–'battle'–5 ⎬		(& *2 Henry IV*, IV. iii.)
	A′: 14–15–14–'lyrical 14' ⎭		
[*parenthesis*]	12/'transition'	Transition	
second interlude	16	Iᵇ	*2 Henry IV*, III. ii.
Fifth rotation (cont.)	*sub2:* 7–3–11–15–14	Pᵃ + Sᵉ	*2 Henry IV*, V. iii.
Coda			
R6 (114:1–130:21)	17–18/1–17/19	Sᴾ: the new king's progress	*2 Henry IV*, V. v.
(Henry V rotation)	3′/4–3–19–1	Pᵈⁱˢ.	
R7 (131:1–end)	17–4–17–11–4–13–19–17	Sᴾ: repudiation	
(repudiation rotation)	5–6–7–1–5–1–5–4	Pᵃ/ᵇ	*Henry V*, II. i.
	16–9–16	Pᵇ + Iᵇ: death	
	3–1–'death'–17–'death chord'	Pᵃ + Sᴾ: 'stern reality'	*Henry V*, II. iii.

Figure 4.2. *Falstaff,* summary of rotational sonata form

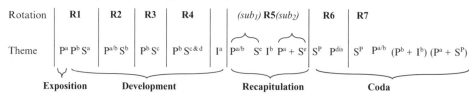

simply spotting allusions is not the primary purpose of this chapter, it is a preliminary requirement. This section is a prop for the two that follow, and its relative comprehensiveness now will obviate the need for further detailed commentary then.

(a) Falstaff and King Henry

The first section corresponds roughly to *1 Henry IV*, Act I Scene ii, in which Falstaff and Hal first appear. It is expository, and consists of a complex of primary themes I call the 'Falstaff complex' in the formal outline of Fig. 4.1; they are boxed together in Ex. 4.1.[56] In this initial presentation the 'P^a' material contains one theme Elgar associated with Hal, but his place at Falstaff's side is later taken by the 'honest gentlewomen'; Falstaff is the focal point of the complex, and so the always slightly inaccurate appellation will do. I shall discuss tonal features of individual themes closely in Section 4, but for the time being it will be sufficient to say that the exposition with its varied repetition gives the first statement of the principal tonal areas of the work: C minor, E♭, and E minor. Falstaff's first theme (motive 1) is a mixture of G major and minor, with a B♭ in its third bar and a suggestive a♯–b♮ in its fourth, which has the higher register to itself; upon its reharmonization the modal mixture is made more apparent (3:4), and minor and major are juxtaposed: we might wonder whether the tune has its own key, possibly G minor, or if it is to function as dominant of C, which the placing of $V_{♭3}^5$/C on the upbeat to the second half of the tune at 3:5 seems to suggest.[57]

The 'witty' Falstaff theme (motive 2), first given at 1:3, in the same moment confirms and thwarts C minor. As shown in Ex. 4.2, the chief melodic g of motive 1 descends through a registral displacement to f^2 at 1:3, while the theme's skittish runs and angular leaps prolong V/C through a hint of B♭ major at 1:7, thereby confirming the dominant implication of the terminal note of Falstaff's initial theme. Once again, though, Elgar mixes G minor and major in the middleground, and gives gentle dominant support to the unfolded B♭, which is soon to be V/E♭. The work's first 'C minor' chord (which has a seventh) then arrives at 2:2, completing a $\hat{5}_V$–$\hat{4}_V$–$\hat{3}_I$ contrapuntal composing-out of the C minor triad

---

[56] In Figs. 4.1 and 4.2 I use references of the form 'P^a' to refer to primary materials, 'S^a' to secondary, and 'I^a' for 'interlude' material. ('S^P' and 'P$^{dis.}$' are special cases, respectively indicating secondary materials that have taken on a primary function, and the disintegrating form of the primary materials, both in the coda space.) Rotations are indicated in the form 'R1' and attendant sub-rotations in the form 'sub1'.

[57] It is likely that on a second or subsequent hearing of the work, a listener will hear the tune of motive 1 as V/c because of its harmonization at 119:12–16 in the coda.

Example 4.2. *Falstaff*, foreground sketch to figure 8

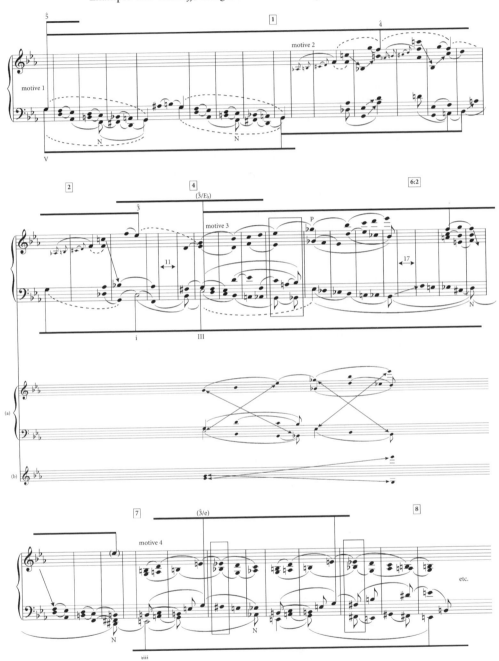

through the first seventeen bars of the piece; but it is already vi^7/E♭, and a graceful ii–V$^{\sharp 5}$–I progression from 2:3 to 4:1 establishes that key.[58]

Elgar carries this modal mixture into Hal's 'courtly and genial' theme (motive 3: *cantabile*, not *Nobilmente*), slightly complicating a mostly diatonic E♭ major with a minor-mode inflexion in the second half of the phrase.[59] The theme is repeated, and its twenty-eight bars constitute almost half of the music so far. Falstaff has more themes, and a subtler harmonic and rhythmic character, but Hal is the centre of attention, the sun to Falstaff's moon. It is perhaps emblematic that both themes are based on a descending scale – Falstaff's G–G$_1$; Hal's (in the bass) E♭–G♮$_1$/G♭$_1$ – but that only Hal's is melodically and tonally strong.

After a sniff of motive 1 (6:5–7:1) a new tune representing a 'cajoling and persuasive' Falstaff (motive 4) is given on E minor. Here, Elgar writes, is the Falstaff who teases the young prince: 'sweet wag, when thou art king' (Falstaff believes Hal will not punish his roguish companions). Again the tune is not straightforwardly 'in' E minor – it has a significant lurch to E♭ – but I shall forgo detailed comment on this matter until Section 4. A reorganized repeat knits the themes together, with the counterpoint between Falstaff's motive 1 and Hal's motive 3 (12:1–13:8) displaying their compatibility. The exposition comes to a close, conventionally, on the dominant.

(b) Eastcheap – Gad's Hill – The Boar's Head, revelry, and sleep

The repeated 'Falstaff complex', rich in thematic content and with a clearly differentiated, because *cantabile*, 'second subject' in Hal's theme, creates the impression on first hearing of a closed formal unit, which emphatic closing gestures affirm (16:1ff.); but Elgar's rhetoric at the start of the next section is decidedly ambiguous. The dominant arrival with its emphatic fermata a bar before figure 17, and the motivic fragmentation in the

---

[58] The 'co-prolongation' of C minor and E♭ in the opening bars has a distinct narratological purpose, which I shall explain in Section 4.

[59] Surface-level mixture of the kind and complexity evinced by the opening pages of *Falstaff* is rare in Elgar, despite being fairly common in music after *Tristan*. For a discussion of its roots see Robert Bailey, 'An analytical study of the sketches and drafts', in *Richard Wagner, Prelude and Transfiguration from 'Tristan and Isolde'* (New York and London: Norton, 1985), p. 116; and for a brief but pertinent analysis of Mahlerian modal mixture, see Kofi Agawu, 'Prolonged counterpoint in Mahler', in *Mahler Studies*, ed. Stephen E. Hefling (Cambridge: Cambridge University Press, 1997), pp. 217–47.

ensuing bars seem to promise rigorous working-out:[60] classic signs of the
beginning of the development space. Yet the motives here are new and
coquettish, and their rakish but perhaps feminine gendering may imply a
second complex of exposition themes on the model of the 'gendered two-
block exposition' typified by the overture to *The Flying Dutchman*.[61]

Is this the beginning of a development or a continuation of the
exposition? I believe it is the former, but there is support in both text
and paratext(s) to come down with reasonable confidence in favour of the
latter. If the first exposition established Falstaff in relation to Prince Hal,
then this putative new one establishes him in the context of the Boar's
Head at Eastcheap, which is populated by bawdy men and 'honest gentlewomen': 'the Tavern where Falstaff is monarch' (figuratively, but more
palpably in *1 Henry IV*, Act II Scene iv). It presents a second side to his
character, which is a function entirely appropriate to a sonata's second

---

[60] The key, too, seems indicative of development. The exposition's bass arpeggiates i–III–
$\natural$iii–V (Ex. 4.3), and the beginning of the second part, which is in B♭ minor, prolongs
the dominant in a fashion similar to that at 1:1–6, where B♭ is reached by a third-
progression in the bass (Ex. 4.2). The development space, on this view, would therefore
open with a prolongation of the dominant, which is entirely orthodox.

[61] On this paradigm see James A. Hepokoski, 'Beethoven reception: the symphonic
tradition', in *The Cambridge History of Nineteenth-Century Music*, ed. Jim Samson
(Cambridge: Cambridge University Press, 2001), pp. 448–50. *Falstaff* does not idealize
the feminine, as in the classic gendered exposition model, but barmaids and prostitutes
are still women. Elgar's Elizabethan female paradigm is similar to Dowden's: 'Woman
was [for the Elizabethans] neither a satanic bait to catch the soul of man, nor was she the
supernatural object of medieval chivalric devotion; she was no miracle, yet not less nor
other than that endlessly interesting thing – woman' (Dowden, *Shakspere*, p. 14). Indeed,
Elgar's exploration of the 'feminine' in music is often rather progressive, despite his
political opinions. One thinks of the louche and self-assertive parallel fifths in Mary
Magdalene's music in *The Apostles* (75:1ff.), and of his feminization of the masculine in
Gerontius, where Newman's male angel (of whom Elgar still has The Soul sing 'I will
address him') is sung by an alto and draws The Soul indulgently into the feminine
spiritual 'homoeroticism' of their Part II dialogue (especially 26:1–28:7). Byron Adams
explores Elgar's music in the context of homoerotic pre-Raphaelite art and late-
nineteenth-century decadence in 'Elgar's later oratorios: Roman Catholicism, decadence
and the Wagnerian dialectic of shame and grace', in *The Cambridge Companion to Elgar*,
ed. Daniel M. Grimley and Julian Rushton (Cambridge: Cambridge University Press,
2004), pp. 81–105 and related issues in 'The "dark saying" of the Enigma: homoeroticism
and the Elgarian paradox', *Nineteenth-Century Music* 23 (2000), pp. 218–35. My
interpretation of the Eastcheap music places me directly at odds with Michael Kennedy,
who claims that Falstaff 'is more likely to idealize the women in the Boar's Head than
pinch their bottoms' (Kennedy, *Portrait of Elgar*, 3rd edn (Oxford: Clarendon Press,
1987) p. 257). If two-bar, tonally fickle musical snippets are not flirtatious, I cannot
imagine what might be.

group of themes. Nevertheless, Elgar's analytical note places the beginning of the 'second movement' at figure 17, and the fermata in the preceding bar cannot be disregarded, since from the first hearing of the work an audience is likely to hear a conspicuous formal disjunction in it. But there is yet another possible interpretation. We might consider the beginning of the Eastcheap section as a counter-exposition within the developmental space of a sonata deformation, which in itself would not be novel. The practice of opening a development section with new material was common enough (albeit unusual) even in the eighteenth century.[62]

What are we to think? Elgar's play here with generic expectations and the implications of his own rhetoric is very witty, but need not be baffling. My own view is that the 'Eastcheap complex' of themes, 'P^{bb}' in Fig. 4.1, continues the expository function begun by the 'Falstaff complex', as the second part of an initial 'rotation' that reaches over into the development space. Elgar's analytical subdivision of the work and the caesura on the dominant at figure 17 are compelling reasons to accept that hypothesis. The entire passage up to the end of Falstaff's 'Arthur song' (20:16) constitutes an initial expository rotation, whose radically different but still primary thematic materials[63] both straddle the boundaries of sonata form and insinuate towards the gendered two-block exposition.

Usually in a rotational structure, primary and secondary materials and perhaps also introductory or closing materials tend to be cycled several times in more or less the same order. These cycles may or may not coincide with classic formal divisions such as exposition, development, recapitulation, and coda. An unusual characteristic of *Falstaff* is that it has no fixed secondary materials. It is, naturally, central to the purpose of the work that the primary materials will be Falstaffian, while the secondary materials will differ depending on the pictorial purpose of the rotation, but the malleability of its material is still unusual.

We find in *Falstaff* that although the primary materials return at the start of each rotation, changes to the secondary materials provided in each case mean that each rotation also contains interpolation from outside; each rotation contains, in essence, a mini-'breakthrough', which realigns the sights, and changes the course of what follows. That is of course true to life, where unexpected things, which tend to be small and unremarkable for most people, constantly guide us in unexpected new directions; but it

---

[62] See Charles Rosen, *Sonata Forms*, rev. edn. (New York: Norton, 1988), pp. 263 and 274–5.

[63] My analysis of the rest of the work will demonstrate that these 'second exposition' materials are primary, not secondary, in function in some later parts of the work.

has a curious musical effect. In his review of the premiere in the *Daily Telegraph*, Robin Legge scratched his head about the extensive use of what I call secondary materials: 'I have not yet fathomed the (to me) mystery as to why what I believe is called in theatrical language the "fat" of the music is applied to other folk and their doings, or to description, and not to the protagonist himself.'[64]

There are seven rotations in *Falstaff*, which together flesh out the sonata deformation. Without exception, each rotation is begun with a varied restatement of primary thematic materials, i.e. either the 'Falstaff' or the 'Eastcheap complex' or a combination of the two. Elgar uses these expositional complexes as referential points in the structure, to clarify the musical argument and jointly endorse and oppose the listener's developing sense of sonata-deformation processes.

In the analytical note he insisted we must read, Elgar carefully makes semantic links between each textual *signifiant* and its paratextual/'meta-paratextual' *signifié*, and his rotational form allows him to present unique pictorial effects like the Gad's Hill robbery in significant referential configurations. This kaleidoscopic arrangement of primary and secondary themes into malleable, interpenetrating complexes allows Elgar to give the material a 'twist' at the start of each rotation, which could not be so easily and comprehensibly achieved with longer-breathed material. A single theme would sound awkward if its bars were even slightly reshuffled, but a complex of themes makes possible a drastic reshuffle or abridgement while still maintaining a clear referential relationship to the first presentation of the themes. This kaleidoscopic rotational phenomenon is not so very different, to take a simple example, from the way we understand the identity of an orchestra. Even though one of the players may sit in different positions from time to time, or be replaced by deputies or even by a new full member when his or her period of usefulness is over, still the identity of the orchestra is recognizable. It may be possible to speculate philosophically about the exact nature of 'the orchestra', but to common sense it poses no difficulty; and this is exactly the case with Elgar's thematic complexes in *Falstaff*. Although the complexes change, we still recognize their underlying musical 'prosopon' (i.e. outward appearance); the 'orchestra' is always identifiable, despite its evolution.[65]

[64] Kennedy, *Portrait*, p. 256.

[65] Elgar's practice here may be derived from the Classical 'synecdochic strategy' (already invoked briefly in Chapter 3), whereby 'references to the presence of a whole (usually, a whole expositional section) through a partial articulation or representation of one or more of its parts' in a post-expositional space of a sonata form allows for abbreviated

In short, the Elgarian rotational form, as seen in *Falstaff*, can be used to forge multivalent semantic constructs out of material that might otherwise have only the very simplest narrative associations, while still leaving the identity of his primary and secondary material, which is introduced in referential configurations before being re-shuffled – beyond question. The possibility of intertextual play with his listeners' expectations of a sonata-form movement frees Elgar to draw in, transform, and in so doing thematicize the whole tradition of sonata composition, with its inherited legacy of extramusical 'meaning', and deal musically not only with Falstaff's character and existential development, but with still greater issues of musical and human importance. I shall come to these in Chapter 6.

The development space initiated at figure 17 takes up part of R1 and the whole of the three following rotations; it ends with the Dream Interlude (76:1–80:7), which stands as a parenthetical enclosure in the work, and was added at a late stage.[66] The 'tavern rotation' (R2, 21:1–29:4) is the shortest of the work. Its brevity is perhaps explained by the 'double function' of the music from figures 17 to 21. The development begins, as we have seen, with a lengthy continuation of exposition materials, and the second rotation has to pick up the expected developmental work of the section quickly, before the reek of the tavern either overwhelms or simply palls on the listener. Nevertheless it follows the practice of the other rotations, by providing its own secondary material (25:2–28:1), a theme for Falstaff's 'colossal mendacity': I designate this as motive 11 in Fig. 4.1.

There is no single Shakespearean source for the beginning of the development (R2 and the end of R1). The scene is the Boar's Head, but Elgar's note is perhaps intentionally noncommittal; his Dowden quotation (see Ex. 4.1, motives 5–8) could point to any Eastcheap scene. But Elgar equates motive 10, the first secondary material – a substantial theme, almost exactly the same length as Prince Hal's in R1, with 'the Falstaff who sings, "When Arthur first in court"'.[67] (I shall say more on the tonality and associations of this 'Arthur song' in Section 4.) Elgar's contrapuntal

recall of musical materials which do not muddy the rhetoric of restatement. (See James A. Hepokoski, 'Beyond the sonata principle', *Journal of the American Musicological Society* 55 (2002), p. 130, n. 57). Elgar's practice is, however, significantly more complex than the examples in Hepokoski's essay.

[66] See n. 82, and the discussion in Chapter 6.

[67] In a letter to Robert Lorenz of 8. xi. 1913, a month after the premiere, he wrote that the theme was composed 'to fit Falstaff's "When Arthur first to court [did come] / And was a worthy king . . ."': Moore, *Creative Life*, p. 647. Falstaff is of course garbling the song, but Elgar's words fit as well to the original as to his own version, i.e. not very well:

interweaving of thematic complexes 'P^a' and 'P^b' (21:3–22:4) establishes Sir John's place in the tavern among the 'honest gentlewomen'; and with motive 11, Elgar's sketch of the protagonist is complete: he is both friend to Hal and bawdy wit of the taverns. The dramatic action can now begin.

The 'robbery rotation' (R3, 29:5–49:1) describes the double robbery on Gad's Hill, with Falstaff's ambush of Gadshill and Hal's of Falstaff being compressed into the same eight bars (43:1–44:1). Falstaff's role during the Gad's Hill robbery is to goad the prince,[68] to boast of his thieving abilities,[69] and, principally, to be a fat and easy target for abuse: hence the appearance of his cajoling and boastful themes (motives 4 and 11) in the secondary material 'S^c' on Gad's Hill (32:1–49:1). Hal's disguise, meanwhile, is presented as an obfuscated version of his theme, motive 3' (41:1–42:8). Since these 'Falstaff complex' themes must feature heavily during the robbery for narrative reasons, it would be have been a mistake to include them in the primary complex of the rotation; as it is, R3 has 'P^b' in its original form, but without motive 9 (see below). The thieves had agreed to meet at Eastcheap before the robbery, and although Shakespeare does not present this meeting, Elgar tidily prefaces the robbery with a suggestion of it (29:5–30:2), to establish this scene's continuity with the redolent music which precedes it.

The 'dozen or fourteen honest gentlewomen' indicated by motive 9 were appropriately shorn from 'P^b' in R3 (they play no part in the robbery), but they feature heavily in the 'revelry rotation', R4, when Falstaff recounts his version of the robbery to them. Again Falstaff's various motives will be required in the narrative secondary space, so the 'Eastcheap complex' is given only in a sketchy form, and without Falstaffian motives (49:2–50:13). All that Elgar must communicate programmatically is the return to the Boar's Head. The primary materials are now sufficiently familiar that musical punctuation can be achieved by the merest suggestion of the complex: we will still recognize their face; and fragmentation of primary materials is in any case expected in the development space of a sonata, even one whose developmental processes are largely driven by characterization. Elgar's rhetoric is apposite and concise.

'When Arthur first in court began
And was approved king
By force of arms great victories won,
And conquest home did bring . . .'
('Sir Lancelot du Lake', in *English and Scottish Ballads*, ed. Francis James Child
(London: Sampson Low, 1861), vol. I, p. 55.)

[68] 'Hang thyself in thine own heir-apparent garters!', *1 Henry IV*, II. ii. 42.
[69] 'I am not John of Gaunt your grandfather, / but yet no coward, Hal', ll. 64–5.

In the secondary thematic space of the 'revelry rotation', Falstaff gives his disingenuous account of the robbery[70] with a recall of the Gad's Hill tune (motive 12, 51:1ff.). His painting of the picture *ff*, when we know it was *ppp* (cf. 32:11ff. and 51:1ff.), makes one think of his hyperbolically spiralling count of his assailants.[71] The prince, however, bursts his bubble[72] and Falstaff quickly reduces his bid to *pp* (53:1–6) before turning his attention immediately to the 'honest gentlewomen'.[73] For them he reserves his most boastful and mendacious countenance in an extra portion of secondary material (54:1–75:8), as Falstaff and Hal act out the coming confrontation between the King and his son.[74] In his note, Elgar draws attention to the form of this role-play episode, which is a self-contained scherzo and trio with a coda:[75]

Scherzo (motive 9)	54:1–62:1
Trio (motive 11)	62:1–67:12
Scherzo (motive 9′)	68:1–71:4
Coda (motives 11 and 1)	71:5–75:8

This episode is formally interesting, because its self-contained form is strongly suggestive of a 'movement within a movement'. Viewed from a purely musical position, the episode comes late in the relatively gigantic development space of a sonata deformation: the development has so far lasted around thirteen and a half minutes, over against the three minutes of the exposition. As such, the scherzo episode is a little troubling; but its paratextual context is instructive. *1 Henry IV*, Act II Scene iv is given over largely to Falstaff's and Hal's role-play in the Boar's Head. There, Shakespeare's modestly disorientating shift of intention – he requires the audience to be aware that characters are acting something, but still 'believe' that the characters themselves are 'real', i.e. he switches between first- and second-order mimesis – finds a parallel in Elgar's modest equivocation in this passage. It is not quite a scherzo and trio, since it clearly springs from one episode and runs into another, without fully establishing itself as an individual movement: yet we are still invited to recognize its generic feints.

---

[70] *1 Henry IV*, II. iv. 110–279.

[71] ll. 172–215.

[72] ll. 220–72.

[73] ll. 272ff.

[74] ll. 371–498.

[75] Daniel Grimley has also identified this structural gesture in a paper which did much to help me clarify my own thoughts on the work, '"Falstaff (tragedy)": narrative and retrospection in Elgar's symphonic study'. This unpublished paper was delivered at the Elgar Conference at the University of Surrey in 2002.

The point is, I think, that Elgar is not attempting to confuse the shape of
the whole, but is playing with the listener's expectations of a modernist
sonata deformation without putting coherence seriously to the test. His
technique mimics Shakespeare's – and Wagner's, too, for the technique of
switching between highly or lowly structured units, changing the implications of each as the dramatic moment demands, is one of the most striking
fingerprints of his style.[76]

The insertion of episodes into the developmental space was in any case a
common practice in the late nineteenth century,[77] and Elgar had used it
earlier in the overtures *Cockaigne*, Op. 40, and *In the South*, Op. 50 (to
adduce only single-movement works).[78] He even defined it, saying that
Op. 50 'follows generally the overture form: new matter (the Roman
section & the Shepherd's song[)] being introduced in the working out
section'.[79] This Falstaffian scherzo episode is best heard as an 'episode
within an episode'; but it has other implications too, such as the reasonable expectation of a scherzo before a slow movement: cf. Elgar's First
Symphony. (And the slow-moving – slow-movement? – Dream Interlude
adds credence to this fleeting expectation.) Yet as in Shakespeare, here the
listener is not required to suspend all of his or her disbelief, viz. that the
whole succession of musical details can be identified with the single-
movement work called *Falstaff*, but only part of it.

Elgar's treatment of developmental episodes in *Falstaff* closely follows
the model of *In the South*, and the Dream Interlude in *Falstaff* plays a
similar role to the 'canto popolare' in that work.[80] The development space

---

[76] See Anthony Newcomb, 'The birth of music out of the spirit of drama: an essay in
   Wagnerian formal analysis', *Nineteenth-Century Music* 5 (1981), pp. 38–66.

[77] See Hepokoski, 'Beethoven reception', p. 451. He notes there that such episodes often
   lead to a 'breakthrough' near the end of the development space, which changes the
   predetermined course of the recapitulation. We shall shortly see that although the Dream
   Interlude, the last of the developmental episodes, fulfils something of that function, its
   purely musical significance, if by that we mean motivic impact on the finale (cf. the
   Heldenthema in *Don Juan*), is negligible. For that reason, I shall not call it a
   'breakthrough' in the Hepokoskian/Adornian sense.

[78] Michael Kennedy compares *Falstaff*'s two interludes with *In the South*'s two
   developmental episodes (*Portrait*, p. 258), but they are not the same thing; it is the
   narrative episodes in *Falstaff*'s development which are really comparable.

[79] Robert Anderson, *Elgar* (London: Dent, 1993), p. 308.

[80] *In the South*, 34:1–39:20. The 'canto popolare' begins and ends with a melodic g tied over
   the bar-line, which begins as $\hat{5}$/C (the key of the shepherd's song) but is later $\hat{3}$/E♭, the
   work's tonic. The one notable difference between these two episodes is that the 'canto
   popolare' develops the primary material of the work (cellos and violas, 37:5–38:8),
   whereas the Dream Interlude does not. Development, in *Falstaff*, is driven more by
   narrative than is the case in the earlier overture.

in *Falstaff* therefore contains three episodes: the Gad's Hill robbery in R3, the Boar's Head 'revelry' in R4, and the Dream Interlude between R4 and R5.

It is notable that each of the developmental episodes throws our attention off Falstaff onto Prince Hal, just as the episodes in Strauss's *Don Juan*, while having the protagonist always somewhere near the centre, successively spotlight his unidentified mistresses.[81] In the first developmental episode in R3, Hal steals from Falstaff after the first robbery on Gad's Hill; in R4, Hal steals from Falstaff again, this time while the knight sleeps behind the arras. In each of the subsequent rotations, as we shall see, our attention is thrown from Falstaff, who opens each rotation with a localized and narratively apposite form of his identifying thematic prosopon, to Hal, whose participation in each of the secondary thematic areas pits him in one way or another against Falstaff. Elgar's structural rotations are also his, and Shakespeare's, narrative rotations; they act as hermeneutic circles in which he ruminates on the same material over again, using each set of fresh discoveries to begin each re-cycle from a more informed angle. I shall show in Section 4 that the work opens with a basic and potentially devastating tension between the knight and the prince, and that from R3 to the concluding R7 this tension is amplified and re-cycled, with a cumulative effect that results in Hal's repudiation and Falstaff's death. Before the Dream Interlude, Hal's attacks on Falstaff seem to the knight, and perhaps also to the prince, entirely playful: whatever money is stolen from him is paid back, and the high priest of wit, who recognizes he is the cause of wit in others, laughingly accepts that the joke is on him. Yet each of these episodes, both musically and dramatically, contributes to his ultimate unravelling. After the Dream Interlude there is no doubt as to the prince's intentions: at his next appearance he will reject Falstaff, and by breaking his heart will kill him. It is a crucial transition.

Despite its intriguing and critical function in the work, it will come as no surprise to anyone familiar with Elgar's working methods to learn that the Dream Interlude (76:1–80:7) was an afterthought.[82] The conclusion of the *Variations*, the second subject of the First Symphony's finale,

---

[81] See Hepokoski, 'Fiery-pulsed libertine', *passim*.

[82] 'The first [interlude] . . . is not mentioned in the plans and there is sufficient evidence in the sketches to support the conclusion that it was not part of the original scheme of the work' (Christopher Kent, '*Falstaff*: Elgar's symphonic study', in *Edward Elgar: Music and Literature*, ed. Raymond Monk (Aldershot: Scolar, 1993), in *Edward Elgar: Music and Literature*, ed. Raymond Monk (Aldershort: Scolar, 1993), pp. 83–107 at p. 84).

and even the astonishing vision of God in *Gerontius* were all last-minute insertions, two of which were owed to the insistence of August Jaeger. It represents a narrative turning-point; from this point Falstaff's love for Hal is never reciprocated again.

(c) Falstaff's march – the return through Gloucestershire – the new King – the hurried ride to London

The air of recapitulation immediately after the Dream Interlude, with the re-appearance of the original 'Falstaff complex' and the tonic C minor (81:1ff.), is tangible. The development had begun each rotation with East-cheap material, but now we return to the Falstaff we were first presented with: except he is now without Hal, and with his main theme, now filled in with scales, motive 1' (82:5–9 etc.), sounding more ridiculous than ever.

The narrative at this point becomes confused. Elgar jumps from the mustering of the 'scarecrow army' (*1 Henry IV*, Act IV Scene ii) and the battle of Shrewsbury (*1 Henry IV*, Act V Scenes iii–iv) to the ride through Gloucestershire to Shallow's house and orchard (*2 Henry IV*, Act IV Scene iii, and Act V Scene i). The 'scarecrow army' is characterized vividly enough by motive 14, with which Elgar associated them, but in Shakespeare's narrative, Prince Hal joins Falstaff on the Coventry road, to inspect and disdain them.[83]

Why is the prince's identifying motive 3 absent from the 'Falstaff complex' at the beginning of R5? I think the answer is critically important. After the Dream Interlude, Hal and Falstaff are not friends in Elgar's study. The knight still daydreams of continued happiness by the prince's side, but there is no confusion for Hal: Falstaff must be shaken off. In this Elgarian context, the King's words before the battle, 'How bloodily the sun begins to peer / Above yon bulky hill!'[84] take on a new significance. Hal/Henry V is consistently associated with the sun, as is his right as a prince and king,[85] while he describes Falstaff as a 'huge hill of flesh'.[86] The royal sun that rises to wake that mountainous Falstaff from his overoptimistic slumber will deal a fatally bloody blow in the next structural rotation. His calculated absence at the beginning of the recapitulation therefore enables Elgar to show his return from two revealing perspectives: first,

---

[83] *1 Henry IV*, IV. ii. 49–75.

[84] *1 Henry IV*, V. i. 1–2.

[85] See, for instance, *1 Henry IV*, I. ii. 192; II. iv. 402–9; III. ii. 79; IV. i. 102; and *Henry V*, IV. 0. 43.

[86] *1 Henry IV*, II. iv. 239.

when Pistol announces his accession (108:1ff.),[87] he is seen with Falstaff's rose tint; second, when Falstaff meets and is rejected by him (127:1ff.), his true colour is revealed.

Falstaff's march to Shrewsbury and the battle there form a ternary structure like the 'role-play episode' in R4:

A   85:6–88:10
B   89:1–95:8
A′   95:9–99:4

But the return of the 'scarecrow army' and Falstaff's march (95:9ff.) does not have the sense of closure the 'scherzo and trio' of R4 had: there the music had come to rest on G major – a dominant to prepare the recapitulation, which the Dream Interlude forestalls – but here it runs immediately into a repeat of the 'ambling' Gad's Hill music (99:5) and the transition to the second interlude. Its function is, then, purely picturesque. The extensive use of the Eastcheap theme 5 during the battle is perhaps a suggestion of Falstaff's tangential involvement. Falstaff's feigned death in *1 Henry IV*, V. iv. would complicate Elgar's narrative here, and there is no suggestion of it in the music; the prince's theme is being saved.

The interlude in Shallow's orchard is in Shakespeare, but that too seems to have been a relatively late addition to Elgar's structural plan.[88] I shall say more on its structural presentation in Chapter 6, and note for the moment only that its purpose is simply to establish Elgar's leap from the first to the second *Henry IV* play, in which the second sub-rotation of R5 will pick up (see again Fig. 4.1).

The recapitulation's 'restart' (107:1) is just as assertive after the second interlude as it was after the first, with a forthright *ff* rush on violins banishing the pastoral ruminations of the previous bars. The primary thematic materials are picked up again, and combined with secondary materials to form the second sub-rotation. With Pistol's announcement, 'King Harry the Fifth's the man', Hal's long-awaited tune, motive 3, returns (108:1). This is of course the most important point of Shakespeare's narrative, as Prince Hal becomes King Henry V, and in purely musical terms this marks the one decisive 'breakthrough' in the work. The announcement, on an unexpected E major – Hal's tune, when undisguised, is usually in E♭ – makes abundantly clear what the Dream Interlude had first hinted at: the dynamic of their relationship has changed completely. It

---

[87] *2 Henry IV*, V. iii.
[88] See Kent, '*Falstaff*, p. 85.

brings about a 'recapitulatory failure' (in Hepokoski's terms), since the music fails now to return to C, and the work of resolving the various tonal tensions in the work is left as a challenge for the coda.[89] Falstaff, of course, still does not see that the new king will reject him. Believing 'the young king is sick for [him]',[90] he rides through the night to greet his beloved friend at Westminster. His scarecrow army, motive 14, goes with him on his march, motive 15 (see Fig. 4.1).

(d) King Henry V's progress – the repudiation of Falstaff, and his death

The new king's progress opens Elgar's final section (114:1). It is the first lengthy and straightforward presentation of the tonic C minor in the entire work; and after the 'failure' of the recapitulation space to establish that key the coda space seems to promise that all will be well. For a moment, Elgar invites the listener to share Falstaff's optimism. Yet this coda – or is it a 'counter-recapitulation'? – opens with *secondary* thematic material. As we have seen throughout the work, Elgar sketches the narrative of each structural rotation with a changing complex or prosopon of secondary materials. In the development space, robbery and revelry had their own self-contained episodes: this is, as I have already noted, a common developmental practice in the nineteenth century, and one that Elgar had already used in major orchestral works. The failed recapitulation followed the putatively triumphant return of the exposition's primary thematic complex, which had tried to re-establish the tonic, with secondary material for the Shrewsbury battle. In combination with the second interlude, there is almost continuity with the development space: the battle and the ride through Gloucestershire could form an 'episode' just as the revelry and sleep had done in R4. In that case, the clear recapitulatory signals of 81:1ff. might be reheard as a false recapitulation within the development; but the resumption of recapitulation at 107:1 gives the lie to that fleeting interpretation, and the recapitulatory failure engendered by Hal/Henry V's breakthrough on E major ten bars later leaves all the musical and narrative resolution for the coda space. Like Falstaff, we recognize the stunningly new revelation of Hal/Henry V on E major, and we hope for the best. We go with him, 'putting all affairs else in oblivion,

[89] In this outline I have deliberately kept specific tonal tensions out of the discussion, since it will make more sense to bring them into the analysis of Elgar's associative tonality, which follows soon in Section 4.

[90] *2 Henry IV*, V. iii. 131.

as if there were nothing else to be done but to see [King Henry V]'.[91] The coda must show whether we hope realistically.

Therefore, the illustrative 'secondary' materials that open the coda space have the function of laying out the answer to our question whether the King will greet Falstaff kindly; and in that important respect they take on a primary function. Tonally we are 'home', and the presentation of a new synthesis of all that has gone before in the piece is begun. A new Falstaff theme, which was actually one of the first to be written for the piece,[92] is introduced at the upbeat to 119:1. Elgar's analytical note draws no links between this and Shakespeare, but it may be plausibly associated with Falstaff's belief that the young king is sick for him (see Ex. 4.1). Yet when materials from the 'Falstaff complex' return (122:1ff.) they are gradually disintegrated; which is to say that the principal ingredient of the complex, Falstaff's motive 1, now takes a definite second place to the finally revealed Henry V motive 3.

The King's *Grandioso* entrance is the young man's apotheosis, but Falstaff's response, although heavily orchestrated, is drowned by rushing quavers on high strings and woodwind (127:1–130:21). Hal's brilliance obscures Falstaff's personal musical prosopon, and by switching the emphasis away from the knight in the thematic complex which defines him, in a sense Hal destroys Falstaff's identity. R6 thus ends the first half of the coda, pregnantly, on V/c. We had hoped, with Falstaff, for a kind acceptance while the King made his progress; when he finally arrives, his glory is blinding, and Falstaff's ability to assert his own personality is taken away: forgetting his own image, he suffers from a kind of musical prosopagnosia.[93] Everything is in the hands of Henry V, who has been handed the basic choice of Falstaff's main theme: to resolve V/c to the tonic or not.

Immediately in R7 Henry V rejects Falstaff with the famously brutal speech from Act V Scene v. Elgar's note says that after

> a brief parley [motives 17 and 4, 131:1–132:14] . . . Falstaff is inexorably
> swept aside by the King's brazen motto [motive 17, 133:1–3], and the last

---

[91] *2 Henry IV*, V. v. 25–6.

[92] See Anderson, *Elgar*, p. 347.

[93] Falstaff's only self-defence would have been the wit that defines his entire being, but the King quickly denies him even that, thus preventing him from putting his case the only way he could: 'Reply not to me with a fool-born jest': *2 Henry IV*, V. v. 55. Falstaff is, as Harold Bloom remarks, 'essentially in receipt of a death sentence' (*Invention of the Human*, p. 277).

pitiful attempt at cajolery [motives 11 and 4, 133:4–134:1] is rudely blasted by the furious fanfare [motive 13, 134:1–5]: 'How ill white hairs become a fool and jester – I banish thee on pain of death.' Immediately the royal march is resumed, and dies away [motives 19 and 17, 134:6–137:12]: the King has looked on his ancient friend for the last time.[94]

Again the formerly secondary materials take on a primary function in this rotation: Hal/Henry V's fulfilment becomes the focus, not Falstaff's. This perceptual shift springs immediately from the joyous but disturbing news of Hal's accession at the end of R5, but its roots are in the Dream Interlude and even (as we shall very shortly see) in the first bars of the piece. The quondam-primary but now effectively secondary materials, 'P$^{a/b}$' (see Ex. 4.2), portray 'the decay of the merry-hearted one'.[95] Babbling of green fields, Falstaff dies on a soft brass C major (141:1–146:10), before 'the King's stern theme is curtly thrown across the picture . . . and with one *pizzicato* chord the work ends; the man of stern reality has triumphed'.[96]

4.4. Associative tonality and the unpicking of identity

The preceding sketch revealed detailed narrative connexions between Shakespeare's plays and the musical themes of *Falstaff*. At the same time, some comments on significant musical gestures such as the E major breakthrough of Hal's accession pointed to more purely musical issues. Having satisfied Hepokoski's requirement that we regard the paratextual content as seriously as the textual one, which in the case of a narrative that pores so subtly and thoroughly through the paratext calls for a very lengthy discussion, we may now proceed to examine the work's 'purely musical details' with the benefit of knowing beforehand their precise relation to the paratext. This re-entry into the hermeneutic circle will also allow for a closer examination of Elgar's role as a minor Shakespearean critic in this (symphonic) study of the history plays.

Since my intention is to hold the now-uncovered paratextual *signifiés* in force during the analysis of their concomitant textual *signifiants*, I shall use as my chief analytical tool the examination of 'associative tonality' which has been a focus of recent writing on Wagner.[97] Through an impressively

---

[94] Elgar, 'analytical note', p. 579.
[95] Ibid.
[96] Ibid.
[97] See the bibliography in n. 49.

tight integration of musical and narrative unfolding, which hinges on his use of associative tonality, Elgar gives us a Falstaff who is 'more' than Shakespeare's, in the sense that Elgar brings his critical acuity to bear on the knight by 'foregrounding' certain elements of his character and of his relationship to and with Prince Hal. He goes some way, I think, to answering Bloom's question about the past history of their love for one another.

I have already noted that *Falstaff*'s exposition is in or on three keys, C minor, E♭, and E minor. Consistently throughout the piece, Elgar associates each of those keys with persons or themes. There are naturally passages on keys other than these three expository keys, but these three are always treated associatively, while the others are not. C minor is associated from the start with Falstaff himself: mellow, frank, gay, easy, corpulent, loose, unprincipled, luxurious; witty, and the cause of wit in others. E♭ is Hal's tonality: courtly and genial, and Falstaff's friend. Note the conventional closeness of C minor and E♭. E (major or minor) is the tonality of 'sweet wag, when thou art King', the announcement of Henry V's accession, and the King's stern military theme: it is associated with Kingship. These associations form the basis of Elgar's psychological narrative in *Falstaff*. I do not propose to discuss each instance of tonal association in the work, since in many cases C crops up simply because Falstaff is on hand, and there is no more to be said of it. But in the exposition, the interludes, the progress of the new king, and most remarkably in the concluding pages, these three tonal associations are used distinctly and importantly.

The exposition is rooted on a bass arpeggiation of a modally mixed C triad (see Ex. 4.3). The dominant of C is not strongly asserted till the end of the exposition (16:1ff.), where a bass B♮ unfolds down to the root of the dominant, G. Till then, the dominant's mode is always minor, and even the exposition repeat is not prepared by a dominant of any colour (9:1). Falstaff's motive 1 theme is in G minor, although a picaresque and prominent, because registrally unique, a♯–b♮ figure suggests something of its putative dominant function (0:4). Echoing Morgann's string of epithets noted above, Robert Anderson considers this mode-changing figure 'the most unprincipled bit of the theme', because its 'A sharp begins by sounding like a B flat'.[98] Perhaps it is unprincipled, but I think even more it is uncertain, or perhaps misguided. The theme is clearly in the minor, yet its key must be parsed as v/c, rather than i/g.

---

[98] Anderson, *Elgar*, p. 343.

Example 4.3. *Falstaff*, middleground sketch of exposition

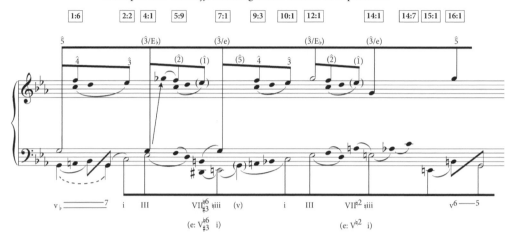

Ex. 4.2 shows a sketch of the first half of the exposition, in which the three associated keys are established. C minor is conceptually operative from the first note of the piece, if only because the piece is styled as a 'symphonic study in C minor'. It is prolonged first by a $\overset{\hat{5}}{v}-\overset{\hat{4}}{v}-\overset{\hat{3}}{I}$ unfolding, in which the tonic makes its rather casual first entry at 2:2, having been assiduously avoided in theme 1 (no subdominant there). Yet as I have already noted in Section 4.4, even from the moment of its first arrival C minor has already taken on the function of vi/E♭. The harmonic language is, in Dahlhaus's terms, both 'centrifugal' and 'centripetal'.[99] C is prolonged 'centripetally' by minor v in the opening theme and the middleground unfolding to $\overset{\hat{3}}{I}$, but 'centrifugal' forces simultaneously carry the harmony away from the centre; Elgar both satisfies and thwarts, confirms and denies.

Hal's thematic arrival (4:1) characterizes him quite brilliantly. As the boy on whom all Falstaff's hope is founded, his confident E♭ springs as a *required* relative major from Falstaff's unsteady tonic C minor, and their relationship as friends is quickly outlined, as is the dynamic of their friendship. But in its fourth bar Hal's theme is inflected by its own minor mode; I draw attention to the bar by boxing it in Ex. 4.2, for reasons that will be seen soon. The prince's ambivalence to Falstaff is immediately apparent, to us if not to the knight. Yet taken as a whole, the theme's

---

[99] See Carl Dahlhaus, 'Issues in composition', in *Between Romanticism and Modernism: Four Studies in the Music of the Late Nineteenth Century*, trans. Mary Whittall and Arnold Whittall (Berkeley, CA and London: University of California Press, 1980; orig. edn 1974), esp. pp. 74–5.

tonality is unproblematic for Falstaff: overall it prolongs 'friendly' E♭ major by means of a voice exchange between the outer voices (Ex. 4.2(b)). It is only in the details that there are problems: two chromatic voice exchanges prolonging a modally mixed E♭ (Ex. 4.2(a)). Falstaff, we take it, takes Hal as a whole, with all his faults, but we who hear the modal mixture are more suspicious.

The C minor prolongation of the first two Falstaff themes relies on a $\hat{5}$–$\hat{4}$–$\hat{3}$ descent (by means of a registral transfer) from the *Kopfton* g, and Hal's own music takes up and reinterprets this same melodic gesture (Ex. 4.3). Filling-in the first step of the descent with the self-concerned g♭^{1} already noted, Hal's form of the third-progression sounds in context like $\hat{3}$–$\hat{2}$–$\hat{1}$ in E♭; but the descent's contrapuntal support complicates the reading. The final e♭ is notated enharmonically as d♯, and functions as the root of V$^{\natural 6}_{\sharp 3}$/e (6:7). Falstaff's self-defining third-progression is, then, usurped by Hal's music, and taken over into the third key area, E minor. The meaning is clear. Hal denies Falstaff his right to self-individualization because it gets in the way of Hal's real concern: his own Kingship. First he 'steals' Falstaff's *Kopfton*, redefining it as $\hat{3}$/E♭ (originally it had been $\hat{5}$/c), then he takes over the C-minor-tonicizing third-descent, g–f–e♭. At the same time, the modal mixture in the smaller-scale voice-exchanges (Ex. 4.2(a)) asserts Hal's own individuality while the larger-scale exchanges (Ex. 4.2(b)) bewitch Falstaff into continued belief in his friend. Elgar's narrative method is as directly ingenuous as the Evangelist's first introduction of Judas Iscariot as 'the one who betrayed [Jesus]'.[100] There are no surprises in *Falstaff*; rather, we are made to watch the slow progress towards Sir John's inevitable destruction, and feel the pain of it more acutely because of our foreknowledge.[101]

The Kingship key, E minor, and its first associated theme, Falstaff's 'sweet wag, when thou art king' (motive 4), are no less interesting than the earlier music. The function of this initial thematic and tonal presentation is to show the interconnectedness of Hal and Kingship, thus separating out the Hal who appears to be Falstaff's friend from the young man whose mind is set on his own future, and who treats Falstaff's with utter contempt. The *Kopfton* is punned on again, now becoming $\hat{3}$/e, which is reached by arpeggiation up the local tonic triad (7:1–2). But in the third bar, a neighbouring g♭, written enharmonically as f♯ for convenience,[102]

---

[100] Matthew 10:4.

[101] My analysis here confirms and expands upon an insight of Tovey's: see n. 42.

[102] The cellists at this point would prefer the notated g–f♯–e–e♭ to the functional g–g♭–f♭–e♭.

suggests E♭ minor. I have boxed this third bar in Ex. 4.2, since it corresponds to the 'Hal-individualizing' E♭ minor chord already discussed (4:4). In fact this chromatic lower neighbour to the *Kopfton* g is central to Elgar's musical gesturing in the exposition. At 4:4 the chord rooted on G♭ asserts a Jungian 'shadow-Hal' to complement the 'persona-Hal' who poses as Falstaff's relative-major 'friend' in the preceding three and a half bars; now at 7:3 it reveals the insidious purposes of the shadow-Hal, viz. his own personal fulfilment, which is based on an inauthentic (because uncaring) Being-with Falstaff. In the 'sweet wag' tune, this shadow-Hal chord can be used to prolong both E♭ minor (7:3–4) and E minor (7:7–8); and Elgar thus inextricably binds the real Hal and his Kingship through the careful use of voice-leading and tonal-association patterns. There are, then, two basic tonal areas: one for Falstaff, a single tonic C, and one for Hal, a double-tonic complex, E♭/e. As long as the stress in Hal's complex falls on the C-minor-friendly key, E♭, Falstaff's identity is safe from harm.

The exposition repeat omits Falstaff's motive 1 tune, switching the emphasis more definitely onto Hal's theme (if, indeed, it was ever of secondary significance) and so the initial $\hat{5}$ for the third-descent is only implied by the switch from E minor to C minor (9:1). It follows the first statement by punning on the *Kopfton* and redefining the Falstaffian third-descent, but differs notably on the reappearance of Hal's motive 3, by omitting the 'uncaring' $g♭^2$ and claiming the high register as its own (12:1ff.). The prince thus stands out finally from the exposition as 'courtly and genial' as Elgar's analytical note suggests, and unspoilt by his shadow; he is totally dominant, but we might expect good things from him.

The friendship whose tragic consummation will form the narrative of the work is, in Bloom's sense, 'foregrounded' in the exposition. What hint does it give of Elgar's view of the roots of their friendship, which Shakespeare does not explain? The choice of the tertial relationship c/E♭ goes beyond mere formal expediency, I think. Elgar had already shown in the First Symphony that a clearly defined bass arpeggiation in the minor mode was not an essential part of his syntax,[103] and his choice to revert to such a conventional classical device in this work corresponds to a basic narrative intent. Composers after *Tristan* could treat the minor and major modes as different sides of the same coin,[104] and an exposition built, like the first movement of Mahler's Ninth Symphony, on an opposition of major and minor modes might be the obvious early modernist response to the narrative desideratum. Elgar does not here wish to suggest an

[103] See Chapter 2.
[104] See n. 59.

identification of Falstaff with Hal, but merely their close friendship, and the traditional 'friendship' between the tonic minor and its relative major could be well used here. Yet, as we have seen, from the start the traditional kinship of those keys is undermined: C minor runs nervously into E♭, and E♭ disparages C minor. What are we to make of this? I think it is reasonable to suppose that by alluding to the tradition of 'friendly' c/E♭ expositions Elgar summons up more than a century of texts – including, significantly, Beethoven's Fifth Symphony – that may have used the same form to say, unproblematically, 'Falstaff and Hal are inseparable friends', and distorts its meaning to say that they were once as close as Falstaff thinks they still are, but that owing to an essential feature of Hal's personality they are no longer. In short, the c/E♭ friendship-paradigm seems to assert that their friendship was once uncomplicated but is now (as from Hal's first entry) doomed. Elgar 'foregrounds' their complex friendship as Shakespeare reveals it in their first scene together, and infers from that presentation the roots of it, in an uncomplicated and potentially fulfilling pairing of C minor and E♭.

The end of R1, the exposition of the 'Eastcheap complex', prolongs the final dominant of the exposition by unfolding to B♭ minor, as a rising third progression G–A♮–B♭ had originally prolonged the dominant before the tonic's first arrival (1:1–7). But the 'feminine' themes are not followed here by a return to the tonic, which would be very curious so early in the development space, and instead run into the 'Arthur song' (19:1ff.). This theme, shown in Ex. 4.4, is more substantial than most of the material so far, but is tonally complex. Modes are mixed repeatedly, with the first four bars mixing D major and minor, and the rest mixing E major and minor (19:1–5 and 19:5–13 respectively). At first E-sonorities act as II or ii in D (19:3–4), but for the greater part of the theme, E is the tonal focus, with two sturdy ii–V–I/i^7 cadences to shore it up (19:8–13). As the words of the song confirm, this is another E/Kingship tonal association, which again hangs guilelessly on Falstaff's lips.

I noted at the beginning of this section that I would not comment on each instance of the tonal associations I have highlighted. Falstaff's appearances on C are easily found on Gad's Hill and in the Boar's Head. Gradually during R3–5, the mode of Falstaff's C tends more towards the major, so that when he falls asleep at the end of R5, the chord held at 75:5ff. is the dominant of C major, rather than minor. The Dream Interlude enters just before the recapitulation, after a very long development section with its two pictorial episodes and constantly changing secondary thematic materials. As such, it denies the listener the expected return of Falstaff and C, but in the most acceptable way. As E♭ was the relative

Example 4.4. *Falstaff*, Arthur song

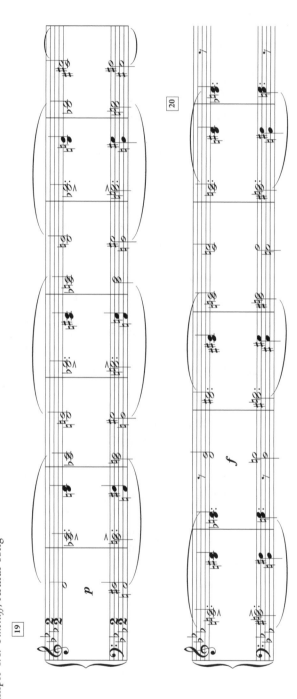

major of the opening C minor, so now A minor is the relative minor of the expected C major. But whereas the original relative had described the relationship between Falstaff and his outer reality, the Dream Interlude probes inwards, into Falstaff's subconscious. I shall discuss the implications of this in detail in Chapter 6 Section 2.

V/C is picked up again, prolonged dissonantly as in the exposition (cf. 1:2–6), to begin the recapitulation, and R5. As we saw above, Hal's motive 3 is omitted from the 'Falstaff complex' at the beginning of the recapitulation, and returns only after the interlude in Shallow's orchard, which recalls the A minor tonality and mood of the Dream Interlude. Once again, Shallow is the Shakespearean source, but Falstaff's subconscious is the Elgarian focus. Yet here Falstaff is awake, and his subconscious imaginings are brought up against the hard realities of his present situation, his relationship with the expectant king. Consequently the Shallow music pairs an interrupted cadence in C major with one in E♭, resolving them ultimately to A minor (see Ex. 4.5). Hence keys associated with Falstaff, Hal, and Falstaff's optimistic subconscious, i.e. A minor, the relative to his tonic major, are brought into uncomfortable alignment. Once again the tertial relationship between Falstaff and Hal is essential to the fabric of the theme; but neither of their keys is straightforwardly asserted, and E♭ now rubs chromatically against Falstaff's increasingly hopeful C major. Harmonies are awash with added sixths but are otherwise clear and functional. The full significance of this theme will only become apparent at the point of Falstaff's death, and I shall return to it then.

R5 resumes after the second interlude, beginning a second sub-rotation of primary and secondary materials (P^a and S^e; 107:1–113:8). This is the moment where Pistol announces Henry V's accession, with Hal's theme appearing on a kingly E major. It is the work's 'breakthrough'; from this point on, the tertial relationship between Falstaff and Hal, which had bound them together through most of the work, is distorted and becomes unsustainable. Already in the second interlude, Falstaff's excessive optimism re his young friend placed his C major uncomfortably alongside Hal's E♭; but when Hal puts on his kingly colours, neither C minor nor C major can come close to E major,[105] and the support Hal-as-E♭ had

---

[105] Except in a hexatonic tonal space, as described by Richard Cohn in 'Maximally smooth cycles, hexatonic systems, and the analysis of late-Romantic triadic progressions', *Music Analysis* 15 (1996), pp. 9–40. I do not doubt that many of Elgar's harmonic moves can be explained along these lines, but I shall add a note of caution, similar to the one on Robert Bailey's observation of the functional singularity of parallel major and minor

Example 4.5. *Falstaff*, Shallow's orchard

103

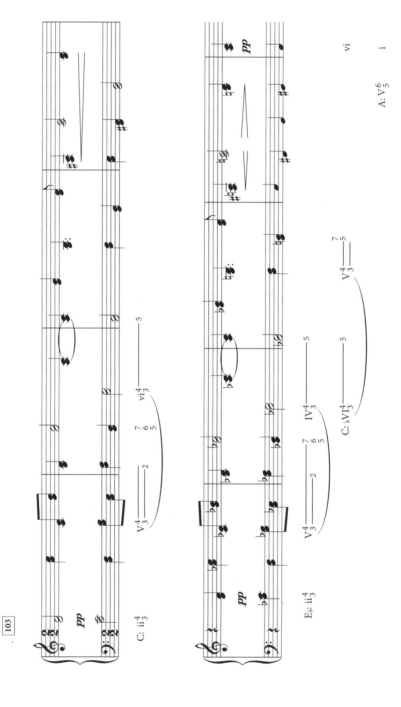

always given Falstaff-as-C minor (recall the way C minor runs insecurely into E♭ in the exposition) is now denied.[106] Hal has chosen a different path, which he had in mind from the first moment his theme was inflected to the minor: recall 4:4 and its ties to the 'Kingship' music that follows (7:3 and 7:7). Not until this moment is his purpose fully revealed to Falstaff, yet still the vast optimist is ignorant, and he mendaciously (motive 11) celebrates the news before heading to Westminster to greet his new sovereign.

The paragraph Elgar called 'King Henry V's progress' (114:1–130:21; R6) is the ultimate musical and dramatic consummation of the tension between Falstaff and Hal, and of the voice-leading structure of the exposition (Ex. 4.6). The three-key musico-narrative structure of C minor–E♭–E minor is recalled, having been absent from the recapitulatory R5. There is no immediate return to the work's principal thematic materials (114:1), so the 'Henry V rotation' cannot be considered recapitulatory, yet it follows the breakthrough Hal-as-E-major in the preceding rotation to completely redefine the remainder of the piece, whose sights are increasingly honed

modes after *Tristan* (Chapter 1, n. 16). That Elgar works in a hexatonic tonal space is evidence of his place in musical history; but the fact that his language was not at all times adventurous does not entail that the meaning of his moves is unsubtle. The significance of Elgar's manipulation of a tonal structure originally based on a Classically familiar c/E♭ to one based on a not-unfamiliar but still (in context) surprising c/E, can too easily be missed if we simply note that in 1913 it was possible and common enough to make the switch. Cohn's system usefully explains *how* Elgar can so manipulate the structure; but I am interested to know *why*. If he sets up a Classical structure then destroys it – forces it to undergo *Destruktion* – I want to find out the reason. Hence my caution, and my avoidance of Cohn's method of analysis.

[106] As I have already noted, Hepokoski links the concept of 'breakthrough' with the *peripeteia* of classical tragedy ('Fiery-pulsed libertine', p. 149); but in the twentieth century Carl Jung added another nuance to the word, which is interesting to note in the present situation. Dreams, on Jung's view, have a definite 'form', 'not unlike that of a drama'; his codification of the different sections into 'exposition', 'development', 'culmination or peripeteia', and 'solution or result' also has a partly musical ring. In the third stage, the *peripeteia*, 'something decisive happens or something changes completely', and redefines the course of the rest of the dream. (See Carl Gustav Jung, 'On the nature of dreams', in *Dreams*, trans. R. F. C. Hull (London: Routledge, 1985), pp. 80–1.) As we have seen, the breakthrough or *peripeteia* in *Falstaff* – which exactly fulfils a function that Hepokoski, Jung, or a classical tragedian would recognize – comes after the second dream interlude. There is almost a suggestion that it is *part* of the dream. Falstaff believes something quite incredible of his friend: that he will be 'sick' for the knight, and desirous of his presence. The whole symphonic study, almost, is a kind of dream, and this breakthrough is merely the point at which it changes.

Example 4.6. *Falstaff*, King Henry V's progress

on Hal.[107] In the exposition space Falstaff-as-C-minor's heavy leaning on Hal-as-E♭ demonstrated the compatibility of the two men, as well as their symbiotic relationship, with Falstaff as parasite, Hal as host;[108] but the tertial relationship, given modal mixture by Kingship/E minor, actually strengthened C minor's position in the tonal hegemony: the exposition as a whole is rooted firmly on a bass arpeggiation. But now in the coda space, E♭ supplants C minor in the hierarchy.

The new king's march theme, motive 17, is the first theme solidly in C minor; a subsidiary Falstaff theme, which I associate with his continued misunderstanding of the new king (motive 18: see Ex. 4.1), continues the tonic prolongation, while the arrival of a dominant (122:1) promises to establish C minor firmly for the first time. But it is not to be, and Hal's mischievous motive 3', the same music as his disguised robbery of Falstaff on Gad's Hill, takes us to E♭. From this point, the coda space follows the

---

[107] *Falstaff* departs from Hepokoski's 'breakthrough paradigm' because the breakthrough actually comes in the recapitulatory space rather than in the development space; but its effect is, as on Hepokoski's model, to reshape what follows, so in 'inbreaking' on E major, the announcement of Hal's accession must rightly be considered a breakthrough.

[108] Parasitic metaphors are a twentieth-century speciality; the sixteenth century would prefer 'whoreson caterpillar' (*1 Henry IV*, II. ii. 81).

exposition space for sixteen bars, moving from III to ♮iii. Falstaff's 'cajoling' Kingship tune, motive 4 (124:1), is joined by the minor-mode inflexion of Hal's motive 3′, still on E minor (124:5). Then an abrupt change from the pattern of the exposition space: E rises a semitone to F (125:1), and the full potential of Falstaff's 'sweet wag, when thou art king' is realized. In a flash iv/c becomes ii/E♭, and C minor itself retroactively becomes vi/E♭. With the King's *Grandioso* entrance, E♭ receives a bolstering considerably stronger than it did in the exposition. E♭'s place in a C minor hierarchy that mirrors the exposition becomes part of the coda space at 123:1, but as the paragraph unfolds Elgar reveals (in an *Augenblick*) that what the exposition space treated as modal mixture in a bass arpeggiation of C minor/major can have a different meaning. III and ♮iii of C minor now function as lower-neighbour and passing note to ii/E♭; E minor is therefore ♯i/E♭, not ♮iii/c. The Falstaff-tonicizing arpeggiation of the exposition is now shown to have been a Hal-tonicizing progression to a strong perfect cadence into his E♭. The potential was always there, unrealized, till after the breakthrough of Henry V's E major accession; the tie of friendship being there stretched to breaking point, now the stronger partner can break free and pull the carpet from beneath the helpless one. A pregnant pause on Falstaff's now desperate V/c, a pale imitation of the realistic and hopeful dominant of the exposition (the *f* cadence at 16:10–11 becomes *pp* at 130:20–1), ends the penultimate rotation.

Elgar deals summarily with C major in R7. The secondary/primary materials, which have now changed places, following Hal's triumph, 'compose-out' the repudiation, as we saw in Section 3; and with the paratextual rejection of Falstaff comes the textual liquidation of C. Kingship and E major reveal their culpability in the tragedy (132:1–14), and as the King departs, having 'looked on his ancient friend for the last time',[109] the plain fact of the victory of the King and his E minor strikes curtly at Falstaff's absurd careens to C (136:7–16; see Ex. 4.7). Three quicksilver V^{6-5}_{4-3}–i cadences in C minor attempt an affirmation of Falstaff's associated key (136:10–11, 12–13, 14–15), but abrupt modal mixture subjugates him once again as VI/e (six times; 136:9–14). His life is waning.

The process continues with the remembrance of Shallow's orchard ('a babbled of green fields'; Ex. 4.8). As in the second interlude (Ex. 4.5), C and E♭ are juxtaposed uncomfortably; but peculiar to this coda-space remembrance are the harp Cs on alternate bars, eight in all (141:1–142:8).

---

[109] Elgar, 'analytical note', p. 579.

Example 4.7. *Falstaff*, E minor/C 'careens'

136:7

Example 4.8. *Falstaff*, liquidation of C/Falstaff

Example 4.9. *Falstaff*, Falstaff's death

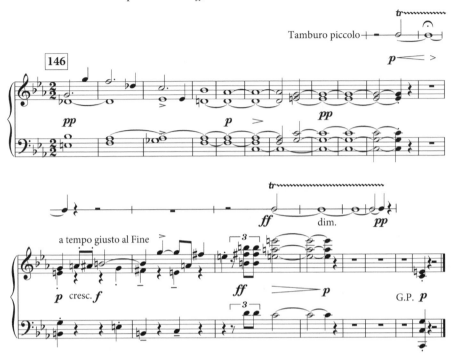

By this stage, Falstaff's C has been so emasculated that speculative cadences (as in Ex. 4.7) are no longer possible; the only available option is to state a unison c^1, which pleads unavailingly against the sour C/E♭ pairing.[110]

The final hammer-blows come in the closing bars (Ex. 4.9). Again there is no surprise that Elgar originally intended to give the piece a different ending. In his second full draft, *Falstaff* ends with the C major chord representing Falstaff's death (146:8); the first draft had ended even more precipitously at 136:7, just before the 'careening' music discussed above.[111] In each case he ends on a chord of C major, despite the fact that key is very weak in the recapitulation and coda, weaker still than it was in the exposition, where E♭ was more charitably disposed towards it: recall that E♭ had allowed itself to be part of a bass arpeggiation instead of claiming tonic status for itself, as it does during the new king's progress.

---

[110] Note that when this music is first heard (104:1ff.), the harp notes are scored for tambourine. This gesture – a voiceless, pitchless one at first – gains a heart-breaking new implication here in the coda space.

[111] See Kent, '*Falstaff*', p. 90.

Elgar eventually decided on the familiar ending, where 'the King's stern theme is curtly thrown across the picture',[112] and so ended with a final juxtaposition of E minor and C major. The result is very curious. The slightly forced resolution onto C major at 146:1ff. at least provides a context for the proposed final chord of Elgar's second draft; the early ending at 136:7 likewise establishes C major in a suitable tonal context, albeit a vicious one. But the final chord in the published score of *Falstaff* is totally dislocated from any C major context, and its highest pitch, e^1, is heard as $\hat{1}$/E, but without harmonic support.[113] We are reminded, I think, of Mistress Quickly's lament in *Henry V*: 'So 'a bade me lay more clothes on his feet. I put my hand into the bed and felt them, and they were as cold as any stone. Then I felt to his knees, and so up'ard and up'ard, and all was as cold as any stone.'[114] The final C major chord is indeed stone cold, and the end of the work is profoundly unsettling. What does it mean? It is the task of Chapter 6 to answer that question; but first I must establish the grounds for my musical hermeneutics, and that is the task of the next chapter.

---

[112] Elgar, 'analytical note', p. 579.

[113] It is instructive to play this final chord as an E minor or major one with e^1 on top.

[114] *Henry V*, II. iii. 21–5.

5 Hermeneutics and mimesis

5.1. Heidegger, Schenker, music, and modern musicology

I begin this chapter by making it clear how the concluding pair ought not to be read. There are two principal reasons why this is necessary. First, the question must arise why I choose Heidegger as a basis for my approach to a musical hermeneutics when the names of J. L. Austin, Hans-Georg Gadamer, Michel Foucault, and Jacques Derrida are more familiar, and have been put to interesting use in recent years in this context.[1] I believe in the binding necessity of acknowledging the hermeneutic circle in the fullest possible sense,[2] but choose to be led round it by Heidegger rather than the others, because I believe that Heidegger is a better grounding than they are for a musical hermeneutics. Gadamer seems to me a more persuasive follower of Heidegger than Derrida, but while some of Gadamer's refinements of Heidegger are valuable, and I shall call on them occasionally, the original arguments are still the most useful guide to hermeneutic enquiry, not least because Heidegger's hermeneutics extend beyond the interpretation of texts into the interpretation of human being and Being as such. I should therefore explain where I disagree with some of the philosophy underlying wings of 'the new musicology',[3] and at the

---

[1] Certain ideas of Gadamer, Derrida, and Austin are central to the argument of Lawrence Kramer's *Music as Cultural Practice, 1800–1900* (Berkeley, CA and London: University of California Press, 1990), the finest recent monograph on the foundations of musical hermeneutics; Foucault's 'archaeologies' are thought through by Gary Tomlinson in his *Music in Renaissance Magic: Toward a Historiography of Others* (Chicago and London: University of Chicago Press, 1993), and there is a strong Foucauldian feel to the burgeoning 'queer musicology', of which the best example is probably still Philip Brett, Elizabeth Wood, and Gary Thomas (eds.), *Queering the Pitch: the New Gay and Lesbian Musicology* (New York: Routledge, 1994)). More recently, Philip Rupprecht has put Austin's philosophical linguistics – incorporating John Searle's elaborations and criticisms – to fascinating use in *Britten's Musical Language* (Cambridge: Cambridge University Press, 2002).

[2] I believe it is a circle formed by human beings and the world, not merely, as on Derrida's view, a circle formed by a text and its reading.

[3] The formulation is hackneyed now, but still comprehensible.

same time pre-empt new-musicological criticisms of my own hermeneutic strategy. My argument is essentially ontological, being concerned with the nature of music, and my claim is that Heideggerian thinking can keep a hermeneutics solidly on track. I have already demonstrated how Heideggerian insights can guide the garnering of 'data' about specific musical works, and in this chapter and the next two, as promised in Chapter 1, I shall show how the same insights can be used to interpret the 'data' thus garnered.

Secondly, the alert reader might conclude, were I to omit this preamble, that my use of Heidegger's conception of an understood, 'projected', ecstatically temporal context for self-individuation, as summarized in Chapter 2 and held in force in the analytical chapters of this book, has connexions, in the musico-hermeneutic discussion of Chapters 6 and 7, with poststructuralist thought in literary studies – i.e. is really no different in kind from new-musicological writing, which is of course inspired in large part by literary studies. But this is a dangerous misunderstanding, and one I am eager to prevent. As a prophylactic, this chapter will provide a literary and philosophical excursus, by now a familiar strategy in musical hermeneutics. I shall return to more narrowly musical issues in the final chapters, although the relevance of my argument to musicology is clear throughout this one. It is also essential to show where I wish to change emphases or make more comprehensive changes to the hermeneutic guidelines of Kramer's *Music as Cultural Practice*, with which I am in broad agreement; otherwise it may be thought that I do not wish to add anything to his 'map'. But my method, while being broadly similar to his, differs quite considerably on one central interpretative point, and I shall explain that here and especially in Section 2.

My central concern is to demonstrate how we may get at musical meaning. I believe, following Heidegger and Gadamer, that works of art reveal meanings or aspects of Being which cannot be grasped in any other way. Furthermore music, as a mimesis of human temporality (see Chapter 2 and this chapter, Section 2) opens up aspects of our own Being. I invoke Heideggerian ideas in connexion with music because I believe music supports and perhaps even calls for them. And those ideas, which I argue are the best way into an understanding of the possibility of all hermeneutics, not merely existential or musical, are an aid to revealing the sorts of things that music says about us, which without Heidegger's analysis it would be difficult to express in words.

But my first concern is to establish what we mean by musical context. (I do not propose to offer a critique of poststructuralist thought, except where it brushes up against my immediate concern here.[4]) This is essential to an understanding of Kramer's third and most powerful 'hermeneutic window', the 'structural trope': 'By *structural trope* I mean a structural procedure, capable of various practical realizations, that also functions as *a typical expressive act within a certain cultural/historical framework.*'[5] The question of how to establish a cultural and historical context for a work of music is an incredibly complex one, and here I part company with Kramer. I believe that poststructuralist discourse is ultimately as terrifying as Kramer finds it exciting, and that what seems a liberation is in fact more like a new enslavement. But fortunately there is a Heideggerian antidote.

Opening a book or a score, we find that not only its contents but the whole dizzying and forever expanding mass of the universe leaps out at us. To understand the one we must grasp the other; but understanding of the other is a prerequisite to an understanding of either: it seems, at first, to be a hellish challenge. Yet this is an old insight: both Schleiermacher and Dilthey were aware of the hermeneutic circle, which dates back to the Reformation. Derrida and Foucault, however, take it to a nihilistic extreme which melds ideas from Nietzsche (the 'will to power')[6] and Marx (alienation) into an impressively pessimistic amalgam. Where common sense tells us that despite the hermeneutic circle we still get by with a sufficient understanding of our immediate surroundings, poststructuralists seem to go against common sense to argue that we are in fact unable to grasp the meaning of anything at all: meanings are, for them, 'fractured' – unstable, uncertain, perhaps even unreal.

An example of this comes early in Lawrence Kramer's study, when he points to what he sees, looking for a moment through Derridian spectacles, as a shortcoming in the Austin–Searle speech-act theory. Having quoted *Hamlet*, Act I Scene ii, the point at which Gertrude asks her son to cast his nighted colour off (for he knows that death is common), provoking the response, 'Ay, madam, it is common', Kramer writes:

---

4 I have found A. D. Nuttall's perceptive critique of structuralism and poststructuralism very useful while preparing this argument: see Nuttall, *A New Mimesis: Shakespeare and the Representation of Reality* (London: Methuen & co., 1983).

5 Kramer, *Music as Cultural Practice*, p. 10, second emphasis mine.

6 Actually this is not, in its influential Foucauldian form, really an idea of Nietzsche's at all, if by 'idea' we mean something fully worked out and ratified by its author. The idea exists merely in Nietzsche's notebooks, the *Nachlass*. Heidegger is to blame for locating the 'real' Nietzsche in the *Nachlass* and considering his published output less important, less authentically Nietzschean. Most modern Nietzsche scholars reject this hypothesis. The 'will to power' as promulgated by Foucault is therefore actually an idea of posthumous Nietzsche.

Austin is ambivalent about this sort of discursive skittishness [i.e. Hamlet's witty pun on 'common']; he alternately unleashes and tries to limit the instability of illocution [in Kramer's sense, the result intended and carried out by a speech-act, i.e. what the joke is driving at]. For present purposes, the most important fact about his proposed limitations is that none of them works. The reason why becomes apparent in a decisive critique of speech act theory put forth by Jacques Derrida. Derrida points out that all acts of communication presuppose the possibility of their repetition in new contexts. In order to function at all, a speech act, like a piece of writing or a visual image, must be *iterable*, that is, capable of functioning in situations other than the occasion of its production, among persons other than those who immediately produce and receive it. In their iterability, speech acts necessarily presuppose the possibility of divergence [*différance*], and hence also the possibility of their being redirected, reinterpreted. The prospect of what Austin thinks of as 'misfire', and 'infelicitous' deviation from the norm, is actually the norm itself. Even though certain speech acts may, and do, recur in typical settings with typical illocutions, we are not spared by that fact from understanding them anew with each recurrence. Speech acts are radically implicated in the situations that they address; they come to life as a kind of improvisation.[7]

This is a typical move: Derrida assumes that the discovered *possibility* is actually a *necessity*. The move seems to run against common sense, but even on a philosophical level it appears unpersuasive. This kind of assertion – that possibility is necessity – actually only applies to one of an infinite number of possible worlds, even to a proponent of modal logic.[8] Be that as it may. In this instance, the argument runs that every speech act, every human utterance, is equivalent to one of the wittiest comments of the greatest intellectual creation in Western literature: even stupid people are as wise as Hamlet. This is interesting, but wrong.

The existence of the Golden Gate Bridge, a destructible man-made structure, presupposes the possibility that a large bomb detonated at the

---

[7] Kramer, *Music as Cultural Practice*, p. 8.

[8] As I understand it, the Derridian (and Foucauldian) assertion that what is *possible* (in one of an infinite number of possible worlds) is *necessary* requires the same iterated modality as Alvin Plantinga's (disputed) proof of the existence of God, the system called S_5. In that system, complex modal statements such as 'it is possible that it is necessary that it is necessary that p' collapse into the final term. So if we write L for 'it is necessary that', and M for 'it is possible that', then '$MLLp$' is equivalent simply to 'Lp', and what begins as possibility becomes necessity. But the choice of S_5, or any other system of modal logic, is by no means inevitable, and it has always been controversial. See A. N. Prior, *Formal Logic* (Oxford: Clarendon Press, 1962), Part III, Chapter 1.

foot of one of its supports could make it fall into the water, but it does not follow that the Golden Gate Bridge *is* about to fall down. A witty man may tear words away from their usual meanings, playfully manipulating the gap between signifier and signified, but it does not follow that meanings themselves are not usually bound up with words or phrases, or that there is a danger, in the absence of a verbal wit of genius, of meanings floating arbitrarily, if at all, or attaching themselves only to words and not to things.

Neither is it the case that a word having multiple meanings, i.e. being polysemic, causes similar problems, because there are always reasonable limits imposed by the context of its use. The polyseme 'Leander' at once refers a thoughtful mind to an ancient love-story, lions, swimming, a Marlowe poem, Henley-on-Thames, a lost symphonic poem by Havergal Brian, and my friend: there is no *certainty* that it can refer to halibut, famine, or income tax. For Derrida, it may mean 'halibut', because for him *différance* contains 'dissemination',[9] and dissemination is potentially infinite. But extreme cases such as Hamlet's wit are not the norm, whatever Derrida may say. Austin's reserve, at this point, is exactly right. Words carry meaning and weight; there is a context, a Wittgensteinian 'form of life', or a Heideggerian and Gadamerian 'horizon', in which things are understood. The question of how much we are to read into them, or how far we ought to look to ascertain the meaning of a thing, depends on our horizon, the way we view things from within our primordial understanding of the world. If someone tells me 'Leander is coming for tea', I don't get out tea cups for a hundred rowers. Derrida's understanding of the hermeneutic circle seems insufficient. Life isn't as baffling as he seems to make out.

Heidegger's argument concerning the hermeneutic circle is simple and ingenious, and causes no offence to common sense. On his view, we are always understanding, never not understanding. As Gadamer puts it: 'Heidegger's temporal analytics of Dasein has, I think, shown convincingly that understanding is not just one of the various possible behaviours of the subject but the mode of being of Dasein itself . . . and hence embraces the whole of its experience of the world.'[10] Furthermore, although all our understanding is circular, the circle is *not* vicious. This is crucial. Heidegger acknowledges that we are 'always already' inside a hermeneutic circle, whatever our object of enquiry. He often powerfully calls this

---

[9] 'Dissemination' means crossing the boundaries of a 'regime of meaning', so that in one 'regime' one may find that 'to poll' means 'to cut hair', while in another 'regime' it means 'to record votes'.

[10] Hans-Georg Gadamer, *Truth and Method*, 2nd edn, rev. trans. J. Weinsheimer and D. G. Marshall (London: Sheed & Ward, 1989), p. xxx.

Dasein's 'thrownness' (*Geworfenheit*). (We cannot, for instance, ask 'what is music?' without having some concept of what music is for us to examine.) Yet day by day we cope with our position vis-à-vis the complexity of our world. How? Heidegger formulates his answer succinctly.

> The ready-to-hand is always understood in terms of a totality of involvements. This totality need not be grasped explicitly by a thematic interpretation. Even if it has undergone such an interpretation, it recedes into an understanding which does not stand out from the background. And this is the very mode in which it is the essential foundation for everyday circumspective interpretation.[11]

The 'ready-to-hand' is, to articulate it very crudely for our narrow scrutiny here, a useful thing I am engaged with (say, a pencil) which is located in a 'totality of involvements', i.e. an infinitely complex network of interrelationships both to other things of like kind and to all other things in the universe. This is the basic understanding of the hermeneutic circle, common now to most thinking people. But Heidegger goes on to say that Dasein *need not* grasp that totality. So for instance, to understand what a pencil is for, i.e. drawing, I do not need to grasp the totality of involvements of which my pencil is part. I simply use the pencil – until it breaks. Even if I think through the complex position of a pencil in the world, I do not, in actually using it, especially care or need to know where it comes from or which other drawing implements are its closest relatives. And this, Heidegger says, 'is the very mode in which it is the essential foundation for everyday circumspective interpretation': it is in this 'everyday', i.e. unreflective, unphilosophical appreciation of a pencil as a thing to draw with that I live my life most usually. It does not destabilize my grip on reality to view my pencil in such an uncritical way, nor does it make the pencil cease to exist – as one can imagine Derrida arguing – simply because another man may not regard the pencil as either a drawing instrument (he might consider it an offensive weapon) or a 'thing' at all (why not a phallic symbol?). To claim these things is to appeal to a sphere 'outside' the hermeneutic circle, which, Heidegger holds, we can never escape, where meanings are 'fractured', an appeal which Jürgen Habermas has criticized. He recalls Heidegger's assertion that there is no 'escape' from the hermeneutic circle, only the possibility of internal reformation. Nor is there actually any point in trying to escape from all possible horizons,

---

[11] Martin Heidegger, *Being and Time*, 7th edn, trans. John Macquarrie and Edward Robinson (Oxford: Blackwell, 1962; rev. edn 1927), p. 191.

i.e. all human traditions, because such an escape would lead, literally, nowhere; and if one does not know where one is going, it is almost impossible to get there.[12]

Each of our understandings has, then, a 'fore-structure', or as one might say, a socio-historically situated hermeneutic structure with embedded preconceptions of the objects we are examining, a particular hermeneutic window which we are predisposed by our socio-historical situation, our 'thrownness', to peer through. The structure is threefold: every interpretation has a 'fore-having' (*Vorhabe*), a 'fore-sight' (*Vorsicht*), and a 'fore-conception' (*Vorgriff*).[13] So to stick with our trivial example of the pencil, I 'fore-have' my *desire to draw*, and I 'fore-see' a way to satisfy it as *using a drawing implement*. Having 'decided', before I even begin to think, to operate on the background understanding that *I wish to draw*, I look around for things that might suit my purpose, and so I 'fore-conceive' my pencil as *a drawing implement*. That basic fore-structure clearly leads me to a firm, basic understanding that I have an object, and a conception of what this object I have actually is.

I cannot escape from the plain fact of my 'pencil fore-structure', even if I examine the object at the molecular level. It will always strike me first as a drawing implement. Dasein is always in a hermeneutic circle with a fairly rigid fore-structure guiding its understanding of everything in its world. For Heidegger, as for Derrida, in many cases, like the case of the pencil, this causes no problems; but in some cases, as in the case of Dasein's (mis)understanding of the history of Being, it can cause terrible problems.

To get to the truth of things, the rigidity of Dasein's fore-structure of understanding – and the fore-structure I have in mind in musical terms is the *Ursatz* – must be prised open or 'destroyed' by hermeneutics. That is Heidegger's 'Destruction' (*Destruktion*). In his account, *Destruktion* 'unveils' the Being of things. Our fore-structure cannot be escaped from, but it can, through *Destruktion*, be modified and improved upon. That is Heidegger's project, and, in a much narrower sense, mine too: I undertake it because, as I suggested in Chapter 2, Elgar's modernist project is the destruction of the Classical–Romantic symphonic tradition.

Destruktion combines two things: the wise man's insight that everything interrelates and we better understand things in particular the more we

---

[12] Jürgen Habermas, *The Philosophical Discourse of Modernity: Twelve Lectures*, trans. Frederick Lawrence (Cambridge, MA: MIT Press, 1987), Chapter 7.

[13] Heidegger, *Being and Time*, p. 191.

know about things in general; and Everyman's conviction that we have a basic idea about things when we come into contact with them and can get along tolerably well without too much hard thinking (as already noted, the hermeneutic circle is not vicious). We might have to radically change our view of what a thing is – as, for instance, happens on the *Antiques Roadshow* when a man who thought his bibelot was a fish-slice learns that it is actually an artist's palette knife – but the fact remains that we always already *have* a fore-structure with which we work to understand everything in the world.[14]

In terms of textual interpretation, Heidegger's hermeneutic mantra is a clear source for Derrida's: 'Hermeneutik ist Destruktion.'[15] Yet they proceed differently from that starting point. On Heidegger's view, and it seems more reasonable than Derrida's, for our interpretation of a text to be a good one, i.e. one which says something about the text and not just about our own psychoses, it must be 'original and genuine', and not imposed on us inauthentically by the mass of popular opinion, 'the They' or 'the One' (*das Man*).[16] Just that: not *best*, not *the only right-headed way,* just authentic to the individual.

I do not wish to suggest that my approach to musicology is 'more authentic' than another. That would be absurd. Authenticity is purely the business of the individual: it cannot by definition be dictated by *das Man*, since it is precisely an escape from that – which draws, however, necessarily on possibilities suggested by *das Man* without giving into them uncritically – that constitutes authenticity. So my approach is not 'more' authentic: but it is, I think, (simply) authentic on this definition; and if it

---

[14] Gadamer holds a very similar position, which is developed from his teacher Heidegger. He holds that we cannot get out of the hermeneutic circle, and that we anticipate our own interpretation of (say) a work of art – 'prejudice' (*Vorurteil*) is an important word for him – but may, if we are aware of our hermeneutic situatedness (within a 'horizon'), gradually wear down the 'prejudice' and form a clearer, more truthful understanding of a work of art. See Gadamer, *Truth and Method*, and Jean Grondin, 'Gadamer's basic understanding of understanding', in *The Cambridge Companion to Gadamer*, ed. Robert J. Dostal (Cambridge: Cambridge University Press, 2002), pp. 36–51: the table comparing Heidegger's and Gadamer's accounts of the hermeneutic circle on pp. 49–50 is especially useful. It is Gadamer's account of the hermeneutic circle which Kramer adopts.

[15] Martin Heidegger, *Ontologie: Hermeneutik der Faktizität* (Frankfurt: Klosterman, 1988), p. 105; trans. J. van Buren as *Ontology: the Hermeneutics of Facticity* (Bloomington: University of Indiana Press, 1995).

[16] Ibid., p. 80.

turns out that my method says interesting things about music, then it will have proved to be worthwhile for others as well as just authentic for me.

Poststructuralist views, now represented in most university music departments, are derived in a chain from Heidegger, but along the way his commonsense approach to the totality of involvements has been distorted. On the poststructuralist view, it seems to me, there is no point of entry into a discussion of a text; cf. Heidegger's 'fore-structure' of understanding, Dasein's finding itself already within an interpretation. Naturally I believe this poses problems for Kramer. On the view he accepts we cannot, for instance, simply read or watch *Hamlet*; we must probe deeper. And neither is it ever enough to know that Shakespeare's *Hamlet* relates to the *Ur-Hamlet*, or whether the author was Kyd or Shakespeare: we must know what the *Ur-Hamlet* relates to, even if we trace its roots right back to the *Pearl* or even *Beowulf* – and even that is not enough, because we need to understand about the development of the English language and the meanings language hides away, and so on. The task of the critic is, on this view, to take us a step closer to realizing how hopeless it is trying to reach an understanding about anything.

We are, on this view, 'alienated' from truth by an exploitative class of people wielding knowledge/power. This strain runs throughout poststructuralist literary theory and musicology: musical works, like cars or coffee tables, are regarded as commodities produced by alienated labour; words and ideas themselves are tainted too by exploitative overtones, and truth, buried forever beneath innumerable patinas of knowledge/power in a variety of forms, becomes irrecoverable. If this is true, and our only purpose in life is to pick apart the history of normalizations with the tools of an 'archaeologist', the consequences for humanity are dire: 'if everyone followed Foucault's advice and became a critic there would be no power–knowledge regimes left to resist and nothing left to do save commit suicide out of boredom'.[17] Although Foucault is right to say that meanings *can* be 'dictated' by a powerful elite, it is unreasonable to conclude that *all* meaning is necessarily ungraspable by dint of the action of an exploitative class. Julian Young writes:

> Though it happens through human language, disclosure is never human 'handiwork', 'will never let itself be mastered either positively or negatively by a human doing' ... Human beings never make their own ultimate horizons of disclosure; conspiracy theories are always false. This, I think, is a matter

---

[17] Julian Young, *The Death of God and the Meaning of Life* (London: Routledge, 2003), p. 182.

not of observation but of logic. Since conspiring or planning is an instance of what Heidegger calls 'calculative thinking', and since thinking of this type always presupposes and happens within a horizon of disclosure, conspiring to create one's ultimate horizon of disclosure would require one to 'calculate' before one could 'calculate'.[18]

Later Heidegger insists that regarding entities as useful objects (a favourite image is of regarding a river as a source of power rather than as a thing in itself) is a misguided understanding produced by 'the enframing' (das Gestell) which characterizes modernity, and has been brewing in all thinking since Plato: our world-view has everything, so to speak, within a 'frame' that makes things appear to us merely as things-for-us, rather than as things-in-themselves. So Alaska is 'oilfield' rather than 'ecological treasure'; everything in the world is the 'means' to something else, productive or otherwise. We do not recognize the 'thingness' of things, only their usefulness to us. This is not peculiar to modernity: it is the essence of the 'fore-structure' of understanding, our basic comportment to the world we live in, and is not necessarily destructive. But what is unique to modernity is that for the first time in history we *don't care* and *cannot be persuaded to care* about the thingness of things: in 'the enframing' of modernity, it strikes us as absurd that a thing might be more than a thing-for-us.

Does that mean that it really is hopeless trying to reach an understanding about anything? Heidegger repeatedly says things *like* that, but does not mean them so hopelessly as, for example, modern deconstructionists.[19] On the other hand, Heidegger has a more conservative estimate of the limits of understanding than the Young Hegelians.

It is difficult to accept Hegel's suggestion that a Utopia of absolute knowledge is ultimately attainable, whether as his Absolute Idea, Marx's vision of the classless society, or Freud's discovery of the meaning of repressed sexual urges. As Schopenhauer noted, 'The oft-repeated doctrine of a progressive development of mankind to ever greater perfection ... is opposed to the *a priori* view that up to any point in time an infinite time

---

[18] Julian Young, *Heidegger's Later Philosophy* (Cambridge: Cambridge University Press, 2002), p. 23. That is also Gadamer's argument against science's claims to hold the only route to truth (see his *Philosophical Hermeneutics*, trans. David E. Linge (Berkeley and London: University of California Press, 1976), p. 410); and what unseats scientism also unseats poststructuralism.

[19] Derrida's *déconstruction* can be seen as an extreme reinterpretation of Heidegger's *Destruktion*: extreme because in Heidegger's original formulation the concept is considerably more hopeful.

has already elapsed, and consequently that all that is supposed to come with time is bound to have existed already.'[20] And modern hermeneutic method does not allow this Hegelian teleology. Heidegger writes:

> In any investigation in this field, where 'the thing itself is deeply veiled' one must take pains not to overestimate the results. For in such an inquiry one is constantly compelled to face the possibility of disclosing an even more primordial and more universal horizon from which we may draw the answer to the question, 'What is "Being"?'[21]

It is the purpose of hermeneutics not to give final answers, but to arrive at a new starting point for further enquiry. Of course this is part of Hegel's dialectical method too, and he often treats a synthesis as the starting point for the next stage of the dialectic. But he also holds that eventually a final synthesis, in the form of the Absolute Idea, will put an end to the dialectical process, when God draws everything into himself. And this proposal Heidegger rejects.[22] There is no ultimate understanding of truth. Truth is not self-evidently 'there'; it comes from Dasein, the primary locus of truth. Truth 'depends' on human beings and their social practices. But does this claim not bring us to the heady Derridian belief that all understanding is cripplingly limited by the play of *différances*? Not at all. Hubert L. Dreyfus writes:

> For both Heidegger and Wittgenstein . . . the source of the intelligibility of the world is the average public practices through which alone there can be any understanding at all. What is shared is not a conceptual scheme, i.e., not a belief system that can be made explicit and justified. Not that we share a belief system that is always implicit and arbitrary. That is just the Sartrean

---

[20] Arthur Schopenhauer, *The World as Will and Representation*, 2 vols., trans. E. F. J. Payne (New York: Dover, 1966), vol. II, p. 184.

[21] Heidegger, *Being and Time*, p. 49.

[22] Robert C. Solomon suggests that Hegel's own view of the Absolute Idea might have been 'schizoid'. 'He conceived of the structure of all his works as a dialectical progression up to and establishing the Absolute, a single idea which encompassed and unified every other idea in the system . . . This apparent consistency of theme and structure hides a tension, however, between the traditional conservative search for an Absolute, and a radical, largely unacknowledged recognition that there may be no such Absolute, but only the possibly endless diversity of different forms of life and consciousness, each of them relative to and dependent upon its own historical, conceptual, and social epoch' (Solomon, *Continental Philosophy Since 1750: The Rise and Fall of the Self* (Oxford: Oxford University Press, 1988), p. 59). Adorno seizes on this Hegelian tension, which is suggestive of a fragmentation of absolute meaning.

version of the same mistake. What we share is simply our average comportment. Once a practice has been explained by appealing to what one does, no more basic explanation is possible. As Wittgenstein puts it in *On Certainty*: 'Giving grounds [must] come to an end sometime. But the end is not an ungrounded presupposition: it is an ungrounded way of acting.'

This view is entirely antithetical to the philosophical idea of *total* clarity and *ultimate* intelligibility ...

Philosophers seek an ultimate ground. When they discover there is none, even modern philosophers like Sartre and Derrida seem to think that they have fallen into an abyss – that the lack of an ultimate ground has catastrophic consequences for human activity. Whereas Wittgenstein, and Heidegger in Division I [of *Being and Time*], see that the nonground is not an abyss. Counting on the shared agreement in our practices, we can do anything we want to do: understand the world, understand each other, have language, have families, have science, etc.[23]

Groundlessness is a licence for freedom in Heidegger's thought, and free human action is essentially disclosive: it reveals aspects of truth. The world is not irremediably fractured: it is full of opportunities, and it is only our chains that are broken, not our spectacles.

We can never know everything, and everything we do know necessarily interrelates: that much is clear. But it does not follow that because we cannot know everything, nothing has meaning. That is a neurotic and nihilist leap. That Derrida seems to make it and Heidegger does not points to a fundamental difference between them.

So, even though it is impossible for any man to completely contextualize it, or even point and say 'there it is', *still* it is meaningful to say that Beethoven's Fifth Symphony exists and has meaning. Of course 'inauthentic' academic-Dasein could perhaps become an orthodox, tunnel-visioned Schenkerian who denies any but the most immediate musical context for the symphony – inauthentic because 'that's just what one does when analyzing music'. It is the duty of an 'authentic' musicologist-Dasein to acknowledge the vastness of its totality of involvements, both musical and extramusical, and to analyze music with a suitably wide eye or, preferably, ear to contextualization: to be aware that the individual musicologist's horizon limits his or her understanding of the piece in question, but to be ready to pursue what seems authentic to the musicologist. The issue here is not 'correctness', of course, only 'authenticity'. In either case, this assertion may at first seem uncontroversial since most people nowadays,

---

[23] Hubert L. Dreyfus, *Being-in-the-World: Commentary on Heidegger's* Being and Time, *Division I* (Cambridge, MA: MIT Press, 1991), pp. 155–6.

especially in poststructuralist musicology, believe that they act in this way. But I do not mean it to be uncontroversial, and believe that many new musicologists act in exactly the opposite way. I think they do 'what one does'. What was originally called the 'new' musicology has solidified into another orthodoxy.

If one is minded to *select* a context for a discussion, to indulge in 'calculative thinking', then the safest bet seems to be to let the context be a musical one. But does this mean that we must retreat into piece-by-piece exegesis, shutting out any notion of 'context' and concentrating on close-reading? I think not.

In a healthy individual there should ideally be a balance, and in this book I argue for a Heideggerian–Schenkerian middle way between formal analysis and hermeneutics: I no more believe that those two musicological traditions can or should be separated than that the mind can or should be separated from the body. Context is important, but *relevance* must be the watch-word: and not all context is relevant. We do not establish the context of a work; it establishes its own context – or, rather, its composer does: to suggest that a work calls itself from nothingness into intentional being is to live in cloud-cuckoo-land.[24] We are not cleverer than a work; it is cleverer than us. So running at it with a predefined hermeneutic goal that it might not share with us is, simply, a waste of time. We should make our approach cautiously, as to a wild beast momentarily cornered, and be prepared to be taken in whatever direction it takes us. So we must analyze, break apart the 'fore-structure' of our understanding, which includes our analytical method, and look for hermeneutic pointers in the Being of the work itself.[25]

Poststructuralists would agree with Heidegger's argument that, as a language-bearing being, man invests the world with meaning, but they run to a different conclusion. For the poststructuralist, it therefore follows that the world is either intrinsically meaningless, or else that such meaning as it has ought not to be trusted, because it was made up by a controlling elite. But Heidegger has not said everything he wishes to say on this point. Meaning, in this limited sense, is (minuscule 'b') being-as-disclosure:

---

[24] I don't mean that a composer establishes the only possible interpretation of a work, or even that he knows all (or anything) of what he is doing. I merely mean that he puts the work into the world, and 'establishes a context' in the way that a somnambulist, ignorant of his nocturnal vandalism of a room filled with china, 'establishes' the state of the room in the morning.

[25] The nature of 'the work itself' is, on my account (explained in Chapter 2 Section 2 and to be elaborated further in Section 2 of this chapter), an intentional object whose supratemporal form is a mimesis of human temporality.

in language, man reveals the nature, the meaning, of things as they present themselves in the world (so he reveals the pencil as a thing to draw with). But the other side of being, and the greater side, is (majuscule 'B') Being-as-concealment: this is the side of things that hides itself away (the moon as dark side; a lover as a person of a richness we can never fully know), in addition to what we have just defined as 'being'; Being is the sum of everything, known or unknown, seen or unseen, the 'plenitude' (*Vollzähligkeit*) of the sides or facets of being.[26]

So although it appears to the poststructuralists, and it is a cause for their concern, that man as language-bearing being prefigures meaning, Heidegger would disagree. Dasein as language-bearing being is prior to being (and meaning) only while finding itself dependent on its social setting, the world which shows everything to it. 'While horizons of disclosure are dependent on social practices and are hence relative to particular cultures, it does not follow that truth (as correspondence) is. That the *medium* of discovery is (for short) "subjective" does not entail that *what* is discovered is dependent on us. And the latter proposition Heidegger denies.'[27] The situation is not as the poststructuralists see it, but more paradoxical. Both man and world *rely on one another* for meaning. The world has no meaning without man to bestow it by language (broadly conceived: all art is language),[28] but man cannot bestow meaning without a world and without an understanding of that world which is given to him by the world – the 'fore-structure' of understanding discussed above. '(Lower case) being and human being are, therefore, to put the point in Heideggerian language, "equiprimordial".'[29]

So being is man-dependent in the sense that as a thing is presented to us its being can be interpreted wrongly – malevolently even, although this is not, contra Foucault, a universal phenomenon – but Being is not man dependent, and includes all the aspects of things which are not presented to us and cannot therefore be abused by us. We need not be

---

[26] Martin Heidegger, 'What are poets for?', trans. Albert Hofstadter, in *Poetry, Language, Thought* (New York: Harper and Row, 1977; orig. edn 1946), pp. 89–142 at p. 124. In his recent study of Heidegger's later philosophy, Julian Young usefully distinguishes between the 'revealed' and 'concealed' forms of being and Being by writing the former with a minuscule initial and the latter with a majuscule; ambiguous or combining forms are written 'B/being'. Having followed the usual practice of capitalizing throughout this book, I shall henceforth differentiate. (See Young, *Heidegger's Later Philosophy*, esp. pp. 10–25.)

[27] Young, *Heidegger's Later Philosophy*, p. 9, n. 5.

[28] See n. 48.

[29] Young, *Heidegger's Later Philosophy*, p. 12.

afraid that we are shut off from meaning because being depends on us; there is Being to safeguard meaning. And Heidegger actually predicts Derrida's nihilistic move by proclaiming that it is part of the 'destitution'[30] of modernity that we are oblivious to Being: we live in a state of 'forgetfulness of Being' (*Seinsvergessenheit*).[31] Heidegger agrees that B/being is as much 'untruth' as it is 'truth', that it hides away as much as it reveals, but it is because the modern mind no longer remembers about Being that, Heidegger holds, we must follow his 'path of thinking' to 'recollect' Being – recollect, that is, precisely the thing that Derridians will argue is not there or cannot be reached because it is irremediably fractured. Derridianism is, on the Heideggerian view, a lamentable but by no means unusual modern affliction.

Adorno's brilliant diagnosis of the 'commodity character' of music and musical material is also part of 'the enframing' of modernity,[32] in which the ontology of music, along with everything else, is debased and regarded with an unflinchingly utilitarian and destructive (because non-worshipful) eye. His analysis of music's commodity character cannot be straightforwardly denied. Trained musicians are often frustrated when they hear classical music described as 'soothing' or 'relaxing', as if it were a homeopathic medicine. Advertising a Beethoven symphony as 'something to help you unwind after a hard day in the office' is to the initiate as absurd as suggesting that a reader or theatre-goer might want to 'bask in the gentle patter of iambic feet in *Hamlet*'. Adorno's instinct does not fail him in identifying an infuriating brainlessness in the commodification of listening.

But one may question whether it is totally impossible to get past the commodity character of, say, a CD by listening to it. A true music lover does not simply own CDs; he listens to them: is he really in the thrall of the recording industry? I do not think so. There is nothing *necessarily* alienating about every aspect of the capitalist system. A musicologist may earn his wage by passing on a love of music to his students. His monetary reward is tied to his essential being as a lover of music. This wage is then partly spent on the purchase of CDs or concert tickets or any other musical commodity. The musicologist therefore exchanges something

---

[30] Heidegger, 'What are poets for?', p. 91.

[31] Martin Heidegger, *Nietzsche, vol. I: The Will to Power as Art*, trans. David Farrell Krell (London: Routledge and Kegan Paul, 1981; orig. edn 1961), p. 194.

[32] For a fuller discussion of 'the enframing' see Heidegger, 'The question concerning technology', trans. with some editorial changes by William Lovitt, in *Martin Heidegger: Basic Writings*, ed. David Farrell Krell (London: Routledge, 1993; orig. edn 1949), pp. 307–41, esp. pp. 344ff., and Young's elucidation of Heidegger's essay in *Heidegger's Later Philosophy*, Chapter 3.

stamped with his personality (the wage earned by teaching) for something stamped just as powerfully with the same personality (the listening experience). A musicologist who collects CDs does not fetishize them: he draws the CDs, so to speak, into his very essence, and holds them close to his heart. It is entirely possible to get past the commodification of musical experience which Adorno so rightly identifies in 'the culture industry'. It does not even require much of an effort.

So another product of the enframing is Adorno's tendency of using the identification of music's commodity character to allow for music and music theory's appropriation in support of a radical social agenda (another symptom of his 'duckrabbititis', first diagnosed in Chapter 1). And, to level the criticism at Heidegger in the spirit of good sportsmanship, yet another product would be a Heideggerian's use of the analysis of the enframing to allow for music and music theory's appropriation in support of the inculcation of Heideggerian ideas. *Mea culpa.*

The difference, of course, is that Heidegger's thought includes itself within its own critique; to convince someone of the rightness of Heidegger's later philosophy is also to convince someone of the dangers of interpreting things in the world in terms of ideologies or comportments to reality which do not do full justice to 'the thingness of things': ideas must not be allowed to congeal as ideologies. Adorno's social agenda, which must like any social agenda be ideologically based, is therefore inevitably less honest in this sense than Heidegger's philosophical agenda (Heidegger himself learnt of the dangers, both philosophical and political, of aligning thought with politics during his brief flirtation with Nazism in the early 1930s), and while I agree with Adorno's historical account of the nature of musical material, I consider the direct socio-political application of his thought to be open to criticism. That is why I prefer existential–ontological critique to sociological critique.

To allow a work to establish its own context we must allow it to show itself, and to observe its self-revelation we must undertake an analysis. In the case of music this may mean performing a Schenkerian analysis, but one brought closer to the Being or essence of the work of music through a (Heideggerian) refinement of the underlying, too-Beethovenian phenomenology of Schenker's system. All this I have done in earlier chapters; the way to assess the findings of such an analysis is the subject of this and the next two chapters.

It should now be fairly clear where I agree and disagree with Lawrence Kramer. Most obviously, I reject Derrida and Kramer does not; but there are more important differences, chief among them being my insistence that music is a mimesis of humankind's temporal existence, a claim I am about to elaborate upon in Section 2. I accept Kramer's three hermeneutic windows ('textual inclusion', 'citational inclusions', and 'structural tropes'), but regard the status of the third differently.

A structural trope, on Kramer's definition, is historically conditioned: its meanings are disclosed from within a specific 'horizon'. A danger, one that Kramer is aware of, is that the horizons of disclosure which condition the interpretation of each structural trope seem not to be generally agreed upon. We tend to have different interpretations of musical gestures: witness the variety of responses Kramer reports being produced by Berlioz's *Grande messe des morts* during a conference.[33] Kramer wisely calls on Gadamer's argument for the 'fusion' of past and present horizons to guard against empty, anachronistic subjectivism in hermeneutics: it is through a 'dialogue' between our horizon (unavoidably partisan and conditioned) and the horizon of the text that this horizal fusion and a sound hermeneutics are possible. But to engage in such a dialogue with a musical work, we must first know what the work is and how its language functions. And that requires the opening of a further hermeneutic window that Kramer does not name, one which is a necessary prerequisite to the hermeneutic analysis of structural tropes but which operates also on its own terms and in a much broader and more powerful sense.

This extra hermeneutic window, in my view the most powerful there is, is opened by an analysis of a piece of music undertaken with a method sensitive to the Being of music, which is a mimesis of human temporality. If we are to engage in dialogue from our horizon with the work of music in its horizon then, to put it crudely, the musical work must be allowed to establish for us what its horizon is. But it is not as easy to get to grips with the structure of a piece of music as it is with the other arts: music's abstract nature calls for great mental exertion before we can even begin to engage in dialogue with it; we must learn its language before we can speak to it. And that means undertaking an analysis which lets the work speak 'as itself': a phenomenological analysis.

I argued in Chapter 2 that Schenker's analytical method, reformulated from background to foreground under a Heideggerian microscope, is a suitable phenomenological method for the analysis of tonal music.[34] Once

---

[33] Kramer, *Music as Cultural Practice*, pp. 18–20.

[34] To understand musical language and allow the music to 'speak' to us and establish its own horizon, we must utilize the most modern tools for analyzing that language; understanding music is, in this sense, no different from understanding a foreign language. In the case of tonal music this means we must take account of the latest developments in Schenkerian theory, including the modifications of the 'duotonal

a musical work's horizon has been opened up to view by such an analysis (as in Chapters 3 and 4 of this book) we may begin to follow Gadamer's dialogic hermeneutic advice and look through Kramer's hermeneutic windows. But we need not stop there: after opening up music's being through phenomenological analysis, we may go on to use Heidegger's analysis of Dasein and the history of Being to greatly expand our own horizon so that it embraces existential and ontological ideas which I have argued music is naturally endowed to communicate in its own language. The resulting horizonal dialogue, enriched by our new intelligence, will produce a fusion that carries even more profound meaning.

Little of this, it is clear, places me in direct opposition to Kramer, who also relies to an extent on Schenkerian analytical methods. He does not, however, insist as strongly as I do on the necessity of such a methodology, nor does he force the methodology to undergo *Destruktion* (as I do in Chapter 2). This is not merely a change of emphasis; it is an entirely different way to motivate a hermeneutics. But my central departure from Kramer is in opening up a fourth hermeneutic window – I shall call it the 'mimetic window' – which I think is significantly more powerful even than his 'structural tropes'. The virtue of the structural trope is that it has the potential to draw into a hermeneutics all of musical history; the power of the mimetic window is that it opens up our view to human temporalizing and the existential and ontological implications of that. Gadamer's philosophical hermeneutics explains the grounds for the possibility of any hermeneutics. But if music is a mimesis of mankind's temporal existence our discussion requires a means of explicating the significance of that mimesis; we need a way of talking about human existence and the question of Being: and this Heidegger provides. I have already demonstrated *that* music is a mimesis of human existence; I shall now explain *how* musical mimesis relates to human existence.

5.2. The mimetic function of sonata form: fairy-stories, the quest narrative, and humankind's historical and temporal existence

I argued in Chapter 2 that music is a mimesis of humankind's temporal existence,[35] and promised to return in this chapter to the specific mimetic

Schenkerians' (see the bibliography in Chapter 1 n. 9), and James Hepokoski's and Warren Darcy's Sonata Theory.

[35] I have already noted (in Chapter 2) that I intend 'mimesis' to be understood in a 'strong' sense: art does not merely represent something that is already there and clearly visible, but uncovers aspects of reality which cannot be discovered in any other way. Art is the *appearing* of what is represented, not just the *reproduction* of what is represented. See

function of sonata form, especially as it relates to the literary 'quest narrative'. Since this issue will underpin my hermeneutics of the First Symphony and *Falstaff* in Chapter 6, it is necessary first to explain the literary function of the quest narrative.

W. H. Auden begins his essay on 'the quest hero' with an existential observation which may have been made (less lucidly) by Heidegger.

> To look for a lost collar button is not a true quest: to go in quest means to look for something of which one has, as yet, no experience; one can imagine what it will be like but whether one's picture is true or false will be known only when one has found it.
>
> Animals, therefore, do not go on quests. They hunt for food or drink or a mate, but the object of their search is determined by what they already are and its purpose is to restore a disturbed equilibrium; they have no choice in the matter.
>
> But man is a history-making creature for whom the future is always open; human 'nature' is a nature continually in quest of itself, obliged at every moment to transcend what it was a moment before. For man the present is not real but valuable. He can neither repeat the past exactly – every moment is unique – nor leave it behind – at every moment he adds to and thereby modifies all that has previously happened to him.
>
> Hence the impossibility of expressing his kind of existence in a single image. If one concentrates upon his ever open future, the natural image is of a road stretching ahead into unexplored country, but if one concentrates upon his unforgettable past, then the natural image is of a city which is built in every style of architecture and in which the physically dead are as active citizens as the living. The only characteristic common to both images is a sense of purpose; a road, even if its destination is invisible, runs in a certain direction; a city is built to endure and to be a home.[36]

Here Auden makes all his central points in their most compact form. To express it in Heideggerian terms, one might say that the literary quest narrative is bound up more than any other with Dasein's ecstatic temporalizing: it is Dasein's 'nature' – insofar as it has one: Heidegger and Auden are agreed that, strictly speaking, it is 'natureless' – to hold the three temporal ecstases (past, present, and future) in force in every moment.

Gadamer, *Truth and Method* and *The Relevance of the Beautiful and Other Essays*, ed. Robert Bernasconi (Cambridge: Cambridge University Press, 1986),*passim*.

[36] W. H. Auden, 'The quest hero', in *Tolkien and the Critics: Essays on J. R. R. Tolkien's 'The Lord of the Rings'*, ed. Neil D. Isaacs and Rose A. Zimbardo (Notre Dame, IN: University of Notre Dame Press, 1968), pp. 40 – 61 at pp. 40 – 1.

Auden's argument here presupposes an authentic present, a 'moment', an *Augenblick* (see Chapter 2 for a definition.) Animals are incapable of quests, or ambitions of any kind, but the quest for *itself* as well as for goals is the very essence of Dasein, whether it accepts the responsibility of making self-defining choices or not.

Being a tree is bliss: clearly one thing and not another – it cannot choose to be a tree-astronaut or a tree-golfer – a tree is rooted in the earth, from which it grows, and into which it will eventually recede. (Dasein enjoys only one of those blessings.) 'To entities such as [trees], their Being is "a matter of indifference"; or more precisely, they "are" such that their Being can be neither a matter of indifference to them, nor the opposite. [But because] Dasein has *in each case mineness* [*Jemeinigkeit*], one must always use a *personal* pronoun when one addresses it: "I am", "you are".'[37] Heidegger holds that this essence of Dasein, its *Unheimlichkeit* – which should be distinguished from Freud's concept of the 'uncanny', so I shall favour 'unsettledness' – is critical to its sense of identity, and it may react to its feeling of unsettledness in one of three ways.

Because 'Dasein is . . . essentially its own possibility it *can*, in its very Being, [1] "choose" itself and win itself; [2]. . . lose itself and never win itself; or [3] only "seem" to do so'.[38] Since Dasein is always already in some kind of social context, for instance, as a child born into a middle-class English family, it must at first and for a considerable time live a life handed down by its society: it must be a schoolboy, say, or a cricket fan. Yet to do so throughout its life would be inauthentic in the extreme: it would 'lose itself and never win itself', the second possibility mentioned above. Possibility 3, 'seeming' to win itself, could be the result of an adolescent rebellion against the dictates of society ('I am no longer a cricket fan, but a skateboarder') which, however, still has the character of uncritical dependence on the possibilities provided by society ('I am a skateboarder not because that is what I should be, but because that is *not* what *my* society wants me to be, and *another* society tells me I can be this way'). Instead of accepting its own possibilities, Dasein identifies with a pre-packaged human nature created by a society, however sharply it rubs against the pre-packaged nature offered by the society Dasein is rebelling against; Dasein does not choose itself, but only *seems* to do so. (This 'teenage rebellion' may happen at any age, and any number of times.) The authentic course, possibility 1, involves the choice of Dasein's ownmost

[37] Heidegger, *Being and Time*, p. 68.
[38] Ibid.

possibilities. Dasein realizes it cannot simply identify with a role – an existentially authentic priest may still curse God, if the need arises (say, when her mother dies suddenly), even though it is not what 'they' consider the behaviour of a priest – but must select possibilities which best suit its ownmost potentiality-for-Being. And in doing so Dasein creatively acknowledges the groundlessness of its own existence, and its unsettledness. It owns up to the fact that it doesn't fit in the world in any preordained way, and forges its own identity from a variety of distinct possibilities. It is a happy and potentially meaning-bestowing thought, quite distinct from Sartre's or Camus's conception.

Auden's image of human existence as a road echoes, appropriately enough (his essay is largely concerned with Tolkien), the simple, recurring 'old walking-song' first sung by Bilbo Baggins in *The Lord of the Rings*:

> The Road goes ever on and on
> Down from the door where it began.
> Now far ahead the Road has gone,
> And I must follow, if I can,
> Pursuing it with eager feet,
> Until it joins some larger way
> Where many paths and errands meet.
> And whither then? I cannot say.[39]

Its immediate context is Bilbo's last departure from home, and journey into a future he cannot predict but chooses willingly, having owned up to his unsettledness, chosen himself, and won himself. But more broadly it is used through the work, as Tom Shippey argues, as Tolkien's way of connecting 'individual time with mythic timelessness'.[40] And this is in line with Auden's codification of the archetypal quest as a combination of six elements, the sum of which is a mimesis of a specific temporal cast:

1 A precious Object and/or Person to be found and possessed or married.
2 A long journey to find it, for its whereabouts are not originally known to the seekers.
3 A hero. The precious Object cannot be found by anybody, but only by the one person who possesses the qualities of breeding or character.
4 A Test or series of Tests by which the unworthy are screened out, and the hero revealed.

[39] J. R. R. Tolkien, *The Lord of the Rings*, Book I, Chapter 1; paginations vary in the innumerable editions of the book.
[40] Tom Shippey, *J. R. R. Tolkien: Author of the Century* (London: Harper Collins, 2000), p. 188; see esp. pp. 188–92.

5 The Guardians of the Object who must be overcome before it can be won. They may be simply a further test of the hero's *arete*,[41] or they may be malignant in themselves.

6 The Helpers who with their knowledge and magical powers assist the hero and but for whom he would never succeed. They may appear in human or in animal form.[42]

This basic template is recognizable in a variety of literary forms (Auden goes on to trace it through genres as diverse as the detective story, the adventure story, *Moby Dick*, and the Kafka novels) as well as some musical ones; but it is also clearly related to our own life experience:

1 Many of my actions are purposive; the *telos* toward which they are directed may be a short-term one, like trying to write a sentence which shall express my present thoughts accurately, or a lifelong one, the search to find true happiness or authenticity of being . . .

2 I am conscious of time as a continuous irreversible process of change. Translated into spatial terms, this process becomes, naturally enough, a journey.

3 I am conscious of myself as unique – my goal is for me only – and as confronting an unknown future – I cannot be certain in advance whether I shall succeed or fail in achieving my goal. The sense of uniqueness produces the image of the unique hero; the sense of uncertainty, the images of the unsuccessful rivals.

4 I am conscious of contradictory forces in myself, some of which I judge to be good and others evil, which are continually trying to sway my will this way or that. The existence of those forces is given. I can choose to yield to a desire or to resist it, but I cannot by choice desire or not desire.[43]

The quest narrative is therefore, in both its purest and most varied forms, a 'literary mimesis of the subjective experience of becoming':[44] and in that sense, as a mimesis of Dasein's ecstatic temporalizing, it is the most 'musical' of literary forms, but one which is, because it has a much looser supratemporal form (if indeed it can properly be said to have one at all),

---

[41] Auden is here referring to the Greek concept of *aretē*, the opposite of *kakia* (badness), the quality of being a good human being. Plato identified four *aretai*: wisdom (*phronēsis*), moderation (*sōphrosynē*), courage (*andreia*), and justice (*dikaiosynē*). It is these *aretai* which Auden suggests are tested in the quest narrative.

[42] Auden, 'The quest hero', p. 44.

[43] Ibid., p. 45.

[44] Ibid., p. 48.

less 'real' or 'accurate' than music. As Auden notes, our consciousness of time, the endless unfolding of 'becoming', is in the quest narrative *'translated* into spatial terms' (my emphasis) as a journey. In music, there is no need for such an inter-dimensional translation: the consciousness of our own 'becoming' is played out mimetically in the very dimension that we experience it in – time.

Music therefore has the advantage over the other arts, and its mimetic structure can more directly mirror humankind's 'nature'. That holds for all musical forms, but the greatest of them in this respect, because it contains within it obvious parallels with the quest narrative, is sonata form. The Object or Person to find and possess (Auden's first element, above) is the conclusive attainment of the tonic in the recapitulation or, in more complex pieces with 'non-resolving recapitulations', the coda.[45] The 'long journey' is, unsurprisingly, the sonata trajectory, and the Hero, an unlikely figure, is the second subject. Recall James Hepokoski's description of the function of secondary materials in the sonata space (Chapter 3 Section 1 of this book): it is the S-material's role to prepare the ground for the essential expositional closure and essential structural closure, the defining structural cadences of the sonata. Of course the primary and secondary materials are not 'characters' in the literary sense, only different aspects of the same character: the sonata itself is, broadly speaking, the Hero; but the secondary materials are the ones with the more explicitly 'heroic' function.[46] Sonata form's goal orientation captures nicely the teleological nature of our lived experience, and the tensions between on- and off-tonic keys represent Auden's 'contradictory forces in myself', which I may choose between, but may not choose not to choose between. The sense of the uniqueness of an individual's future is captured in the *way* the choice of how to resolve the tension between contradictory forces is made: classically, by upholding a monotonal hegemony. In earlier chapters I show this through reference to the musical form of Heidegger's *Augenblick.* But Auden's (ontological) analysis of the quest narrative, like

---

[45] We do not 'possess' the tonic at the beginning of the sonata: it is merely promised. Were that not so, then everything that follows the opening tonic section would be tautological at best, redundant at worst. Cf. Auden: 'one can imagine what [the desired thing] will be like but whether one's picture is true or false will be known only when one has found it'.

[46] 'Otherness' is central to the sonata principle: it generates the 'tension' that must be 'resolved'. And the Other material, i.e. the secondary material, is the most powerful music in the form. Without the S-materials, there could be no sonata, because there would be no need for tonal resolution; without the S-materials there is only bombastic, flaccid sterility. The basis of sonata form, then, itself the basis of musical thought for two centuries, is (on one interpretation) a self-asserting triumph of Otherness over Sameness.

traditional explanations of sonata form, does not explain *why* resolution comes, or what brings it about; for that one must turn to Tolkien's own analysis of the quest narrative.[47]

The greatest medium for the quest narrative in literature is, on Tolkien's view, the fairy-story, which is a catalyst and perhaps the principal literary focus of what he calls 'Recovery'. This is a kind of re-sacralization of the world, a reinvestment of the world with meaning. Derridians will snort but Heideggerians will purr, seeing that it closely mirrors Heidegger's conception of art revealing things as they are, for the first time, in the full, awesome complexity of their Being.[48] Speaking metaphorically of fairy-stories as leaves 'from the countless foliage of the Tree of Tales, with which the Forest of Days is carpeted', Tolkien says that each story, each 'leaf, of oak and ash and thorn, is a unique embodiment of the pattern, and for some this very year may be *the* embodiment, the first ever seen and recognized'.[49]

Mimicking Heidegger's characteristic zero-derivation of verbs from nouns, we might summarize Tolkien thus: fairy-stories allow trees *to tree*, and hills *to hill*. They do this by creating a believable Secondary World which is neither the same as nor different from the Primary World, and which in fact depends crucially on it. The structures of the Secondary World are found in and must be read off the Primary World, but they cannot ever be fully evidenced in it, just as music's supratemporality is found in and must be read off worldly temporality, but cannot ever be fully evidenced in it. Speaking phenomenologically, one might say that Tolkien's Secondary World is an intentional object of stupendous complexity founded on observation and experience of the world. And expressed thus one can see parallels with Roman Ingarden's analysis of music (see Chapter 2 of this book). Tolkien's fairy-story has a 'worldly' form; Ingarden's music a 'supratemporal' form: the one is a mimesis of how the most 'worldly' thing, i.e. the Primary World, is or might be; the other a mimesis of how the most 'temporal' thing – on Heidegger's view and definition, Dasein – is or might be. One could say that music allows man *to man*.

The crux of Tolkien's argument addresses the questions, raised earlier, of *how* and *why* events resolve themselves in particular ways – the questions

---

[47] J. R. R. Tolkien, 'On fairy-stories', in *The Monsters and the Critics and Other Essays*, ed. Christopher Tolkien (London: Harper Collins, 1983), pp. 109–61.

[48] Art, as 'poetry' (defined specifically by Heidegger as a means of communicating), 'alone brings beings as beings into the open for the first time'. See Heidegger, 'Origin of the work of art', trans. Albert Hofstadter, in *Martin Heidegger: Basic Writings*, ed. David Farrell Krell (London, Routledge, 1993), p. 168.

[49] Tolkien, 'On fairy-stories', p. 145; cf. Heidegger quotation, preceding note.

which should be at the heart of every good hermeneutics. Finding no answers elsewhere, he creates his own term, one which I have used already in Chapters 1–4, but without explanation.

> Tragedy is the true form of Drama, its highest function; but the opposite is true of Fairy-story. Since we do not appear to possess a word that expresses this opposite – I will call it *Eucatastrophe*. The *eucatastrophic* tale is the true form of fairy-tale, and its highest function.
>
>   The consolation of fairy-stories, the joy of the happy ending: or more correctly of the good catastrophe, the sudden joyous 'turn' (for there is no true end to any fairy-tale): this joy, which is one of the things which fairy-stories can produce supremely well, is not essentially 'escapist', nor 'fugitive'.[50] In its fairy-tale – or otherworld – setting, it is a sudden and miraculous grace: never to be counted on to recur. It does not deny the existence of *dyscatastrophe*, of sorrow and failure: the possibility of these is necessary to the joy of deliverance; it denies (in the face of much evidence, if you will) universal final defeat and in so far is *evangelium*, giving a fleeting glimpse of Joy, Joy beyond the walls of the world, poignant as grief . . .
>
>   In such stories when the sudden 'turn' comes we get a piercing glimpse of joy, and heart's desire, that for a moment passes outside the frame, rends indeed the very web of story, and lets a gleam come through.[51]

There are tangible Adornian resonances in this description of eucatastrophe: is it not the *Durchbruch* under another name? Both ideas were formulated at roughly the same time: Tolkien's essay originated as a lecture in March 1939, beating Adorno's Mahler book by twenty-one years, but 'the rupture between self and forms' (*der Bruch zwischen Ich und Formen*) had concerned Adorno since the 1920s,[52] and the form it takes in 1960 is merely a fully unfurled form of an early idea. In that book, and in words redolent of Tolkien's (quoted above), Adorno says of the *Durchbruch* that 'The rupture [*der Bruch*] originates from beyond the music's intrinsic

---

[50] Tolkien has no truck with those who sniff at the 'escapism' of fairy-stories – or, by extension, the 'escapism' inherent in any artistic mimesis, music not least. 'Why should a man be scorned, if, finding himself in prison, he tries to get out and go home? Or if, when he cannot do so, he thinks and talks about other topics than jailers and prison-walls? The world outside has not become less real because the prisoner cannot see it. In using Escape in this way the critics have chosen the wrong word, and, what is more, they are confusing, not always by sincere error, the Escape of the Prisoner with the Flight of the Deserter' (ibid., p. 148).

[51] Ibid., pp. 153–4.

[52] See Max Paddison, *Adorno's Aesthetics of Music* (Cambridge: Cambridge University Press, 1993), pp. 21–5.

movement, intervening from outside.'[53] For him, the outside is the Other (or New) set over against 'the world's course' (or tradition), the deliberately internecine, 'mediating' binary opposition which governs his interpretation of Mahler's music. In fact the rupture between Self and Form is not so very different from the gulf between the 'authentic Self' and inauthentic 'they-Self' or 'One-self', or the rift between 'earth' and 'world' in the Heideggerian philosophy Adorno found so objectionable. But the crucial difference between the (*Durch*)*bruch* and the eucatastrophe, as will soon become abundantly clear, is that Tolkien's conception is subtler: he allows for eucatastrophe *and* dyscatastrophe, while Adorno's 'breakthrough' retains a certain narrative ambiguity that is not, beyond its application to Mahler's music, very helpful.[54]

But what of eucatastrophe in music? Scott Burnham's interpretation of Schenker in particular and post-Beethovenian music theory in general (*Beethoven Hero*) leads one to wonder whether tragedy, as in the first movement of Beethoven's Fifth Symphony, the movement which gives us the *Ursatz*, is also 'the true form of music, and its highest function'.[55] Or perhaps music is tragedy and fairy-story in one, for in that symphony we also clearly have a traditional eucatastrophic happy ending. The beginning of the 'turn' is, of course, the transition to the finale, the *evangelium* the glorious final bars of C major. And in the Ninth Symphony, eucatastrophic 'Joy' is proclaimed explicitly in words, while the 'turn' is prepared by 'O Freunde, nicht diese Töne'.

Examples of truly dyscatastrophic endings are quite rare, but Mahler's 'Tragic' Sixth Symphony is a powerful example. The three dyscatastrophic hammer-blows in its finale arguably pack a punch even mightier than Beethoven's trombone bombardment in the finale of his Fifth Symphony – a moment which is, so to speak, the Last Trump, or in German *die letzte Posaune* (the last trombone), at the sound of which God reaches over into the space of the universe, changing each one of us, and calling everything into Himself.[56] But of course none of that would do (in 1903–4, at least)

---

[53] Theodor W. Adorno, *Mahler: a Musical Physiognomy*, trans. Edmund Jephcott (Chicago and London: University of chicago Press, 1992 orig. edn 1960), p. 5.

[54] To be fair, this criticism may also be levelled at Heidegger's differentiation between inauthentic and authentic temporalizing. The attainment of authenticity can still be bad news for the individual (see further, Chapter 6, in my discussion of the First Symphony's *Augenblick*, and the brief discussion of *Peter Grimes*).

[55] Nietzsche was once persuaded that this might be the case.

[56] In Luther's 1545 translation 1 Corinthians 15:52 reads: 'in einem Nu, in einem Augenblick, bei der letzten Posaune; denn posaunen wird es, und die Toten werden auferweckt werden, unvergänglich sein, und wir werden verwandelt werden'.

for Mahler, who himself called the Sixth Symphony 'tragic'.[57] God doesn't even get a look in.

So are we stuck with just 'catastrophe', whether for good or ill? Or is the meaning and potency of each more subtle, less black-and-white? I think that the conflation of tragedy and fairy-story, the bifurcation of the goals of eucatastrophe, is not as impossible as Tolkien seems to suggest. At least one writer has argued that eucatastrophe has a literary function in tragedy as well as fairy-story. His focus is *King Lear*, and its relation to its source, *The True Chronicle History of King Leir*, an anonymous tragedy with a 'fairy-tale' happy ending. In Shakespeare's play,

> The fairy-tale eucatastrophe of the earlier anonymous drama of *Leir* is smashed. Indeed, to borrow Berowne's words, this tragedy doth not end like the old play. Consider the majesty – the moral majesty – which Shakespeare has chosen to destroy . . .
>
> In the Chronicle [i.e. *King Leir*], when Cordelia returns with the French army, she wins and places her father on the throne. It might be thought that Shakespeare exercised his maximum destructive energy, when he turned this victory into defeat. The truth is a good deal more painful. For Shakespeare continues the music of eucatastrophe, beyond the point of material defeat, thus giving it an inescapably spiritual power – a Christian power. Lear and his daughter, hauled off to prison, are in charity both with each other and with their captors. The emotional tyrant of Act I now wishes to kneel to his own daughter and is luminously benevolent to his very gaolers. It is possible to think at this point of the play, 'Nothing that these people can do to them now can destroy this love, itself formed from an extremity of suffering; because it transcends material humiliation it is full Christian charity, something stronger than pain or death.'
>
> But as we all know, something more can be done to them, and is done . . . It is the ending Johnson could not bear, the killing of Cordelia. When Lear enters, howling, with Cordelia dead in his arms, which is he more like, the archaic King of the opening (now carried to much greater power), or the figure of universal charity we saw at the beginning of V. iii? . . . It is as if, by killing Cordelia before the King, Shakespeare has quickened ancient moral energies which Christianity cannot, after all, effortlessly transcend.[58]

---

[57] The programme for the third and last Mahlerian performance of the work on 4 December 1907 – almost exactly a year before the premiere of Elgar's First Symphony – bore the title: 'Sechste Sinfonie (Tragische)'. See David Matthews, 'The Sixth Symphony', in *The Mahler Companion*, ed. Donald Mitchell and Andrew Nicholson (Oxford: Oxford University Press, 1999), pp. 366–75 at p. 371.

[58] A. D. Nuttall, *Why Does Tragedy Give Pleasure?* (Oxford: Clarendon Press, 1996), pp. 90–3.

Here is eucatastrophe 'poignant as grief', as Tolkien says, a glimpse of something that, no matter how beautiful and joyous, cannot ultimately triumph over the ills of this world. The eucatastrophe of fairy-tale can 'never ... be counted on to recur', he says, and in *Lear* it does not. Lear is broken and seems to be remade; but (divine) help does not come a second time.

This is the unrealized tragic *conclusion* latent in the musical narrative of Beethoven's Fifth Symphony and its many imitations. Eucatastrophe, such as the transition to the finale and the joyous explosion of its opening bars, can bring with it a joy that reaches in from beyond the frame of the world; but it cannot be counted on to recur, and should the narrative *continue* – 'for there is no true end to any fairy-tale', Tolkien notes – it may be that its eucatastrophe will be superseded by dyscatastrophe, or that it implodes, as in *Lear*.

The discountenancing of the breakthrough in the Rondo-Burleske of Mahler's Ninth Symphony is not quite the same as the tragic use of eucatastrophe I am discussing here.[59] In the Ninth Symphony it is proposed that a breakthrough in the trio section might lead to redemption; but very shortly, in the mocking woodwind liquidation of its material, the quickly reached conclusion is: '*this* breakthrough *can't* lead to redemption'. Its recall at bb. 73ff. in the finale, on D♭ instead of D major and *pp subito* after a massively hopeful upbeat, confirms its impotence. That, properly understood, is breakthrough failure, *not* tragic eucatastrophe. For the latter to occur in the Ninth Symphony, the breakthrough would have to effect some form of redemption (say, a D major opening to the Adagio) which later events – maybe the *ersterbend* of the closing page – turn on its head, just as Lear's 'redemption' in prison is turned agonizingly to tragedy by the end. And it is this second kind of rupture, I suggest, that Elgar uses in his First Symphony and *Falstaff*. It marks him out even from Mahler.

Like Elgar, both Auden and Tolkien are aware that if the narrative just goes a stage further, *evangelium* may be impossible to maintain, and victory may turn to defeat.

> 'And so they lived happily ever after' is a conventional formula for concluding a fairy tale. Alas, it is false and we know it, for it suggests that, once Good has triumphed over Evil, man is translated out of his historical existence into eternity. Tolkien is much too honest to end with such a pious fiction. Good has triumphed over Evil so far as the Third Age of Middle-earth is concerned, but there is no certainty that this triumph is final.[60]

---

[59] cf. Adorno, *Mahler*, p. 165.
[60] Auden, 'The quest hero', p. 60.

Shakespeare might have 'got through' eucatastrophe to an intensified tragic height five centuries ago, but it would not be till the twentieth century that the emptiness of the happily-ever-after formula would become almost impossible to condone. Despite their alleged conservatism, both Tolkien and Elgar avoid it, and both do so by working inside traditions that have explicitly and for many generations accepted the happy-ending thesis *in toto*. As such, they are both modernists, although the learned may balk at the suggestion. But to the learned we need simply say that a man may be a revolutionary even if his means of communicating are reactionary: he can change the world order even if he prefers carrier pigeons to text messages.

The beliefs expressed in the Beethovenian heroic narrative, when boiled down as in my summary of Burnham's analysis above, are precisely those which lead countries like nineteenth-century Britain or twenty-first-century America to build up vast international empires. The justification for pillage and enslavement of weaker foreigners – if that is what empire-building is, and Edward Said argues that it is[61] – comes from the deeply held belief that through struggle, even if it must be against one another, human beings can progress to a significantly better, perhaps almost perfect, world. Disney makes the suggestion warm, but it is easy to make it inhumanly, sepulchrally cold. Such a belief, taken to its most chilling extreme, can be seen to lie behind events like the Russian Revolution, or even the bombing of New York and Washington with passenger jets. It is disastrous.

Elgar was, probably for 'inauthentic' reasons, a superficial imperialist who flourished at the height of the British Empire and wrote the odd jingoistic tub-thumper. If a mind of Elgar's scintillating intelligence had cared deeply – or, frankly, at more than the most puerilely superficial level – about empire, he would have written a substantial and intelligent body of work in support of it. That he did not speaks volumes. Whatever it can be said to amount to, at least Elgar's relation to empire is now being examined thoughtfully, not brushed aside. Hot potatoes need to be dealt with, and if they can be passed from hand to hand, so much the better.[62]

---

[61] Edward Said, *Orientalism* (London: Routledge and Kegan Paul, 1978).

[62] For a sub-Saidian analysis see Corissa Gould, 'Edward Elgar, *The Crown of India*, and the image of empire', *Elgar Society Journal* 13 (2003), pp. 23–35; and for subtler interpretations, see Charles Edward McGuire, 'Functional music: imperialism, the Great War, and Elgar as popular composer', in *The Cambridge Companion to Elgar*, ed. Julian Rushton and Daniel M. Grimley (Cambridge: Cambridge University Press, 2004), pp. 214–24, and the chapter on Elgar in Jeffrey Richards, *Imperialism and Music: Britain 1876–1953* (Manchester and New Yark: Manchester University Press, 2001). For very

One old story, and not an especially credible one, reads his imperialism in a wholly negative light. In 1935 the young and passionately political Benjamin Britten wrote of Elgar's First Symphony: 'I swear that only in Imperialist England could such a work be tolerated.'[63] The irony is that two months after this summary judgement, on 6 November 1935, the first full performance was given of Walton's First Symphony, a work which unlike Elgar's symphony reinforces the Beethovenian heroic *per aspera ad astra* narrative with a classic final eucatastrophe.[64] Elgar's First Symphony, which, like his Second, can be heard on one interpretation to make mock of a hundred years of hope in human progress, i.e. the entire history of Victorian imperial expansion, was and perhaps still is derided as a work that upholds the old world order, while a work in a more reassuringly modern idiom, which can convince one to believe that it carries a 'modern' meaning, expresses the same old beliefs but with an appealing new tang: Beethoven plus horseradish. It would palter with the truth less to say that Walton is the reactionary imperialist and Elgar the revolutionary.[65] In the following chapters I shall attempt to support this claim.

different treatments, which follow along the lines outlined in Chapter 1 Section 3, see Bernard Porter, 'Elgar and empire: music, nationalism and the war', in *'Oh, My Horses!': Elgar and the Great War* (Rickmansworth: Elgar Editions, 2001), and my 'Elgar's deconstruction of the *belle époque*: interface structures and the Second Symphony', in *Elgar Studies*, ed. J. P. E. Harper-Scott and Julian Rushton (Cambridge: Cambridge University Press, forthcoming).

[63] Diary entry, 5. ix. 35, quoted in Humphrey Carpenter, *Benjamin Britten: a Biography* (London: Faber and Faber, 1992), pp. 68–9.

[64] The first three movements had been premiered on 3 December 1934, exactly twenty-six years after the premiere of Elgar's First Symphony.

[65] Britten soon became aware of this irony. He wrote in his diary that the premiere of Walton's First Symphony was a 'great tragedy for English music. Last hope of W. gone now – this is a conventional work, reactionary in the extreme & dull & depressing.' (diary entry, 6. xi. 35, quoted in Carpenter, *Benjamin Britten*, p. 70). Whether the 'tragedy' was, for Britten, musical or ideological we cannot be certain, but it is certainly possible that he heard in it the atavistic pro-imperialism I have suggested. He did not, however, change his opinion of Elgar until he conducted what is probably the finest recording of *The Dream of Gerontius* towards the end of his life.

6 The annihilation of hope and the unpicking of identity: Elgarian hermeneutics

6.1. 'A nice sub-acid feeling': the First Symphony

Before beginning a hermeneutic interpretation of the First Symphony, it will be useful to be reminded, briefly, of its structural outline.

In the first movement, an Ideal Call in a confident but rather unconvincing immuring A♭ is challenged by the sudden entrance of a tonally unstable but A-minor-inflected Sub-Acid Theme, the first of the primary exposition materials. The exposition's trajectory to an immured A minor, and an essential expositional closure in that key at 17:8 with the Amfortas Tune, hinges on a pivotal F major, which acts as a dual agent: VI/A♭ and VI/a. With the full arrival of the immured tonic, the *Kopfton* is punned on and its structural function called into question. The rhetorical ESC (essential structural closure) at 44:8 is into the F minor of the Amfortas Tune's recapitulatory guise (NB this is the 'pivot' key in the minor mode): it is a 'crisis' in the movement, a non-resolution. The coda attempts unsuccessfully to re-establish the immuring A♭ as the movement's final tonic: the final recall of the Amfortas Tune in the closing bars, during which the stasis of the *Kopfton* is re-emphasized, undoes the coda's work.

The second and third movements are directed teleologically towards the D major 'Heaven Tune' of the latter's coda, the theme which establishes the immured tonic as the stronger of the symphony's two tonalities by a considerable margin. On the way to this final *telos* there are other important events. The first *telos* is the arrival of the first D major tune in the Adagio, a slow form of the F♯ minor tune of the second movement, which recalls some of the thematic contours of the Ideal Call, especially the rising fourth (see below, in my discussion of *Parsifal*-derived materials). The second subject too recalls material from the first movement. In this case it is the Amfortas Tune, the tune which first affirms the immured tonic, and here appears as a counterpoint to the second subject, now in A major. Its effect is to draw the first movement's immured A minor into the orbit of the work's immured tonic, D major, as dominant to tonic.

The finale sets about abandoning the immured tonic and re-establishing the immuring tonic. Opening in D minor, a minor-mode rebuttal of the immured D major, Elgar brilliantly re-presents that opening D minor as a 'secondary' key in the exposition by making it seem 'unhomely' after the medial-caesura material immediately preceding it. This allows him to abandon the movement's first tonic and move towards a resolution in A♭. The first *telos* (130:1–133:12) gives the march-like S^2 theme in an edulcorated form on e♭/G♭, 'quashing' its 'coarseness' (Elgar's words), and the recapitulation begins on E♭ minor, v/A♭. As in the first movement, the recapitulation is non-resolving, and again the rhetorical ESC is in F minor. But this point is also the *Augenblick*, the moment which focuses the possibilities of the work uniquely, revealing the 'future' that is most its own. Based on this moment, with its grammatical and structural implications (see Chapter 3 Section 2), the second and final *telos* is possible: the return of the Ideal Call and of A♭. The work closes with a satisfactory tonal ESC, and the completion of the *Ursatz* in the very last bars, this being the first point at which the *Urlinie* descends in the whole work. But there is a sense in which the work ends only because Elgar decides it should: the ending is not, in purely musical terms, absolutely the end of all argument. It could conceivably go on, and things could end differently.

That formal summary is intentionally riddled with lacunae and provocative generalizations, but it gives a good basic idea of the 'horizon' of the work itself, and proceeding from it we may now begin the long-promised hermeneutics, starting with perhaps the most obvious way 'in'. The first of Lawrence Kramer's 'hermeneutic windows' is what he calls a 'textual inclusion'.

> This type includes texts set to music, epigrams, programs, notes to the score, and sometimes even expression markings. In dealing with these materials, it is critical to remember – especially with the texts of vocal pieces – that they do not establish (authorize, fix) a meaning that the music somehow reiterates, but only invite the interpreter to find meaning in the interplay of expressive acts.[1]

Apart from the texted works, such as *The Dream of Gerontius*, in which textual inclusion is obvious to every listener, Elgar's scores, manuscripts, and letters – not to mention his analytical note on *Falstaff* – are often a rich source of literary allusions which may open this kind of hermeneutic window. Brian Trowell has written a magisterial study of them.[2] But the First Symphony, as Trowell notes,

---

[1] Lawrence Kramer, *Music as Cultural Practice, 1800–1900*(Berkeley, CA and London: University of California press, 1990), pp. 9–10.

[2] Brian Trowell, 'Elgar's use of literature', in *Edward Elgar: Music and Literature*, ed. Raymond Monk (Aldershot: Scolar, 1993), pp. 182–326.

bears no epigraph, unlike its sister [symphony], and I know of only one
literary connection, which was not made public, though it may have been
confided to a friend. Significantly, it is the dying Hamlet's last words, 'The
rest is silence', copied in a sketch over the beautiful theme at fig. 104 that ends
the slow movement. This, and the general emotional progression of the work,
would suggest that it reflects Elgar's favourite cycle of a life interrupted by
loss and even self-extinction, but regenerated by hope, by faith, by a
determined resumption of artistic activity, forward-looking if not always
happy.[3]

Hamlet is certainly 'not always happy', yet if this quotation – above a
theme which August Jaeger said brings the listener 'near Heaven': people
have tended to hear something 'otherworldly' in it, even without the
Shakespearean allusion – indicates that Hamlet (or *something*) dies at this
point (why else quote his *dying* words?), then I would question Trowell's
suggestion that the quotation points to 'regeneration' and the rest. At any
rate it might be useful to trace what connexions we may between the
symphony and the play.

An obvious parallel between the two works is that both have an agonizing
indecisiveness as a central thematic concern. Hamlet must decide how or
whether to avenge his father; the symphony must decide how or whether to
restore A♭ to the tonic function it seemed to claim at the beginning of the
first movement. Yet there is a subtler connexion, an existential one, which
probably the most famous crux in Shakespeare draws out:

> So, oft it chances in particular men
> That for some vicious mole of nature in them,
> As in their birth, wherein they are not guilty
> (Since nature cannot choose his origin),
> By their o'ergrowth of some complexion,
> Oft breaking down the pales and forts of reason,
> Or by some habit, that too much o'erleavens
> The form of plausive manners – that these men,
> Carrying, I say, the stamp of one defect,
> Being Nature's livery or Fortune's star,
> His virtues else, be they as pure as grace,
> As infinite as man may undergo,
> Shall in the general censure take corruption
> From that particular fault. The dram of evil

---

[3] Ibid., p. 254. I have already drawn attention to this sketch in Chapter 3 Section 2.

Doth all the noble substance often dout
To his own scandal.

$$(Hamlet, \text{ I. iv. } 23\text{–}38)^4$$

A♭'s livery is meretricious and transparent: it cannot quite conceal its feeble bearer, or disguise its shoddy manufacture; and the 'dram of evil', the 'mole of nature' represented by the Sub-Acid Theme is more than strong enough to dout (meaning 'to put out or extinguish') the noble substance of the work's fairy-tale, eucatastrophic 'happy ending'. As has been pointed out, *Hamlet* is a play about rot that sets in not only in states like Claudius's Denmark but in all societies, and all individual humans – a rot that stinks.[5] And the symphony is, in some sense, also rotten. The worldly dignity of the Ideal Call is eaten up by the corrosiveness of the Sub-Acid Theme and the immured tonality of the first movement, which one might almost therefore call the 'putrefying tonality'. The juxtaposition of A♭ and A minor in the closing bars of the opening movement is therefore, insofar as music is capable of synaesthetic olfactory suggestion, 'smelly'.

Elgar will have read in Dowden's *Shakspere* – a work he cited in his analytical note on *Falstaff* – that

> In several of the tragedies of Shakspere the tragic disturbance of character
> and life is caused by the subjection of the chief person of the drama to some
> dominant passion, essentially antipathetic to his nature, though proceeding
> from some inherent weakness or imperfection – a passion from which the
> victim cannot deliver himself, and which finally works out his destruction.[6]

And Elgar carries this over directly into his own work. There are, both in *Hamlet* and the First Symphony, contradictory forces within a single

---

[4] The reference, with the unusual but convincing 'dout', is to Harold Jenkins's important edition of *Hamlet* for Arden (London: Methuen, 1982).

[5] 'The stink that rises from dead flesh emblematizes the sheer loathsomeness of the sort of evil, cunning and lecherous, with which Claudius has corrupted the whole kingdom; the fact that once begun, the process of rotting gains inexorable headway and the odor it generates spreads far and wide, suggests the dynamic and infectious quality of sin; and the further fact that the process transforms the beautiful human body into a horrid, malodorous mass of corruption is symbolic of the dread effect of sin upon the human soul.' See Richard D. Altick, '*Hamlet* and the odor of mortality', *Shakespeare Quarterly* 5 (1954), pp. 167–76 at p. 167.

[6] Edward Dowden, *Shakspere: A Critical Shidy of this Mind and Art* (London: Henry S. King, 1875; 20th edn London: Kegan Paul, Trench, Trubner & Co., n.d.), p. 129.

'personality', seditious psychological 'moles' (twentieth-century overtones of espionage are appropriate here) that threaten to overthrow reason and logic as it applies either to the character of a human being or the grammar of a symphony. In the symphony, the Amfortas Tune and immured tonality are antipathetic to the Ideal Call and the immuring tonality: the Amfortas Tune robs the Ideal Call of its defining melodic pitch (the *Kopfton*), its cruel pun turning $\hat{3}/A\flat$ into $\hat{3}/a$ – the Jungian 'shadow' aiming to assert itself as 'persona', destabilizing the psychological balance with a spot of mad humour – while the immuring tonality, with its strong harmonic, thematic, and structural support, claims the centre ground in the battle for tonal supremacy. (Combative imagery, which can sound hackneyed in discussions touching on sonata form, nevertheless does not seem out of place here.) Contradictory forces of this nature are, of course, present in every human being, and to a greater or lesser extent in every musical work; they are the Hero and those who test him in the literary quest narrative (see Auden's quest archetype in Chapter 5 Section 2, above), or the tonal tensions in the sonata: but in *Hamlet* and the First Symphony they are elevated to a much grander, almost cosmic, level.

When Elgar writes at the end of the slow movement, even if it is only for his own benefit, that 'the rest is silence', we may be invited to reflect that D major, the beautiful 'heavenly' hope at the centre of the work, has died. And with it does hope die *altogether* in the symphony? What can bring redemption in *Hamlet* or the First Symphony after the protagonist dies? Let us turn now to another intertextual dimension of this symphony, its curious and subtle relation through Kramer's 'citational inclusions' to *Parsifal*. It may be that the answer to the question 'what brings redemption?' may be found there.[7]

I know of no pointer in Elgar's own words to establish a solid link between Wagner's opera and this symphony, but the evidence of our ears

---

[7] Aidan Thomson has an engrossing thesis of *Parsifal*-influence in Elgar. By marking motivic and tonal associations between the works, he reads the First Symphony as 'creatively associated with the narrative strategy of *Parsifal* – and, by implication, with its contemporary ideological message of reclaimed idealism' ('Elgar and chivalry', *Nineteenth-Century Music* 28 (2005), pp. 254–75 at p. 264). This is, for Thomson, a culturally conservative rather than a progressive move, albeit a complex, dialectical conservatism with regard both to society and to his own creative process; see also his discussion of *Falstaff* in the same essay (pp. 267–74). In his D.Phil. thesis he widens the net to consider Parsifalian resonances in *The Black Knight*, *The Banner of St George*, *The Dream of Gerontius*, and *The Apostles* ('Re-reading Elgar: hermeneutics, criticism and reception in England and Germany, 1900–1914', D.Phil. thesis, University of Oxford, 2002).

is sufficient, and people have been hearing sounds redolent of *Parsifal* in the First Symphony for seventy years. A. J. Sheldon, in his posthumously published *Edward Elgar*, writes that the Ideal Call is 'such a theme as the Knights of the Grail might have kept step to in their solemn progress through Monsalvat',[8] and one can hear an echo of the fourth to sixth bars of the first-act prelude of *Parsifal* in the third to sixth bars of the Ideal Call (Ex. 6.1), while at the end of the first movement, where the stasis of the *Kopfton* is emphasized, the likeness is even more remarkable (Ex. 3.7). And an element of the first *Parsifal* theme, the 'spear motive', a stepwise rising fourth, is especially prominent in the Adagio theme (Ex. 3.1). In his essay on Elgar's symphonies James Hepokoski notes the Ideal Call's indebtedness to Wagner, and also points to the 'Amfortas-like brass cries'[9] of what I therefore call the Amfortas Tune in the first movement – the first arrival of the immured tonic, in its as-yet-not-fully-realized form, A minor.

But is the key structure not more suggestive for our hermeneutics than these thematic hints? Hepokoski spots an 'A♭-ness' that the *Parsifal* prelude and the Ideal Call have in common, and it seems to me equally interesting that *Parsifal*'s 'Good Friday Music' and the immured tonic in the symphony have a (spiritual) 'D-major-ness' in common. It is by examining the suggestiveness of these commonalities, and the progress in both works from A♭ to D major and back again, that we may find Elgar's (complex) answer to the question, 'what brings redemption?' His answer is, it seems to me, both surprising and unnerving.

Recall Elgar's words: 'the opening theme [of the First Symphony] is intended to be simple &, in intention, noble & elevating . . . the sort of *ideal* call – in the sense of persuasion, not coercion or command – & something above everyday & sordid things'.[10] It is possible that the 'ideal call' he speaks of is the call of God, a vocation; a calling that offers a real choice, not the semblance of one: it is the kind of choice, in short, that Amfortas has.[11] As a Knight of the Grail, Amfortas is of course a Christian, and one convinced more than most, one imagines, by the grace of the repeated miracles he witnesses to believe in the earthly manifestation of divine power to redeem and save. Yet at the same time he is 'wonderfully' wounded by the 'wunden-wundervoller heiliger Speer' that he had tried to use to put an end to the lasciviousness of Klingsor – who was

---

[8] A. J. Sheldon, *Edward Elgar* (London: Office of 'Musical Opinion', 1932), p. 48.

[9] James A. Hepokoski, 'Elgar', in *The Nineteenth-Century Symphony*, ed. D. Kern Holoman (New York and London: Schirmer, 1997), p. 331.

[10] Elgar, *Edward Elgar: Letters of a Lifetime*, ed. Jerrold Northrop Moore (Oxford: Clarendon press, 1990), p. 200.

[11] It is also the kind of choice that Hamlet has.

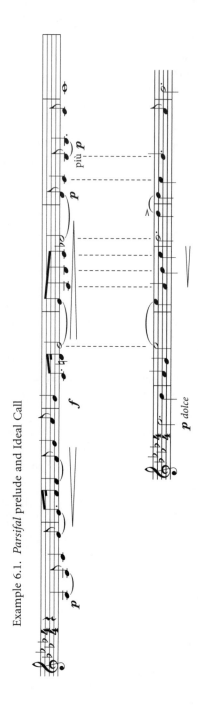

Example 6.1. *Parsifal* prelude and Ideal Call

excommunicated by Titurel, one presumes, for sexual indiscretions; the magician castrated himself to atone – and his wound can only be healed by mortal agency. Celebrating the Grail Mass, the supreme iterable earthly miracle, reopens his wound and intensifies his misery, but if a witless youth touches the wound with the spear he guilelessly retrieves from Klingsor Amfortas will personally be saved.

Wagner's curious theology here seems to suggest on the one hand that universal salvation, as represented by the Grail and the powerful love of God, is incapable of saving Amfortas, and on the other hand that the actions of a Hero, which are powerless to save humanity, are nevertheless the only way that Amfortas qua individual can be saved – i.e. that God is powerless to save Amfortas without additional human agency. It is a theology played out in *Tristan* too, as Roger Scruton has recently shown. In Scruton's view, we humans 'can achieve the transfiguration for which it is in our nature to yearn with no help from God'.[12] God is powerless to bring about redemption, or rather is unnecessary, because 'man makes himself by *sacralizing* himself, and . . . by sacralizing himself he also sacralizes the world . . . And once we recognize that the sacred too is a human invention, redemption becomes a possibility'.[13]

In her interpretation of *Parsifal*, Lucy Beckett suggests that 'Amfortas's sin and repentance . . . belong to a different story from Amfortas's unhealed wound, although the sexual guilt with which Wagner binds them together is a triumphant psychological and dramatic invention'.[14] I assert, by contrast, that rather than being 'a different story', Amfortas's sexual guilt is the central component of his sin, and the only route to absolution is therefore necessarily through the joint action of the deity and the wholly human saviour, Parsifal. Beckett goes on to say that the human element of the saving act has a Schopenhauerian source, and that while, 'for the Christian, salvation comes from God through Christ, for Schopenhauer it is a purely human achievement'.[15]

[12] Roger Scruton, *Death-Devoted Heart: Sex and the Sacred in Wagner's 'Tristan und Isolde'* (New York: Oxford University Press, 2004), p. 185.

[13] Ibid., pp. 182–3.

[14] Lucy Beckett, 'A proposed interpretation', in *Richard Wagner: Parsifal*, ed. Lucy Beckett (Cambridge: Cambridge University Press, 1981), pp. 129–49 at p. 133.

[15] Ibid., p. 134. She argues that in the man-led redemption Parsifal *reveals* Christ's redemptive power (p. 146), but I insist that Parsifal does not merely 'reveal' divine redemption, but actually mediates it (even if he cannot actually be said to *enact* it). And mediation is more involved than revelation, since it requires a specific agent performing certain acts to bring about a redemption which would not otherwise come to pass. If Parsifal merely 'revealed' Christ's redemption, i.e. made it open to view, then the redemption could happen without his agency.

In fact, I suggest that this 'Schopenhauerian' human role in salvation *is* fully compatible with Christian belief, and that the theology is not actually even idiosyncratic to Wagner. The theologian John Macquarrie, one of the translators of *Being and Time*, characterizes Christianity in his Heideggerian systematic theology as the only 'existential–ontological theism' because it requires both at its heart and in every individual case the active participation of human being ('existence') *and* God (Being).[16] At the heart, there is Jesus, a man, offering himself, and God, Being, receiving the offering and working with it; and in each particular case of Christian existence, the individual must choose and act in certain ways, while God acts on and with those chosen actions. Wagner brings out this two-sided existential–ontological theology in a subtle and very personal way in both *Parsifal* and *Tristan*. Elgar's 'call' is much less complex than Wagner's, and while being therefore somehow less Christian it nevertheless makes him more modern, because less confident that man's nature is essentially good. Elgar's 'ideal call' draws man away from – draws man *above*, as he says – 'everyday & sordid things'. His vision is therefore fairy-tale: the eucatastrophic happy ending requires outside help; salvation is entirely by divine agency, not existential, but purely ontological.

The Ideal Call seems 'in intention' to be rather like Heidegger's *Ereignis*, the 'happening' (in a work of art, for instance) which re-sacralizes the world and reveals the awesome, ungraspable Other of Being.[17] The *Ereignis*, or as I call it the 'mimetic window', shows us the 'thingness' of a thing, revealing that our view of things in 'the enframing' is banausic, which is to say mechanical, and restricted to immediate use-value – it shows us that our understanding is 'everyday & sordid'. And it shows not only that there is more to things than we tend to think, but also that we

---

[16] John Macquarrie, *Principles of Christian Theology*, 2nd edn (London: SCM, 1997). 'Existence' or 'standing-out' is, on Heidegger's definition, unique to Dasein, while the ground for the possibility of any ontology at all is Being, or God: hence Macquarrie's 'existential–ontological theism'. Other religions stress human or divine agency separately (as regards the specific issue of salvation), but not together. Julian Young too is clear (in *Heidegger's Later Philosophy* (Cambridge: Cambridge University Press, 2002)) that Being 'is' God in Heidegger's philosophy, although unlike Macquarrie he stresses that it is not the God of Christian theology. Herman Philipse, meanwhile, goes so far as to characterize Heidegger's Being as 'post-monotheistic' (in *Heidegger's Philosophy of Being* (Princeton, NJ: Princeton University Press, 1998), esp. pp. 172–210). But all are agreed that the self-presencing of Being requires man to nurture the presencing, and in this sense Macquarrie's argument holds: man and Being work together.

[17] This is precisely the effect of artistic mimesis in Gadamer's usage (and mine).

have a way of getting through to the truth.[18] It is, as I have been arguing, a calling or vocation, a way of making a gestalt switch in our understanding of the world. But in this symphony the Ideal Call never functions fully like the *Ereignis*, never wakes us up to the mysterious Other of Being, because it never quite achieves its potential: it always falls short just as it promises to open up sublime new vistas. And furthermore, the Ideal Call is not the only potential *Ereignis* in the work; there is also the Heaven Tune: recall Jaeger's Heideggerian-sounding words on that bringing us 'near Heaven'. For the *Ereignis* to 'happen', therefore, A♭ and D – and their two principal associated themes, the Ideal Call and the Heaven Tune – must be somehow conjoined in a concerted act of musical 'happening', whatever Elgar's way of conjoining the tonalities and themes might be.

The difference between Wagner's and Elgar's conception of redemption and salvation, or of an individual's self-discovery and self-definition, is therefore nowhere more apparent than in their respective handling of the tritonal opposition of A♭ and D, which constitutes the *Ereignis* in each of the works in question – or one such 'happening' of the revealing of truth, for there are always many in great art. Those keys are set as far apart as man and God. Both are separated by a devil: the keys by *diabolus in musica*, God and man (in traditional Christian teaching) by Satan himself, whether an embodiment of evil is believed literally or only symbolically as the power of sin. In *Parsifal*, 'A♭-ness' and 'D-ness' join hands in the saving act of the final scene, when the D major of the supreme existential sacrifice symbolized by the Good Friday Music becomes the key of Parsifal-as-redeemer, and the A♭ of the Grail underpins his second redemptive act, the death of Kundry. God and man, both clearly distinct, nevertheless work the two redemptions together; and D and A♭, also clearly distinct, also work together as one, a tonal paradox made into a very great virtue. But in Elgar's First Symphony, the teleology of the immured tonality is in the end discountenanced, and the eucatastrophe of the Heaven Tune allowed to pall and lose its power to turn events to a happy conclusion. We return 'home', to A♭, i.e. to the beginning, to the *past*, not to the consummation of the D major teleology so scrupulously prepared by Elgar. By the end of the symphony A♭ and D are still opposed to one another inconclusively; because A♭ is simply restated, albeit grandly, and does not emerge from the processes of the music as a *necessary* goal (it is merely a *possible* one), there is nothing like the long-range tonal and thematic 'completing and perfecting [of] the musical form as an

---

[18] The reader is referred back to the discussion of the hermeneutic circle and horizons of disclosure in Section 1 of Chapter 5.

audible symbol for the utopia of redemption' which William Kinderman elucidates in *Parsifal*.[19]

It is critical to this potted interpretation of *Parsifal*, and through it my exegesis of Elgar's treatment of the tritonal tension between A♭ and D, that Parsifal's heroism be understood as active, not passive (the latter being Dahlhaus's belief).[20] As Kinderman argues,[21] at the moment of Kundry's kiss Parsifal undergoes a transformation that comes to three other great Wagnerian redeemers-through-love, Tristan, Isolde, and Siegfried, only at the end of their lives. As the 'replay of the earlier seduction scene'[22] between Kundry and Amfortas, which occurs before the drama begins, this kiss becomes Parsifal's *Augenblick*. It awakens him to his destiny as redeemer, in the context of a tragedy linked to his *Augenblick* which stretches back into his youthful nescience. He therefore draws in potential from before the beginning of the drama and projects it on, from the moment of the kiss, to the end. He is no lifeless tool of the drama, no *deus ex machina*, but a resolute individual projecting his own future, in this case for the sake of others. Furthermore, and on the more purely musical level, complex thematic and tonal connexions stretching from the opening of the drama are all drawn together in the final A♭,[23] and the promise of the active hero is fulfilled. Elgar's peroration in A♭ has no such massive or compelling preparation. What does this mean? Profound things, if we can perform the difficult task of viewing the symphony as a four-movement unity with a definite truth-giving purpose.

But the colossal structure of Elgar's First Symphony, a single argument ranging over about an hour of music, demands much of the listener, although not perhaps much more than Beethoven's Op. 131 Quartet.[24] Elgar's dramatization of important moments by use of the various devices

---

[19] William Kinderman, 'Dramatic recapitulation and tonal pairing in Wagner's *Tristan und Isolde* and *Parsifal*', in *The Second Practice of Nineteenth-Century Tonality* (Lincoln, NE: University of Nebraska Press, 1996), pp. 178–214 at p. 210.

[20] See Carl Dahlhaus, *Richard Wagner's Music Dramas*, trans. Mary Whitall (Cambridge: Cambridge University Press, 1979; orig. edn 1971), p. 147.

[21] Kinderman, 'Dramatic recapitulation', pp. 202–6. Lucy Beckett also believes it is 'a mistake to regard Parsifal . . . as "a passive hero"' (Beckett, 'A proposed interpretation', p. 144).

[22] Kinderman, 'Dramatic recapitulation', p. 204.

[23] Ibid., pp. 206–10.

[24] It should be pointed out that, unlike Beethoven's quartet, the movements of Elgar's symphony do not sacrifice their individual autonomy to the whole piece in the same way; Elgar's movements are at the same time both autonomous and subsidiary parts of a whole, like American States.

discussed in the analysis in Chapter 3 aids the listener as he or she tries to follow the various threads of this densely plotted work. Although the surface of his music may well seem 'violently switched about',[25] when the end comes Elgar's grammar is impeccable, and concentrated reflexion on what has passed will explain how that end has been reached.

But good grammar is not the same as a convincing argument. The conventional close in A♭ proves that, despite what he might have said with the tendentiousness of the partially inverted snob, Elgar certainly knew how to follow the rules. He presents the listener with a return of the opening theme, in the opening key, and with a satisfactory harmonic closure; but the listener has every right to object that this opening theme and its immuring tonic have by various means been emasculated, and the gloriously eucatastrophic light of the third movement, which brought him 'near Heaven', hidden under a bushel. Why must we accept it is A♭ and all is well when most of the work has been playing a different tune and pointing to a different locus for hope? (A♭ stands for human hope, not divine.) Just as the single flat in the key signature at 5:2 is, as Elgar says, 'convenient for the players',[26] the closure of the *Ursatz* is convenient for the analyst; but only a fundamentalist would claim the end really is a conclusion.

At the beginning of the symphony Elgar seems to say, 'I can write a symphony in A♭ – can't I?' At the end he merely repeats the question. The return of the Ideal Call is not affirmatory: it is palliative. It is perhaps superfluous to note that the immuring A♭ is less bright than the immured D. But does all this actually *mean* anything? What is the symphony *about*?

My intertextual discussion of it alongside *Hamlet* and *Parsifal* gives some suggestion, and Elgar himself gave a hint to Walford Davies, when he wrote of this symphony that there 'is no programme beyond a wide experience of human life with a great charity (love) & a *massive* hope in the future'.[27] These are also commonly understood as Beethoven's concerns in the *Eroica*, but Elgar's symphony is a distinctively twentieth-century creation. There is no final victory, but only 'a massive hope'. Elgar's quest ends, like Tolkien's in *The Lord of the Rings*, with the hero (if there is one at all) scarred and enfeebled by his travails; superficially happy, but deeply unsettled at heart. Elgar's preference for immuring–immured tonality over against directional tonality reflects this narrative structure. Directional tonality can result in triumph because it can absorb

---

[25] Michael Kennedy, *Portrait of Elgar*, 3rd edn (Oxford: Clarendon Press, 1987), p. 248.

[26] Letter to August Jaeger, in Edward Elgar, *Letters to Nimrod: Edward Elgar to August Jaeger, 1897-1908*, ed. Percy M. Young (London: D. Dobson, 1965), p. 276.

[27] Letter to Walford Davies, 13. xi. 1908, in *Lifetime*, p. 205.

tensions and decide on a final outcome, but Elgar's immuring tonality merely swallows tensions and leaves them rumbling inside; and since after a struggle things can never be changed back to their former state, the result must be negative. In *Gerontius* Elgar makes no pretence the story has ended, because the poem makes it clear the story goes on; but in the First Symphony he does pretend the story is over, that eucatastrophe leads to evangelium, which is why unpicking his argument is so profitable.

The symbolic implications of Elgar's structural technique are, then, antiheroic and thoroughly modern. None of the seven structural devices of the first movement (see Chapter 3 Section 2) strives *for* something, as Beethoven's music strives to overcome difficulties; each device strives *against* something: the 'quest' of the First Symphony is not to find or gain the immuring A♭, but to lose or destroy the immured D. (The difference between this and Wagner's goal is striking.) Beethoven's heroic music, and later music in the same style, seeks to absorb contradictions and complexities into a final, glorious apotheosis; the hero grows through his trials into something far greater than even he could have hoped. And to the nineteenth-century mind such an idea was conceivable: to cite a single example, its renewed veneration of saints would have been unthinkable if it was not believed that miraculous power could be used entirely for good, and to the benefit of its user. But in the twentieth century, whose greatest power struggle led only to Auschwitz, this belief was turned on its head. The heroic ideal is in important ways less easy to take seriously now, and while the saintly hero with miraculous power used to be called Prometheus or St George, nowadays the closest we can get is Harry Potter.[28] There are no heroes in Elgar, or at least none Beethoven would recognize. Elgar said his symphony offered *hope*, but he presents it as a rather forlorn one. His musical hermeneutics of human existence is rather bleak, but it invites us to confront difficult issues – issues which in 1908 he was prescient to raise.

Most of Elgar's mature music was written before the First World War, but even without the personal experience of the chief evils of the twentieth century he would eventually have, he composed knowing that 'power tends to corrupt, and absolute power corrupts absolutely'.[29] Therefore, his refusal to grant A♭ the unambiguous structural power the tonic had traditionally expected – and still got, ultimately, in the directional-tonal

---

[28] This point has been made by Tom Shippey in *J. R. R. Tolkein: Author of the Century* (London: Harper Collins, 2000), pp. 112–17.

[29] Lord Acton, letter to Bishop Mandell Creighton, 3. iv. 1887, in Louise Creighton, *Life and Letters of Mandell Creighton* (London: Longmans, 1904), vol. 1, chapter. 13.

structures of Mahler – can be read as an authentically twentieth-century scepticism. If the concluding A♭ is deemed weak, then Elgar would appear to say that human victory, whether over personal anxiety or political antagonism, is impossible, because all that can be effected is man's return to his starting point, and from there tragedy will inevitably ensue. On this view all human endeavour leads ultimately to ruin; and in his way Elgar makes his point as powerfully as post-War writers of fantasy such as Tolkien, Golding, and Orwell. If the pessimistic interpretation is, on balance, the one that despite the symphony's lingering ambiguities is the one which must be preferred, then the First Symphony's 'motto' theme, the Ideal Call, is misnamed: the Sub-Acid Theme, which symbolizes the anxiety over the necessity to choose between possibilities it has itself created, and the ultimate failure to find unproblematic resolution, is really the motto of this symphony, and perhaps of all Elgar.

To understand how this point is made, however, we must get to grips with how the 'hero's victory' in this symphony is presented in an ironic and cynical way, and it is the *Augenblick* that allows for that understanding. Recall Heidegger's definition of the *Augenblick* as the moment of vision that brings Dasein in its Present away from 'distraction' (*Zerstreuung*) with immediate concerns, and carries it – holding in force future and past – to the possibilities most distinctively its own, which are then projected resolutely into an authentic future. The *Augenblick* changes the form of Dasein's everyday activity, but not the content.

Elgar's object of concern in this symphony is the resolution of the tension between immuring-A♭ and immured-D tonalities. A Dasein in an inauthentic present is, on Heidegger's account, over-concerned with immediate things, to the extent that it is Being-*alongside* them in a way that limits Dasein's potentiality-for-Being itself. Over-concern in music, then, might manifest itself as a 'distraction' – or, more literally, 'scattering' – with or in immediate syntactic questions such as the 'key' of the Sub-Acid Theme. (If one is blind even to the possibility of falling in love then one's 'distraction' or 'scattering' in the popcorn and Coca Cola of a cinema trip will limit one's potentiality-for-Being oneself, i.e. a lover, in the romantic example from Chapter 2. It may lessen the pain of acting on the *Augenblick*, and inauthenticity is the supreme existential palliative medicine: but one will scarcely be oneself.) When taken on to the level of the entire structure (i.e. the *Ursatz*) such distraction is counterproductive, and we must look 'deeper', to the sixth-unfolding sparked off by the Sub-Acid Theme rather than just at the theme itself, or to the effect of the immured D rather than just to the levelling-off of that key as an engorged contrapuntal-structural chord.

But at the same time we must not imagine that 'distraction' is wholly wrong. Even an authentic individual can enjoy popcorn qua popcorn. It would be a poor early modernist symphonist who did not acknowledge and work with the symphonic tradition, and for Elgar that largely means Beethoven and his powerful influence in the nineteenth century. For Heidegger it is the 'anticipating' 'repetition' of the past that allows for an authentic consummation of the possibilities for individuality glimpsed in the *Augenblick*: seeing the future Dasein 'anticipates' it – *makes* it – by projecting useful possibilities from the past (as its vision of the future permits it to reinterpret them); it 'repeats' them in a way which will serve a new, authentic purpose. In Elgar's case the acknowledgement of the past of the tonal and, especially, the symphonic tradition (if bound up with a fore-conception of the possible goals of the piece, most likely a resolution in either A♭ or D) can allow him to 'repeat' the *Ursatz*, which codifies the Beethovenian symphonic model, or specific musical devices in this work or others, in such a way that his First Symphony projects an entirely distinctive identity. The *Augenblick* does not by itself disentangle the knotty contradictions of the work, since, as Heidegger says, nothing 'happens' 'in it'; it just focuses the possibilities for disentangling them which, if projected resolutely, can eventually lead to a solution, however complex that may be.

Without taking into account the *Augenblick* we risk concluding that the symphony 'repeats' the *Ursatz* in an inauthentic way: the work ends in A♭ after a satisfactory harmonic closure, after all. Is that not a 'happy ending'? But such a misprision is based on a 'scattering' in the tonal tradition, and especially in Beethoven's heroic goal-orientation, as if that style were a thing to be grasped, like a security blanket. In the First Symphony's *Augenblick* the work's 'hero' realizes that his only means of grace lies in the seizure of the powerful tools that tore him apart in the first movement: to become as powerful as he promised he must use the same malicious machinery of his enemy. Here Elgar wrestles with the ineluctable problem of evil that would concern so many twentieth-century artists. Things may indeed triumph over other things, but brute strength does not obey moral rules.

That is what the symphony seems to say in interpersonal terms, but for an individual existent it voices a similarly uncomfortable warning. No matter how clearly we see our future, our supreme possibilities for being – D major in this symphony, so carefully prepared and so beautifully presented – because of some 'vicious mole of nature' in us we will find it impossible to realize our potential. We see the *summum bonum,* but we cannot get to it. Hope, Elgar says, is palliative, not effective; we cannot escape from our limitations, cannot attain the ambition we see so clearly, because our nature is cursed, 'carrying . . . the stamp of one defect'. We are not at home in the world, as Heidegger consistently points out, but – and here Elgar is pessimistic where Heidegger is not – even if we are wise enough to recognize this, by seeing that our proposed A♭ is really not our 'nature' (D is our ownmost Self), we cannot act authentically on our wise realization. Dasein cannot, on Elgar's account, '"choose" itself and win itself'; it can 'only "seem" to do so'.[30] We are stuck with our 'unsettledness' in the world, and permanent, useless angst is all our hope.

It is clear that the *Augenblick* does not just lead us to hermeneutic conclusions that illuminate a single work, composer, or period, i.e. lead us 'to say something about music'. Because of music's temporal similarities with Dasein's temporal 'projection' it actually brings us nearer to understanding what music seems to be saying about us, which is precisely what draws us to the art form in the first place. And Elgar's message is not comforting.

6.2. Elgar's invention of the human: 'Falstaff ([micro-]tragedy)'

If the First Symphony is an exploration of two contradictory forces within one person, which create the impression of two actual combatants, *Falstaff* is an exploration of the relationship between two actual people, which however also stands for the nature of an individual's own relation to his possibilities and choices. The two works are, in a hermeneutic sense, mirror-images of one another. The following Heideggerian reading of the work, based on the existential structure of Being-with, will open out into a discussion of what Elgar's rumination on Falstaff and Hal, played out in the context of musical history, might mean in a less restricted sense. I shall outline the structure of Being-with first in the abstract, and then through an example taken from Britten's *Peter Grimes*, which demonstrates the kinds of musical pointers one might look for in this connexion, before entering into a detailed hermeneutic of *Falstaff*.

The opening co-prolongation of C minor and E♭, as discussed in Chapter 4 Section 2, makes a fundamental existential point about Falstaff which must be grappled with from the outset. Falstaff's identity is bound up with Hal and their loving relationship; his very being is dependent on Hal's, having at its core (on Heidegger's terms) dependent Being-with Others, rather than, at the moment at least, Being-its-Self. A dependence on others does not necessarily preclude an individual Dasein's existentially

---

[30] Martin Heidegger, *Being and Time*, 7th edn trans. John Macquarrie and Edward Robinson (Oxford: Blackwell, 1962; orig. edn 1927), p. 68.

'authentic' self-fulfilment, but Heidegger notes that an individual's 'own-most possibility is *non-relational*, in the sense that surrendering all one's Being to the manipulation of others – the 'they-self' or 'One-self' – leads to the sheepish behaviour of the unimaginative. Authentic Dasein must realize that its life is its own business, its own responsibility, and should strive for the resolute self-definition which is founded chiefly on awareness of its ownmost death. The supreme example of this realization comes in the *Augenblick*. But despite the potentially inauthentic effects of 'losing oneself' in Being-alongside things and Being-with Others in the world, e.g. being too wrapped up in work or the expectations of others to be oneself, both existential structures are essential to Dasein's normal life. He goes on:

> As structures essential to Dasein's constitution, these have a share in conditioning the possibility of any existence whatsoever. Dasein is authentically itself only to the extent that *as* concernful Being-alongside and solicitous Being-with, it projects itself upon its ownmost potentiality-for-Being rather than upon the possibility of the they-self. The entity which anticipates its non-relational possibility is thus forced by that very anticipation into the possibility of taking over from itself its ownmost Being, and doing so of its own accord.[31]

Being wrapped up with things and other people are facts Dasein cannot escape from: they are structures of its Being, and it is by dealing *authentically* with those structures that Dasein can discover and achieve its authentic, individual Self. This dealing with things and other people manifests itself as 'concern' or 'solicitude'. Heidegger's concept of 'solicitude' (*Fürsorge*) in relation to others is part of his basic structure of 'care' (*Sorge*), which refers to our relations to things and other persons, and may have either positive or negative connotations. An individual – say, Hal – might 'care' for the Other, Falstaff, in one of two ways: he could either '*leap in* for him' in the sense that Falstaff 'is thus thrown out of his own position' and has his being shaped by another; or conversely Hal could '*leap ahead* of him . . . not to take away [Falstaff's] "care" but rather to give it back to him authentically as such for the first time'.[32] The distinction is essentially between treating the Other, Falstaff, as a real and potentially authentic individual or simply as a lifeless tool, a means of accomplishing some end or other.

[31] Ibid. p. 308.
[32] Ibid., pp. 158–9.

The difference can be illustrated by considering two university teachers. One spoon-feeds his students, always knows what is best for them, wants them to get Firsts, because they are his little 'projects' and he wants them to fulfil the potential *he* has decided they have, and he does not let them waste time on frivolous things that will not serve them well in final exams, like indulging their love of acting. That tutor 'leaps in' for his tutees, denying them the right and responsibility to find their own way and make their own choices, to stand or fall by their own actions. Kind though his intentions are, he presents them with no real choices, no opportunities to define themselves, and so, like a mother who 'always knows best' for her son, he does not treat them as fully human.

Another teacher tells her students which books they ought at least to know, and suggests other interesting avenues of research when asked specific questions; she asks terrifying questions in lectures which force her students to find their own ways to an answer whose argumentative strength she assesses but whose veracity she neither confirms nor denies. That tutor 'leaps ahead' of her students, trying to clear a space for them to move into as best she can, and looking out for their interests, but not coercing them into doing things they do not choose to do or limiting their right and responsibility to make such choices. If after all her efforts to enable them to take a First they fritter away entire terms on plays, so be it.

A good example of what I mean by musical 'Being-with' is *Peter Grimes*. In that opera Ellen 'leaps ahead' of Peter but he 'leaps in' for her: it is one of the principal causes of his tragic end. Early in Act I, in their unaccompanied duet, Ellen encourages, but does not coerce, Peter to join her in E major at the end of a bitonal struggle (see Ex. 6.2). The pitch E then forever becomes crucial to Peter's sense of Self. In the 'Great Bear' soliloquy it could hardly be stressed more obsessively (Ex. 6.3), yet as Peter Evans points out, this is the most obvious presentation of Grimes's alienation from the Borough in the whole work.[33] But that is exactly the point: for Peter to be Peter he must be alienated. He cannot be part of the Borough and they will always either deride or hate him: note the Nieces' mockery of his E immediately after the soliloquy. Ellen 'leaps ahead' of him and shows him how he can be, should he choose to be, but that revelation is not a hopeful one for him.[34]

---

[33] Peter Evans, *The Music of Benjamin Britten* (London: Dent, 1979), p. 109. E is important too in 'What harbour shelters peace?' (Fig. 49 in Act I) and, somewhat less so, in 'In dreams I've built myself some kindlier home' (Fig. 60 in Act II).

[34] It is during the 'Great Bear' soliloquy that he becomes certain of the meaning of his E. What at first seems either $\rightarrow\hat{3}/c\sharp$ or $\hat{3}/C$ becomes finally $\hat{1}/E$.

Example 6.2. Britten, *Peter Grimes*, authentic Being-with

Example 6.3. Britten, *Peter Grimes*, 'Great Bear' soliloquy

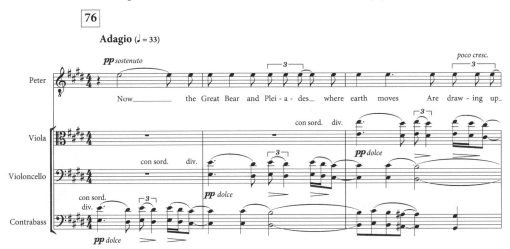

The Borough is *das Man* – note that Peter is part of *das Man* too, as is every Dasein – and its horizon of disclosure runs between A and E♭.[35] Before his final 'mad scene', when the oboe takes his desire to 'begin again', B–A–G♯–F♯–E – his resolution into E major, just before Fig. 77 in Act I – into a horribly high register and converts it into the octatonic tritone descent, A–G♯–F♯–E♯–D♯, his identity is placed into the only context the opera understands: the Borough's A/E♭ (the boundary pitches of the oboe version). His final scene is an internal battle for him, the horrible choice between his 'alienated' E or the Borough's 'mad', 'outlaw' E♭. He ultimately decides on the latter. Even his remembrance of Ellen, the source of his E, is on an E♭ chord.

So Ellen's 'leaping ahead' does not lead to a happy conclusion, just as in our example above an academic's 'leaping ahead' might mean that her undergraduate, making the wrong choices (in terms of the exam, not life), takes a Third. Peter, though, never 'leaps ahead' of Ellen: he always 'leaps in', reducing her from the fully human to the merely equipmental. She is a means to an end for him: acceptance by the Borough. She is the only person who makes him even remotely acceptable in the eyes of the Borough, but he rejects her because she seems to lose her 'usefulness'. After their first duet there is hope, but after his prayer, 'So be it, and God have mercy upon me!' – his *Augenblick*, the point at which he sees his future as outcast and resolves to fulfil that potential – there is none.

Because both Falstaff's and Hal's Being-with the other is inauthentic, in *Falstaff* the tragedy is even more inevitable. There is never any hope. Hal regards Falstaff as little more than an entertaining instructor in personal freedom, welcome and useful during his youth but obnoxious and unwanted in his regal splendour. We saw in Chapter 4 Section 2 that on Dowden's view Hal's involvement with the tavern was 'provisional' and that he stays at arm's length from Falstaff and his associates, 'hold[ing] his truest self in reserve for the life that is best, and highest, and most real'.[36] But the face he presents to the tavern does not reveal this; his soliloquy in *1 Henry IV*, Act I Scene ii makes clear his intentions to the audience, but his 'friends' are off-stage and insensible. Hal is Falstaff's 'sweet wag' and Falstaff Hal's 'sweet beef'.[37] The promise understood from Falstaff's perspective is that this sweet boy who will be King will keep with Falstaff and banish the others.[38] He expects, in short, to have life given back to him in

---

[35] See Evans, *The Music of Benjamin Britten*, Chapter 5, *passim*.

[36] Dowden, *Shakspere*, p. 212.

[37] *1 Henry IV*, I. ii. *passim* and III. iii. 176.

[38] *1 Henry IV*, II. iv. 424–5.

even greater fullness after Hal's accession; and fullness of life is all Falstaff understands or values. Hal regards Falstaff as useful before his accession; Falstaff regards Hal as useful afterwards. Both are, or were (recall Morgann's and Bloom's insight), in love, but their love is based on inauthentic Being-with and as such is doomed.

In the opening paragraph of *Falstaff* Elgar's deft handling of tonality – the co-prolongation of their two associated keys – cannily makes the point, as I noted above, that Falstaff cannot stand up on his own; his music has no major-mode dominant support and the arrival of the tonic is immediately subservient to the interests of E♭ and since that is Hal's key, the point is simultaneously made that Falstaff's usefulness to Hal is strictly limited. Moreover, and most devastatingly, the way C minor leans towards E♭ suggests that Falstaff actually interprets Hal's inauthentic Being-with as authentic. Whatever the failings of his own love for Hal, he believes Hal's love is authentic. It is a tragic irony that Hal's actual Being-with Falstaff is so horribly misunderstood, and that irony is focused especially well in the Dream Interlude.

The interlude is the principal example in *Falstaff* of Elgar's 'foregrounding' (Bloom's term) of character; in it he most obviously refers to the lost hopes of the young boy Jack Falstaff, but also a little more abstrusely to the uselessness of childish dreams, whether they are dreamt in adulthood or not.

In Shakespeare the interlude is the reminiscence not of Falstaff but of Justice Shallow; its substance comes from much later in the history plays, in the scene that also provides the source for the interlude in Shallow's orchard.[39] Shallow recalls Falstaff's insouciant youth, which he failed to live up to, in terms of the worldly 'facts' that Dowden makes so much of; and Shallow's ironic reappearance, in Elgar's setting, not in Shakespeare's, just before Falstaff's death seems to underline the futility of his adult existence. By transferring these reflexions to Falstaff's unconscious Elgar makes a tragic personal addition to the character, which is part of his grander project in this work.

The function of this dream interlude is almost the antipode of Verdi's parallel treatment of the same material in his opera (Act II Scene ii). There Falstaff hides behind a curtain after the 'interlude material', but in Elgar he hides first, *then* falls asleep. In Verdi, his pursuer is the husband of a woman he intends to steal (figuratively), whereas in Elgar (as in *1 Henry IV*) the theft is not figurative but literal: he hides from a sheriff who comes to question Falstaff for the robbery on Gad's Hill. Finally, and most

---

[39] *2 Henry IV*, III. ii. 24–9 and 80–214.

importantly, in Verdi's opera the conscious remembrance of his svelte and virile youth is intended to stimulate Alice and get himself into a situation; but in Elgar's symphonic study the unconscious remembrance is a wish-fulfilling dream, intended to get him out of a situation – and I do not mean the sheriff's enquiries.

According to Freud, wish-fulfilling dreams 'are usually short and simple dreams, which afford a pleasant contrast to the confused and exuberant compositions that have in the main attracted the attentions of the authorities'.[40] Falstaff's dream could not be simpler. 'He was page to the Duke of Norfolk': it is a pastoral idyll. As a boy, good service was offered for fair reward; the duke, his employer, was no threat to his stability. Now with adulthood's higher stakes the duke is replaced by a prince, and the service Falstaff offers is nothing less than a kind of Socratic instruction that opens the door to individual freedom.[41] It is reasonable for him to expect the wage of Hal's loyalty, and the wish-fulfilling dream Elgar drops in here, at the very point where Hal's mischievous treatment of Falstaff turns imperceptibly but irrevocably to wickedness, is both acute and subtle.

As Freud explains, dreams of wish-fulfilment tend to replace the subject of a dream, often conveniently, so that for instance a dream about drinking may obviate the need to wake up and have a real drink.[42] Falstaff dreams of being content in his employment, and in no danger of having his contentment ended. His wish is fulfilled in his dream, but he wakes up to a different reality which reveals itself insidiously until the moments before his death.

The sketches for *Falstaff* show that the Dream Interlude was pasted into an earlier sketch, which tied the G major of 75:8 across the bar-line; the resumption of the original sketch, now displaced by the Interlude to 81:1, omits the two beats of G major (V/c) originally planned.[43] Ex. 6.4 reproduces Christopher Kent's transcription of an early sketch for *Falstaff*, which shows how Elgar tropes the interlude into the work's structural dominant.

In effect, the interlude is a parenthesis in the larger structure. The prolongation of V/C, which the interlude interrupts, is conceptually

---

[40] Sigmund Freud, *The Interpretation of Dreams*, trans. James Strachey (London: Pelican, 1976), p. 205.

[41] Cf. Bloom's interpretation, Chapter 4 Section 1, above.

[42] He gives numerous examples in *The Interpretation of Dreams*, pp. 200–13.

[43] See Christopher Kent, '*Falstaff*: Elgar's symphonic study', in *Edward Elgar: Music and Literature*, ed. Raymond Monk (Aldershot: Scolar, 1993), pp. 83–107 at p. 84.

Example 6.4. *Falstaff*, early sketch for music around Dream Interlude

effective from the bar before the interlude to the bar after it. William
Kinderman has drawn attention to Beethoven's use of parenthetical enclo-
sures in his later music, which is of exactly this sort: the parenthesis could
safely be removed without creating an uneasy join.[44]

Yet the implications of the parenthesis here are more complex. In
Falstaff Elgar follows the example of his own First Symphony, to
whose finale he had added the Brahmsian theme at figure 114 only after
fully scoring the movement.[45] The Dream Interlude's position as a kind
of splice into a structural dominant makes it function in some ways as
a cadenza. Yet it is not merely a cadenza; Elgar's frame is still more
suggestive.

It seems to me that this particular parenthetical enclosure comes even
closer to Christopher Lewis's analysis of Bruckner than to Kinderman's of
Beethoven. Lewis argues that several distinct tonal strata run through the
Adagio of Bruckner's Seventh Symphony, and compares their implication
of separate chronologies with Maurizio Nichetti's film *The Icicle Thief.*[46]
Bruckner's movement is founded on a tonal pairing of C♯ and E, and
Lewis traces these tonal strata through the movement, arguing that the
surface's frequent changes of focus are a result of a switch between
chronologies comparable to the switch of scene in a film. Referential
sonorities announce the beginning of each switch and establish a clearly
audible link with the end of the last period of that chronology's unfolding.
Elgar was also interested in weaving different threads like this, but more
usually on a larger scale; the gigantic opposition of immuring and immured tonalities we saw revealed in the First Symphony in Chapter 3 is an
example of this. But in the Dream Interlude we find something of the
disturbance of more localized chronology that interests Lewis. The narrative here, which *Falstaff* has but Bruckner's symphony does not, is
switched for a while to another thread. So far we have followed Falstaff
through robbery and revelry, but as he sleeps we are jerked out of that
continuous time-frame into an altogether different one. It might seem that
the interlude has little to do with the rest of the work, but by seizing on its
rereading of Falstaff's past Elgar projects it through the rest of the work.

---

[44] William Kinderman, *Beethoven* (Oxford: Oxford University Press, 1995), esp. pp. 240–3
and 300–2.

[45] Robert Anderson, *Elgar (London: Dent, 1993)*, pp. 329–30.

[46] Christopher Lewis, 'The mind's chronology: narrative times and harmonic disruption in
post-Romantic music', in *The Second Practice of Nineteenth-Century Tonality*, ed. William
Kinderman and Harald Krebs (Lindon, NE: University of Nebraska press, 1996),
pp. 114–49.

The referential V/C sonorities on either side enclose this somnolent parenthesis and identify it with a different chronology, but eventually the time-frames are spliced into one another with a violence that destroys Falstaff.

In Shakespeare's context Sir John falls into a drunken sleep behind a curtain while Hal defends him from a sheriff who comes to charge the knight with the first robbery on Gad's Hill. His sleep comes, then, amid reasonable confidence in his friend's intentions, so Elgar's suggestion that he would dream happily is entirely plausible. But nostalgic feeling and diatonic language, both identifying marks of the Dream Interlude, are rarely presented straightforwardly in Elgar even when they do not represent dreams: they are usually tools for shaping his profoundest musical cynicism. It is for this ulterior motive that Elgar transplants Shallow's much later reminiscence to this early stage. A bonhomous snooze that allows Hal once again to pilfer from his friend's pockets is at the same time a trenchantly cynical Elgarian statement, perhaps the defining moment of the work.

Michael Allis has drawn attention to the resonances of Elgar's description of the Dream Interlude in his analytical note.[47] Falstaff's recollection of 'what might have been' echoes the quotation from Charles Lamb in the score of Dream Children, Op. 43: 'We are nothing; less than nothing, and dreams. *We are only what might have been.*' Allis uses this observation to tie *Falstaff* in with what he calls 'Elgar's retrospective aesthetic'.[48] He writes that Charles Lamb was part of a Victorian literary tradition that had an idealized view of childhood, and a regret at its passing: the tradition of the Romantic Child. Through *Dream Children* Elgar established a link with this tradition, which resulted in a focus on nostalgic or retrospective concerns in a number of mature pieces. Among Victorian idealizations of childhood Allis cites the work of Blake, Wordsworth, Coleridge, Tennyson, and Dickens alongside Lamb, with J. M. Barrie's *Peter Pan* being the *opus classicum*.[49] He argues that for these Victorian writers, as well as for Elgar, childhood '[embodies] understanding and receptivity . . . [and] produces a creative renaissance'.[50] Referring also to Elgar's incidental music for the Blackwood/Pearn stage play *The Starlight Express* he suggests that in various mature works, including *Falstaff*, Elgar uses a variety of retrospective narrative techniques to play

---

[47] Michael Allis, 'Elgar and the art of retrospective narrative', *The Journal of Musicological Research* 19 (2000), pp. 289–328.

[48] Ibid., pp. 309–13.

[49] Ibid., pp. 292–5.

[50] Ibid., p. 296.

with the listener's sense of his music's representation of chronological time, and by so doing 'suggest[s] that the past is superior to the present'.[51] Allis suggests that by playing narratively with our sense of chronology Elgar idealizes the past, sadly reflecting that it cannot be regained. I think this is only partly true.

One little figure whom Allis does not mention, but whom I consider much closer to Elgar's view of childhood than all his examples, is Little Father Time in Hardy's *Jude the Obscure*. He stands out as a most remarkable Victorian literary infant who hangs himself and his siblings *'because we are too menny'*; and I believe he is the child in literature that illuminates Elgar's retrospective music best. Preternaturally wise, Little Jude's childish insouciance and optimism are turned pessimistic by experience he is too young to have had. Unlike the Victorians and Edwardians who idealized the too-soon-corrupted 'innocence' of childhood, I believe that Elgar would have shared W. H. Auden's later insight that 'no boy is innocent, [and] he has no clear notion of innocence, nor does he know that to be no longer innocent, but to wish that one were, is part of the definition of an adult'.[52] One critic believes that one of Auden's most thoughtful friends held a very different opinion.

> It seems that Britten was captured at many levels by the notion of return to a perfect state symbolized by childhood – it has been called 'innocence', but a more useful concept is that of the 'pre-symbolic' explored by disciples of Lacan or of 'nescience' in the words of Hardy's poem 'A time there was' (set in *Winter Words*). The entry into the 'symbolic' (language) and the patriarchal order make this state impossible to recapture, and much of Britten's music is about the difficulty and pain of separation from it, but it is arguably his principal fount of non-verbal inspiration. Lack produces desire (in the already lost adult); and the sexual element that occasionally obtrudes, and can never satisfy or be satisfied, is a symptom of that lack.[53]

The Victorian trait Allis points to is, if Brett is right, more characteristic of Britten, and tied up at least as much with sexuality as with artistic context. For Elgar, whose Oedipal, uxorious sexual makeup (at least on the traditional interpretation) could not exercise quite the same influence,

[51] Ibid., p. 307.

[52] W. H. Auden, 'Dingley Dell and The Fleet', in *The Dyer's Hand and Other Essays* (London: Faber and Faber, 1963), pp. 407–28 at p. 409.

[53] Philip Brett, 'Britten, Benjamin', in *The New Grove Dictionary of Music and Musicians*, ed. Stanley Sadie and John Tyrrell, 2nd edn (London: Macmillan, 2001), vol. IV, pp. 367–8.

childhood is not as it appears to the Victorians; returning to the past is not blissful, but painful.[54]

It was a typically Victorian folly to hope that even if the steady march of progress did not lead directly to utopia – and only the very wisest doubted that it would – then at least there would be hope of a fresh start through an imaginative return to the prelapsarian state of childhood. Mid- to late-twentieth-century artists were forced to the realization that the unmitigated evil of Auschwitz had closed a vast iron door on all hopes for human progress,[55] and although Elgar did not live to see the Second World War, the death of Edward VII, the last end of the Victorian age, and his experience of the First World War, quite apart from the musical revolution on the continent, were sufficient: the early twentieth century's unpitying changes – the destruction of his musical and political world – could to some extent have poisoned Elgar's view of humankind.

In mature works which contain nostalgic passages or are concerned almost exclusively with retrospection, and here one thinks particularly of *The Starlight Express* and the First Symphony, Elgar's opinion of the child's relation to the man could scarcely be further from the comfortable Victorian idealization of *Peter Pan* or Lewis Carroll's stories about Alice. Elgar certainly treats childhood with a kind of fantastic fascination, seeing in it things that disgrace the state of adulthood as he perceived it, but one could argue that he did not see much real hope in retrospection, since childhood itself is imperfect and no guide to the future. Later in the same article on Dickens from which his earlier words were taken W. H. Auden suggests a fruitful way of grasping the dichotomy between differing fantasies that led to the Victorian exploration of childhood.

> Our dream pictures of the Happy Place where suffering and evil are unknown are of two kinds, the Edens and the New Jerusalems. Though it is possible for

[54] Later in the twentieth century there are more examples of the kind of childhood representations that Elgar explores. Several of the boys on Golding's island in *Lord of the Flies* fit the requirements of Elgar's wise and tragic youth; so too does the diminutive (but not childish) tragic hobbit Frodo Baggins, in Tolkien's *The Lord of the Rings*. In both cases, after a struggle with hitherto unexplored 'grown-up' things, the return to a former state is heartbreaking, and in no way redemptive.

[55] William Golding wrote: 'Before the second world war I believed in the perfectibility of social man . . . but I must say that anyone who moved through those years without understanding that man produces evil as a bee produces honey must have been blind or wrong in the head.' See Golding, 'Fable', in *The Hot Gates, and Other Occasional Pieces* (London: Faber and Faber, 1965), pp. 85–101 at pp. 86–7. The same sentiment runs through Britten's post-war operas, *Peter Grimes* and especially *The Rape of Lucretia* (see Evans, *The Music of Benjamin Britten*, p. 144).

the same individual to imagine both, it is unlikely that his interest in both will be equal and I suspect that between the Arcadian whose favourite dream is Eden, and the Utopian whose favourite daydream is of New Jerusalem there is a characterological gulf as unbridgeable as that between Blake's Prolifics and Devourers.

In their relation to the actual fallen world, the difference between Eden and New Jerusalem is a temporal one. Eden is a past world in which the contradictions of the present world have not yet arisen; New Jerusalem is a future world in which they have at last been resolved. Eden is a place where its inhabitants may do whatever they like to do; the motto over the gate is, 'Do what thou wilt is here the Law.' New Jerusalem is a place where its inhabitants like to do whatever they ought to do, and its motto is, 'In His will is our peace.'[56]

Allis unequivocally plants Elgar in the arcadian category, and on the usual estimation of Elgar's social and musical atavism – note those starched shirts and pretty spats and the familiar-sounding tonal language – Elgar scholarship has traditionally come down on his side. I am not convinced.

Little Jack Falstaff, page to a duke, might well dream about 'what might have been', but his own childish thoughts are not primarily Elgar's concern: more fool the boy for dreaming so idly. Elgar plants those boyish hopes in the beer-muddled head of a repellently fat and tragically optimistic vulgarian who is meanwhile having his pockets picked by an emotionally dependent but unthankful young prig. If Elgar were really the arcadian that Allis, in common with many other commentators, seems to suggest, this Dream Interlude would come in its proper Shakespearean place in Shallow's orchard; but Elgar was neither arcadian nor utopian, for such persons need hope, and Elgar had little of that, as his many despairing letters bear witness. The little boy's foolish ambition, regurgitated in a drunken slumber, is mocked by the prince and by Elgar. The listener who does not know the *Henry IV* plays might miss the irony of this interlude, but recall that Elgar would have no sympathy with him. The interlude does not merely take Falstaff back to his youth, there to allow him to idle in bliss; it shows up the folly of fantasy, and specifically the kind of Victorian idealization of childhood Allis writes about.

Commentators have often remarked that the Dream Interlude is the most stable point of the work, with its thirty-nine bars of clear and unchallenged A minor tonality, which are introduced by seven hazy bars that seem to function like the wobbling pictures of 'flashback' sequences in

---

[56] Auden, 'Dingley Dell', p. 409.

old films. Yet this 'appeal to diatonicism', as it were, is merely the most obviously cynical of Elgar's compositional practices. In the First Symphony, as we have seen, the simplicity and ostensible 'reliability' of a diatonic A♭ major set over against the crunching chromaticism of much of the rest of the work is in the end powerless to refute the challenge it faces. In *Falstaff* Elgar's surface musical language comes as close to the dissolution of tonality as it ever did; and the placement of the unassuming diatonicism of the Dream Interlude with its regular periodic phrases (another rare thing in *Falstaff*) at the heart of such turmoil, not to mention its position in the narrative, cannot but communicate a certain cynical intent. I have already noted that the interlude is a kind of 'breakthrough' in the work, although its actual musical content does not play any further part.[57] The breakthrough is narratively and, as we shall see, musically crucial. Although we might look generously on much that he has done so far, from this point in Elgar's symphonic study Hal's actions are unquestionably cruel, and we are made to watch Falstaff's agonizing destruction as it unfolds. Elgar probably wrote no more potent passage of music.[58]

We saw in Chapter 4 how Falstaff's paratextual mortal illness is 'composed out' by the textual liquidation of C. In *Henry V* it provokes the following exchange:

> HOSTESS: As ever you come of women, come in quickly
> to Sir John. Ah, poor heart! he is so shaked
> of a burning quotidian tertian, that it is most
> lamentable to behold. Sweet men, come to him.
> NYM: The king hath run bad humours on the knight;
> that's the even of it.
> PISTOL: Nym, thou hast spoke the right;
> His heart is fracted and corroborate.
> NYM: The king is a good king: but it must be as it
> may; he passes some humours and careers.
> PISTOL: Let us condole the knight; for, lambkins, we will
> live.
>
> (*Henry V*, II. i. 117–27)

---

[57] Nor should we expect it to, since the interlude was added late in the process of composition.

[58] I explore Elgarian nostalgia and his thematic treatment of childhood further in 'Elgar's unwumbling: the theatre music', in *The Cambridge Companion to Elgar*, ed. Julian Rushton and Daniel M. Grimley (Cambridge: Cambridge University Press, 2004), pp. 171–83, and 'Henry and the *Gräfin*/Grinder: Elgar and *The Starlight Express*', *Elgar Society Journal* 13/4 (2004), pp. 15–23.

This conversation in the Boar's Head certainly squares with Prince Hal's hard-nosed soliloquy in *1 Henry IV*, Act I Scene ii, Warwick's assessment of Hal's reasons for frequenting taverns (*2 Henry IV*, IV. iv. 67–80), and the rejection speech itself (*2 Henry IV*, V. v. 47–70). It is not an entirely unbiased presentation of the young monarch, but as we have seen Elgar gives the listener little room to choose a reading that flatters him more: we are forced onto the side of Mistress Quickly and the others.

And what are we to make of the C major ending that is 'as cold as any stone'? I believe that Wagner, Mahler, or Strauss would have ended their *Falstaff* with an E minor or major chord in place of Elgar's C major. As Adorno notes, 'Hope in Mahler always resides in change.'[59] That is precisely why Mahler and Strauss prefer directional-tonal structures, in which developments at the heart of a work necessitate a change of goal. In a directional form, there is hope for victory, even if it turns out to be less glorious than was originally hoped for or requires the eucatastrophic inbreaking of a deity to bring it about. Yet Elgar was almost alone among early modernist composers in insisting on a return to a work's opening tonic *regardless of the cost*; and I believe that in so insisting he makes a uniquely cynical point. For Elgar, the grace of eucatastrophe is 'never to be counted on to recur';[60] a *King Lear* ending is always possible.

Elgar's returns to the original tonic have the effect of disfiguring what seemed at first beautiful and promising. His music does not earn its return home but simply retreats there, away from challenges. In the Dream Interlude I drew attention to Elgar's idiosyncratic view of childhood, innocence, diatonicism, and nostalgia. At the end of *Falstaff* the cynical insights of that interlude are given their most marmoreal presentation in Falstaff's tombstone C major. The return, or retreat, does not lead to a prelapsarian state of bliss and security: in Elgar a return to childhood leads to Little Father Time; and a return to a simple diatonicism leads back only to a sound world whose destruction we have just witnessed.

At the end of *Falstaff* the tone might have been lightened by an E minor or major chord such as I believe other modernist composers would have provided. At least then we could accept the change in focus, just as Shakespeare's audience regrettably accepts Sir John is dead, and girds itself for Agincourt and one of England's most remarkable victories. But Elgar does not allow Henry V to claim at the end the position he has earned by

[59] Theodor W. Adorno, *Mahler: a Musical Physiognomy*, trans. Edmund Jephcott (Chicago and London: University of Chicago Press, 1992; orig. edn 1960), p. 6.

[60] J. R. R. Tolkien, 'On fairy-stories', in *The Monsters and the Critics and Other Essays*, ed. Christopher Tolkien (London: Harper Collins, 1983), pp. 109–61 at p. 153.

right, as well as by manipulation of the tonal structure of the work. Michael Kennedy has wondered 'if Elgar was ever tempted to call the work "Henry the Fifth" as Verdi was once tempted to call *Otello* "Iago".'[61] One sees his point, but I doubt that the thought ever crossed Elgar's mind. Such a title would make us instantly more sympathetic to Hal/Henry V, in whose accession and glory we could delight; but Elgar does not wish us to delight. We might hear: 'the King is dead; long live the King', but Elgar gives us: 'Falstaff is dead', and no more – a moment of grim jocularity.

Elgar's *Falstaff*, like Shakespeare's, is finally 'shaked / of a burning quotidian tertian'. The work's 'death' is engendered by a tonal malaise, centred on a self-redefining tertial relation which turns a feverish colour in the breakthrough of Hal's tune on E major. Whether this is a eucatastrophic or dyscatastrophic moment depends on whether we take Hal's or Falstaff's side. Pistol's observation that Falstaff is 'fracted and corroborate' is a contradiction in terms, but is an exact description of Elgar's *Falstaff*, in which Sir John's identity is unpicked – fractured beyond recognition – by the selfish and self-corroborating actions of Hal/Henry V, whose inauthentic Being-with Falstaff is in the end deleterious to the latter's health. It is easy to see why, in a copy of the score Elgar gave to Alice Stuart-Wortley, a sketch attached to the fly-leaf reads, 'Falstaff (tragedy)'.[62] Yet the tragedy is not merely Falstaff's. Elgar wrote to Ernest Newman:

> I only want you to understand – as I think *you* will already – that *Falstaff* (as programme says) is the name but Shakespeare – the whole of human life – is the theme. A theatre conductor cd easily have given a heavy scherzo and called it Falstaff – but you will see I have made a larger canvas – & over it all runs – even in the tavern – the undercurrent of our [sic: not 'Falstaff's'] failings & sorrows.[63]

These scarcely credible words immediately raise a difficult question: how can a single symphonic poem discourse on 'the whole of human life'? It seems fairly clear that no single piece of music, with its complex and unreliable interplay of sounds that may or may not have extramusical significance, can approach 'the whole of human life' in any but the most superficial manner. Yet a single piece of music may have a better chance of grappling with such universal questions if it presents not only itself but itself-as-commentary on a vital and paradigmatically 'meaningful'

---

[61] Kennedy, *Portrait*, p. 257.
[62] Kent, '*Falstaff*, p. 100.
[63] Letter to Ernest Newman, 26. ix. 13, in Elgar, *Lifetime*, p. 263.

musical tradition: the symphonic tradition of Beethoven, and particularly the *per aspera ad astra* narrative typified in the first instance by his Fifth Symphony.[64] If *Falstaff* is in dialogue with that tradition, what does its interpretation of the tradition seem to indicate?

Elgar's play with a sonata deformation runs directly against many of the expectations of an informed listener – and recall that Elgar had little time for any other kind. Exposition we have, with a superabundance of material; development there is too, although the work's primary themes are treated a little haphazardly in the long development space; but it is in the recapitulation and coda that expectations are thwarted. The tonal structure of the recapitulation space is 'wrong'. Owing to his insertion of another narrative episode (the battle), a mildly confusing allusion to the practice of the development space, Elgar does not offer the expected tonal resolution of his expository materials. Indeed, the exposition's grandest theme, the one for Prince Hal, returns on a staggeringly inappropriate E major. The whole is a uniquely disturbing 'non-resolving recapitulation' (Hepokoski's term) which contains a hermeneutically ambivalent 'breakthrough' that will change the course of what follows.

The burden of resolution into one of two *evangelia* – either Hal's E or Falstaff's C – rests, then, on the coda space; and the informed listener's knowledge of the achievement of Beethoven's *Egmont* Overture allows him or her to hope for success. Yet the coda begins by turning the work's thematic hegemony on its head. Secondary materials, i.e. 'narrative' materials, now become primary, not simply by virtue of their placement at the beginning of the last two rotations but because of their rhetorical function. The tonal focus expected before the breakthrough – the tonic C minor, or, in accordance with the minor-to-major paradigm, C *major* – is replaced during the new king's victorious progress by E♭, which is itself in the final variation supplanted by E minor, the key of the Kingship. In the closing pages there are hints of C major everywhere, but they are liquidations, each weaker and more ridiculous than the last. The final chord scoffs at our informed listener's expectations by granting him or her the tonic chord that the sonata archetype promises, but only as a totally emasculated and stone-cold vestige. And even the 'booby-prize' *evangelium* of Hal's kingly E minor is denied us: despite the heavy emphasis on the key at the end of the coda, a concluding chord of E minor or major is not forthcoming. In short, Beethoven's Victory Symphony has become a Defeat Symphony.

---

[64] Elgar makes similarly stupendous claims about the 'meaning' of the First Symphony in relation to human striving, as we saw in the first section of this chapter.

So much for Elgar's play with single-movement sonata conventions; but his dialogue with the multi-movement symphonic tradition, whether the movements are actually or only implicitly separated, is equally meaningful. It may be that Elgar's key-scheme in *Falstaff*, C minor to C major, was chosen deliberately to set the work in direct relation to Beethoven's Fifth Symphony, just as the A♭/D pairing of keys in the First Symphony might be intended to bring *Parsifal* to mind. As Scott Burnham has shown, Beethoven's heroic style in general and the Third and Fifth Symphonies in particular have come to be understood as musical expressions of human identity, striving, and victory, teleological forms which affirm mankind's possibilities and his hopes of progress.[65] The rhetoric of *Falstaff* is very different, of course, from that of the Fifth Symphony; Falstaff's opening themes cannot be compared to Beethoven's. But in its four implicitly separate 'movements' *Falstaff* follows the same course and promises the same result, albeit in Elgar's own musical language. And the outcome is a resounding failure – death – expressed in archly cynical terms with the final sardonic presentation of the C major goal fractured and impotent; on Elgar's interpretation of the heroic narrative self is negated, hope in progress is smashed, and the *telos* is merely a sudden, absurd extinction. If Beethoven Hero, with its grand teleological thrust, is (as Burnham suggests) 'the exemplary expression of the unmediated self',[66] then I would suggest that modernist music – and Elgar's in particular – is the exemplary expression of the existentially absurd or contingent self.

A third way that Elgar's music may have something to say about 'the whole of human life' is in its function as a musical existential study. As we have seen, the tonal pairing of C minor and E♭, which redefines itself as the study goes on, is a subtle and deeply moving exploration of the nature of existential Being-with others, which Elgar seems to view in a rather bleak way. But the projection of Falstaff's and Hal's associated keys through the work brings the study down from the cosmic eucatastrophe of the heroic narrative to the level of individual humans pursuing their own existential possibilities, one of them authentically (Hal), one of them inauthentically (Falstaff). The work can therefore be heard as a study of how we as individual humans define ourselves for ourselves and among others in the world. I shall return to these critically important issues in the final chapter.

---

[65] Scott Burnham, *Beethoven Hero* (Princeton, NJ: Princeton University Press, 1995).

[66] Ibid., p. 151.

Thirty years after *Falstaff* Strauss would revivify the funeral march from the *Eroica* in his *Metamorphosen*, as if to shake the cadaver at his stinking, rotten world and proclaim the death not only of musical art, for which Beethoven principally stands, or just of Germany, but of the very possibility that there could ever be real humanity after that moment. Although Strauss had experienced a war Elgar did not live to see, still this proclamation came before the full horror of the extermination camps was brought to notice. The later revelation of the enormities at Auschwitz and Treblinka arguably confirmed Strauss's contention. Humankind continues to inhabit the world, but only lives a kind of 'half life'. As with someone who suffers a stroke we can identify the real point of 'death' much earlier than the actual physical expiration.

We cannot with certainty say that Elgar intended to proclaim anything more than the death of the protagonist in *Falstaff*; but in his idiosyncratic use of diatonic/childlike nostalgia in the Dream Interlude and Hal's theme one cannot mistake a tinge of regret that is as purely musical as it is psychological and narratological. In much of his mature music, and increasingly after *Falstaff*'s poor reception and the long years of war that followed, Elgar seems to ruminate on the death of a musical language to which Amfortas had administered Extreme Unction. As he 'foregrounds' the tainted love between Falstaff and Hal in the (meta-)paratextual aspects of *Falstaff*, so he 'foregrounds' the disintegrating system of tonality, which the Schoenbergians were concurrently doing in a more optimistic (because vivacious) way on the continent.

In Elgar, as in Mahler, tonality 'becomes a medium of modernism'.[67] But whereas Mahler's sharpening of tonality rests, according to Adorno, on his play between major and minor modes,[68] for Elgar it does not: he takes up another element of late-nineteenth-century tonality, the double-tonic complex, and uses it for his own ends. In the immuring–immured structure of the First Symphony, two tonics achieve the previously unthinkable job of both being on the throne and both being pretenders to it; and the crucial third-relationship between C minor and E♭ in *Falstaff*, troubled by the doubling of the secondary tonic into a complex of E♭/e, fulfils the same function. But the rhetoric in both cases depends on tonics

---

[67] Adorno, *Mahler: a Musical Physiognomy*, p. 26.

[68] Adorno writes as if this is a distinctively Mahlerian tendency, or even a Mahlerian invention, but this is misleading. Robert Bailey has convincingly demonstrated that all post-*Tristan* music functions with a double-sided view of the tonic's mode (see his 'An analytical study of the sketches and drafts'). Mahler did not do the sharpening, then; but he certainly used the tools.

being heard as tonics. Only then can rugs be pulled from beneath feet. Without tonal centres Elgar's modernist argument would be impossible. Mahler takes Wagner's modal mixture into modernism; Elgar does the same with his double-tonic complex.

Falstaff says: 'banish plump Jack, and banish all the world',[69] and there is a real sense in Elgar's presentation of Falstaff's tragedy – intermingled as it is with a discussion of the nature of tonal resolution, aspects of sonata deformations, the eucatastrophe of the heroic Beethovenian symphonic tradition, and a study of human Being-with others and existential self-projection – that in Falstaff we are to see *ourselves*; as Everyman he shows us what life is, and in dying explodes our hopes. Harold Bloom may have identified Falstaff with 'the invention of the human', and his rejection with the implicit rejection of human life itself, but in his unassuming way Elgar got there first.

[69] *1 Henry IV*, II. iv. 473–4.

7 Modern music, modern man

It is because Elgar's symphonic narrative style, which my emphasis on the *Augenblick* brings into focus, is so contra-Beethovenian that total reliance on the *Ursatz* as a structural prop simply will not suffice. We can ask again the questions at the beginning of this book: is early modernist syntax basically Beethovenian–Schenkerian, and is Schenkerian analysis of it appropriate? Clearly there are vital elements of the common-practice syntax in Elgar, for instance his contrapuntal prolongation of diatonic triads and the dramatic opposition of subsidiary keys; but the syntax is taken to extremes that make an orthodox Schenkerian reading inadequate. First, contrapuntal prolongation will very often be off the triad rather than on it, either before or after an arrival: so, for instance, in the first-movement exposition of the First Symphony, the triad of A minor is prolonged first by a VI–V–i cadence, where VI is itself established so painstakingly that it almost sounds like a tonic, then in the development V/a is prolonged contrapuntally. A minor itself, however, only appears for a very short while (11:4 and 17:1). It is the movement towards and then sharply away from a goal that takes up all Elgar's time.[1] Since in the pristinely cynical world all possibilities are equally undesirable, the only acceptable option is to procrastinate, which is precisely what he does. Second, in Elgar's immuring–immured tonal structure the opposed key is prolonged to such great lengths, and with its own subsidiary keys and *Ursatz*, that it becomes a tonality itself.

So Elgar's syntax does rely basically on the Beethovenian–Schenkerian model, although his mutation of this model, which is revealed by my existential reinterpretation of Schenker's theory, is probably more interesting than his dalliance with it. Formal archetypes and Elgar's play with them are, then, critical to our understanding of the composer. Adorno (via Lukács) calls musical forms 'second nature', a mirror of one segment of the fragmented world objectified by the equally fragmented composing Subject. That understanding offers a shade of meaning to my assertion that

---

[1] We see this also in *Falstaff*, where C's arrival in the exposition is already pointing towards E♭, and when that key (Hal's) is revealed in the recapitulation to have been the real focus all along, it is in turn quickly left behind in favour of the Kingship key, E, which is the root of the work's difficulties.

musical forms are each a mimesis of one sort or another of humankind's temporal existence. Regardless of its historical or social situation, Dasein exists in time; time is its mode of existence: therefore each 'fragmented' understanding contains within it a universality of outlook which it is unhelpful to deny.[2] Musical forms are not, I would argue, as radically problematical as Adorno wishes to make out, and the 'rupture' he identifies between 'self and forms' (or 'the Other' and 'the world's course') can, if viewed through a Heideggerian lens, be regarded profitably as a hermeneutic tool to open up music of all historical periods, not just the modernist – although like Adorno that is my principal concern in this study.[3] Therefore it cannot be stressed too strongly that to understand how Elgar works we must understand him in terms of the models he works from and with, the 'form of life' or disclosive 'horizon' which is his: which means analyzing from the viewpoint of the tonal tradition he inherited and used, however critically. The same holds for every other early modernist composer.

Another methodological concern of this book has been to examine how a multi-movement piece works structurally, to offer a personal answer to the question of why works have as many movements as they do, and in which order. In the First Symphony answers are ready to hand. The *Urlinie*'s failure to descend at the end of each of the first three movements and the lack of strong tonic statements in all but the third movement (whose D major, as we have seen, has problems of its own) are two notable ways Elgar carries the argument on without a break. This technique is not Elgar's, though: it reaches back at least as far as Beethoven, who habitually (and increasingly, as he aged) channelled energies towards recapitulations, codas, and finales, with early implications worked out only in the closing stages. Hence, to take some well-known examples, major-mode auguries in the opening movements of the Fifth and Ninth Symphonies must wait till the finale for full explication, and real confirmation of a work's tonic

---

[2] That is not to say that the sonata form, for example, provides the only universal view of human temporality. Were that so, then a small North European formal predilection would receive undue favour. Sonata form is only one interpretation of human temporality; but it is by intention one 'universalizable' view of it, an interpretation put forward as one possible way of temporal being common to all human beings. Other forms, like Stockhausen's 'moment form', put forward alternative 'universalizable' interpretations.

[3] It will be demonstrated below that the concept of the Other, if restored to its Hegelian roots, can also have much to say about the meanings inherent in musical forms, especially the sonata.

only comes in the finales of the Op. 102 No. 1 Cello Sonata and Op. 131 String Quartet.

On its own the *Ursatz* can rarely help to answer the question of why a work has a number of separate movements, which is one of its principal failings: with its four-movement *Ursatz* Elgar's First Symphony is anomalous in this respect. But an existential interpretation of the *Ursatz*, twinned with a narratological realization that the point a movement – or indeed a work – *stops* is not necessarily where it *ends*, allows us to stand back from the analysis and ask questions of it. A particular statement has been made, which carries a particular meaning and a particular weight: when an *Ursatz* closes, it makes the utterance grammatically coherent – but does it necessarily conclude the argument? Bearing in mind the *Augenblick*, I think we should say that it does not. After the eucatastrophe of the First Symphony's 'Heaven Tune' or the accession of Henry V in *Falstaff* the musical argument continues and leaves its happy ending far behind.

We may ask whether my analytical method, however far it stretches the methodology, is still recognizably Schenkerian. In the First Symphony the *Ursatz* (although spread over four movements) still closes; in *Falstaff* and some other works, notably *Gerontius*, it does not.[4] Using a Heideggerian–Schenkerian method, however, a closed *Ursatz* is no longer essential. What is essential is that the *possibility* of ending ('heroically') is available as an option to be explored and worked with and, principally, that a revelation of the authentic Being of the individual piece is glimpsed and held in the *Augenblick* and projected resolutely to the end. If that means that after a duotonal struggle the piece will complete a contrapuntal descent, all well and good; but an existential analysis allows for a more nuanced reading, one that reveals the empty futility of the supposed 'victory', the limits of eucatastrophe. The *Ursatz* will always be there in the background, as the guiding principle of the tonal language, but we cannot disregard the indebtedness of its 'fore-structure' to the Beethovenian heroic style, or its insufficiency for analysis of much music of later periods and of multi-movement works. The foregoing discussion suggests one possible way out of this particularly restrictive hermeneutic trap. But what sort of hermeneutics does it lead us into?

---

[4] In the Second Symphony the nature of its closure is extremely ambiguous. See my 'Elgar's deconstruction of the *belle époque*: interlace structures and the Second Symphony', in *Elgar Studies*, ed. J. P. E. Harper-Scott and Julian Rushton (Cambridge: Cambridge University Press, forthcoming).

One way to begin to answer this question might be to decide on the general material thrust of Elgar's music, i.e. whether he is reactionary or progressive. Max Paddison offers a useful summary of Adorno's argument on this issue in 'Reaktion und Fortschritt'.

> Adorno maintains that it is purely in terms of the demands thrown up in the course of [the historical dialectic of musical material] that the question of progress or reaction is decided – in other words, the work's *consistency*. The reasoning appears to be along the following lines: (i) 'consistency' means the full realization in the structure of the work of its motivating 'idea' or concept; (ii) however, all 'authentic' works of art are the concrete manifestation of an adequate response to the historical demands of the material, the structuring idea of the work being also of necessity an inseparable aspect of this response; (iii) to respond adequately to the historical demands of the material is to be progressive; (iv) thus any work which strives to achieve consistency in its response to the historical demands of the material will thereby show itself to be progressive.[5]

The motivating 'idea' of Elgar's mature modernist music is, I have argued (although some ambiguity remains), the ironic, pessimistic deconstruction of the heroic *per aspera ad astra* narrative. Elgar clearly responds to the historical demands of the material – the unfolding of the heroic *Ursatz* and the upholding of the monotonal hegemony – at the level of the work's deep structure. Ergo on Adorno's careful definition Elgar's music is 'progressive'. It resists its fate as commodity at the level of form, if not at the level of surface musical language. His rebellion is more understated but every bit as single-minded as the more radical-*sounding* music of other modernists. To change minds, a composer requires other people to listen to his or her argument. It is sometimes better to argue suavely than abrasively, although both have their merits, and Elgar prefers the former.

If we are to summarize the hermeneutic core of Elgar's music we must understand how he works with the 'meaning' of sonata form, how this 'progressiveness' or 'modernity' is played out. And one interpretation of the form's Classical 'meaning' will probably be recognizable to most readers. The two tonic areas of the traditional sonata require each other if they are to have any identity, just as in Hegelian philosophy every self-consciousness requires the recognition of an external object. And just as a self-consciousness ideally requires the recognition of another self-consciousness, so the tonic area requires the recognition of an equally

---

[5] Max Paddison, *Adorno's Aesthetics of Music* (Cambridge: Cambridge University Press, 1993), p. 89.

well-grounded secondary tonal area, classically tonicized by the essential expositional closure.[6] In the usual terminology used of Hegel's dialectical model, the tonic is the *thesis*, the dominant or other non-tonic key is the *anti-thesis*, and the resolution of the latter into the former in the recapitulation, at the point of the essential structural closure, is the *synthesis*.[7] In the traditional sonata an Other is posited in distinction to the tonic in order that it may be recognized; and once recognized the tonic in turn recognizes the Other as another part of itself, draws it back into itself, and ends in a state of contented self-consciousness. But Elgar's take on sonata form brings to mind another Hegelian analysis, the dialectic of master and slave.[8]

In the immuring–immured structure, one musical self-consciousness ultimately rules over the other; in the First Symphony, A♭ is master and D slave. But exactly what is their relationship? In Hegel's dialectic, a struggle, intended to be to the death, between two self-consciousnesses results in continued coexistence. This is necessary because the death of one combatant would be of no use to either, since the 'victor' would find himself without the means of recognition he entered into the battle for in the first place. So one must be slave to the other: this is the first synthesis.

But the slave works for his master, producing artefacts, and by so doing he, unlike his master, creates objects external to himself which carry his stamp and allow him to recognize his own consciousness: and through this process he gains a Stoical sense of freedom. But then his hostile master, who unlike the Stoic lives in the real world, takes this consciousness-defining object away from the slave, thereby alienating the slave from his objectification of himself. It is Marx's contention that this arrangement pertains universally in capitalist societies, and that the master, the capitalist, goes still further, actually using the slave's objectified essence against him, by using it to increase his own wealth and by extension his power to oppress the slave further. Balance may be restored by the abolition of private property and alienated labour, i.e. the imposition of communism.

---

[6] In the directional-tonal structure, the synthesis is not the reaffirmation of the first tonic but the happy termination in a secondary tonic: it is still a clear resolution of the problems of the work.

[7] This tripartite understanding of Hegel's dialectical method is not the only way to grasp it, although Hegel himself saw some use in the formula. For a lucid and detailed account, see Michael Forster, 'Hegel's dialectical method', in *The Cambridge Companion to Hegel*, ed. Frederick C. Beiser (Cambridge: Cambridge University Press, 1993), pp. 130–70.

[8] This negative or inauthentic mode of Being-with others brings Elgar closer to Sartre's pessimistic analysis of the essential nature of interpersonal relationships than to Heidegger's sunnier vision. I shall return to this point in conclusion.

At what stage in the dialectic does Elgar's symphonic music rest? If the immuring tonic is the master and the immured tonic the slave, then we clearly see that one ends up being subservient to the other: A♭ is master at the end of the First Symphony.[9] But have the artefacts produced by the D-slave been smashed, or used against him? I think not. The D major Heaven Tune which closes the third movement still rings in the ears at the end as the crucial focus of the symphony (just as Hal's glorious final entrance on E♭ towards the end of *Falstaff* rings in the ears after the stupefying final chord). But the dialectic is much more complex than that.

The immured slave's original form, A minor, sits so uncomfortably alongside the immuring master's A♭ that at the end of the first movement the two combatants seem to lie side-by-side, breathless, on the battlefield, neither capable of further action. One has triumphed – but only just. In the middle movements the master is absent and we are thrust into the world of the slave. And there we witness something quite remarkable: the slave redefines himself through the teleological labours of the second and third movements so that his world and identity are centred on D major. The hierarchy of master and slave has not changed, but the slave has created for himself a new identity, and one which takes on some of the characteristics of his master – note the motivic similarities between the Heaven Tune and the Ideal Call – while still remaining Other. In objectifying his own existence, the slave has produced an effigy of his master which while purloining some of the identifying marks of his oppressor has also stamped them with his own identity. The slave has at once created an imperishable symbol of his own freedom and taken control of the freedom of his master by labelling it as his own handiwork. Elgar's dialectic ends with the slave in control, no matter what the master's bluster in the closing pages might suggest. (I trust there is no need to tease out further parallels in *Falstaff*.)

In psychological terms the result is a shocking schizophrenia. The dualism of master and slave, combined in one person, results in a musical example of what Hegel calls 'the unhappy consciousness': a consciousness striving against itself, half aiming for transcendence, half realizing its materiality. In the traditional sonata the musical self-consciousness recognizes that the tonal Other which the structure has proposed in opposition to the tonic is in fact a quality of its own self, capable of being drawn back

---

[9] For the sake of clarity I shall examine the parallel between the master–slave and immuring–immured-tonic dialectics almost solely with reference to the First Symphony, in which Elgar's view of the sonata dialectic is presented very clearly and dramatically. But as we have seen in *Falstaff*, and is also the case in the Second Symphony, the situation is largely the same, even if the nuances are different: one tonic is still slave to another.

into unity. (In Schenker's system, this overarching unity is never doubted.) In the reconciliation of tonic and non-tonic the traditional sonata creates a psychological bliss: absolute self-recognition. But Elgar's consciousness is irremediably unhappy. The immuring tonic master is not reconciled to its immured tonic slave.

On Hegel's account, any religion which separates God entirely from man, and this includes a Christianity which locates the Incarnation solely in the person of Jesus Christ, divides each human consciousness against itself by projecting human attributes onto God and failing to acknowledge them within himself, thereby inculcating through the (unnecessary) comparison feelings of sinfulness or worthlessness. And I believe that that is precisely what the immuring–immured structure does to Elgar's music and to the self-consciousness of which it is a mimesis. The radical instability of the master–slave relationship in his version of the sonata form leads to the psychological phenomenon whereby a questioning inner voice in an individual mind, here the immured tonality, gains in strength so compellingly that by the end the immuring tonality, the centre of the work's identity, can do nothing but babble madly to itself: 'I'm the king of the castle, and you're the dirty rascal.' We may smile atavistically at the childish taunt, but if we examine it seriously we know it is nonsense. Elgar's sonata form is a mimesis of neurosis; and it is not just the neurosis of one human mind.

As we have seen, the heart of Elgar's oeuvre, his symphonic music, ostensibly embraces the Beethovenian tradition. But it is the murderous embrace of a python. Elgar's symphonic style speaks directly against Beethoven's: and since a Beethovenian or Elgarian symphony is equally a mimesis of human temporality, that means they say starkly different things about each lived human existence.

As I conclude, now is the time to pick up the words that stand as a vaguely mystical epigraph to this book.

> Song is existence,

> says the third of [Rilke's] *Sonnets to Orpheus*, Part I. The word for existence, *Dasein*, is used here in the traditional sense of presence and as a synonym of Being. To sing, truly to say worldly existence, to say out of the haleness of the whole pure draft and to say only this, means: to belong to the precinct of beings themselves. This precinct, as the very nature of language, is Being itself. To sing the song means to be present in what is present itself. It means: *Dasein*, existence.[10]

---

[10] Martin Heidegger, 'What are poets for?', trans. Albert Hofstadter, in *Poetry, Language, Thought* (New York: Harper and Row, 1977; orig. edn 1946), p. 135.

It has been my contention throughout this book that music is a mimesis of human temporality: a revelation of how we are. Music brings us close to the only beings for whom B/being is an issue; in it we step into a 'clearing' in which the full richness of our temporal existence is illuminated by a light that reaches in from outside the everyday sphere. And if the clearing is impalpable, that does not make it any less powerful. Seamus Heaney tells of the day of his mother's death, when the space (temporal, spiritual, physical) opened up by her passing brings about a 'pure change' in the family surrounding her bed.

> Then she was dead,
> The searching for a pulsebeat was abandoned
> And we all knew one thing by being there.
> The space we stood around had been emptied
> Into us to keep, it penetrated
> Clearances that suddenly stood open.
> High cries were felled and a pure change happened.[11]

This absence which 'suddenly [stands] open' is unaccountably a presence, profound because in it the unknowable side of the mother's Being is revealed for the first time. In this poem, and elsewhere in Heaney's work, 'the world is defined not by the presences moving within it, but by the etched absences of the *realia* that used to be there'.[12] The clearance is a presence with power to transform the dead woman's family, a space 'utterly empty, utterly a source'.[13] Stepping into that clearing is, in later Heidegger's language, stepping into 'the precinct of beings'. His language verges on the occult, but there is a different formulation of the idea in *Being and Time*.

Truth, for Heidegger, is usually hidden or concealed, and he designates (not altogether reliably) states of unhiddenness or unconcealedness which apply to different kinds of beings.[14] Things ready-to-hand or present-at-

---

[11] Seamus Heaney, 'Clearances' 7, *The Haw Lantern* (London: Faber and Faber, 1987), p. 31.

[12] Helen Vendler, *Seamus Heaney* (London: Harper Collins, 1998), p. 111.

[13] Heaney, 'Clearances' 8, *The Haw Lantern*, p. 32. For a discussion of Heaney's poetry alongside Heidegger's philosophy see Irene Gilsenan Nordin, 'Nihilism in Seamus Heaney', *Philosophy and Literature* 26 (2002), pp. 405–14, and the discussion of this sonnet sequence on pp. 410–11.

[14] The following three-paragraph exposition draws heavily on Michael Inwood, 'unhiddenness, disclosure and lighting', in *A Heidegger Dictionary* (Oxford: Blackwell, 1999).

hand in the world, i.e. the entities which are not Dasein, are revealed in *Entdecktheit*, 'discoveredness' or 'uncoveredness', as if a veil has been lifted from them. But the hidden Being of Dasein is revealed in *Erschlossenheit*, or 'disclosedness'. The term comes from *erschliessen*, meaning 'to open up or explore'.

The *Entdecktheit* of things in the world is grounded in the *Erschlossenheit* of the world, but Dasein does not need that grounding. Dasein is its own ground: 'disclosedness [*Erschlossenheit*] is that basic character of Dasein according to which it *is* its "there"'.[15] The 'there' of a thing is a place for it to 'be', a ground on which its 'truth' – all the aspects of its Being, fully revealed and no longer hidden – stands firm; the 'there' is where a thing is clearly and richly itself.

Heidegger also calls this 'there', with picturesque intent, *das Offene*, 'the open', or 'the clearing' – a clearing not unlike the painfully bright open space of Heaney's poem. In modern German, 'clearing' or 'glade' is *Lichtung*, but Heidegger returns that word to its severed etymological root by saying that Dasein is a light which illuminates other entities, itself, *and* the clear space which provides the ground for Dasein's disclosedness. In a dark place, we can only see a light by the light it itself sheds, and on Heidegger's account, Dasein is such a self-illuminating light. The image is an old one, acknowledged by Heidegger to come from Plato's story of prisoners in a cave who at first see only shadows cast on the walls, but discover when they leave the cave the source of their shadowy images: the sun.

This formulation is perhaps more quotidian than the later talk of 'the precinct of beings', but it conveys the same thought. Dasein's way of being, its temporality, opens up a space in which its temporality can be brought into focus. Stepping into that clearing *is* being human. And by leading us into an impalpable temporal clearing, music too illuminates our being there, *Da-sein*, in the clearing. The space it opens up is 'emptied into us to keep': in listening to it we step into an appreciation of our temporality, and through it and with it we see ourselves. A 'pure change' happens, and we become clear to ourselves. But the transformative impact of the step into the space opened up by Elgar's music is quite terrible.

Every human being is 'thrown' into a historical situation populated by others in which he or she must make existential choices. Existence possibilities are provided by the individual's historical and social situation, but 'projection' of them – living with them and fitting them into one's own

---

[15] Martin Heidegger, *Being and Time*, 7th edn trans. John Macquarrie and Edward Robinson (Oxford: Blackwell, 1962; orig. edn 1927), p. 263.

being – requires individual choice, which may be authentic or inauthentic. On Beethoven Hero's account, especially in the middle period, authentic choices may be made and may lead ultimately to fulfilment for the individual and, which follows from that, true community among all human beings. But on Elgar's account human beings are either too scared to make self-defining choices or else get so bound up with the needs and demands of individual others or the expectations of society as a whole that they fail to break free and find themselves. They do not 'own up' to their existential responsibilities, and merely regard themselves as less-than-fully human objects within a grander scheme which itself is the highest reality.

And Elgar does not present his philosophy as a positive one, i.e. as the truest form of human existence. Rather, by setting it so directly in altercative dialogue with the Beethovenian tradition and philosophy he acknowledges our immurement in this state, but argues that such living is considerably beneath our full potential. This places Elgar's philosophy alongside later Heidegger's analysis of the 'destitution' of modernity, in which human beings live within 'the enframing',[16] incapable, without a total change of heart in the world (a 'world-turning'), of regarding anything, even themselves, as anything but 'resource': every human being is mere 'equipment', something whose character lies in its use-value rather than in a rich and mysterious Being capable of transcending itself (which is Beethoven's view). And in both Elgar's and Heidegger's cases the diagnosis seems alike: we get into this state by relating inauthentically to others in the world, and by failing to own up to our own existential responsibilities, both individually and as societies.

Moreover, by carrying his music on after the point of eucatastrophe – e.g. the arrival of D major in the First Symphony, or Hal's accession (eucatastrophe for one, dyscatastrophe for the other) in *Falstaff* – Elgar, like Shakespeare in *King Lear*, denies the possibility that even God can help.[17] Grace may well come, surprisingly and without bidding, but it

---

[16] The frame is now more than ever mercantile, and people speak delphically of obeying 'the markets' (which are reified, if not actually deified), rather than the thoughts of their own heads.

[17] This takes him a step beyond Heidegger, or even the un-Hegelian Christian who separates out God from man (propagating 'the unhappy consciousness'), because they both hold out at least *that* last hope. Roger Scruton, like the later Heidegger, believes that by resacralizing ourselves and the world through artworks we can bring about our own redemption (see his *Death-Devoted Heart: Sex and the Sacred in Wagner's Tristan und Isolde* (New York: Oxford University Press, 2004), especially Chapter 7 and the Epilogue). I would argue that even if Elgar believes we *can* achieve this, it is our nature that through weakness – or 'bad faith', as Sartre would say – we choose not to.

cannot be relied upon to return; and even when it does come, humankind tends to press on regardless, ultimately bringing even divine help to a bad conclusion. As noted in the previous chapter, Elgar realizes the unrealized tragic conclusion latent in the heroic Beethovenian narrative. The realization that after victory comes a hopeless and unending struggle is an old English conclusion: as old as *Beowulf*, one of whose themes it is.[18]

Elgar's music was written during a time that, in Ezra Pound's apt phrase, men walked eye-deep in hell believing in old men's lies.[19] Such times breed pessimistic opinions, but maybe the Elgarian view of truth really is the only truth in a post-Auschwitz, post-Hiroshima world. On Elgar's musically expressed understanding of human existence, which was as much informed by his view of the march of human and musical history as by his own personal existential struggles, there really seems to be little hope for a positive outcome. No matter how clearly an individual sees what he or she must do to attain full, authentic humanity, he or she will always ultimately fail, by shying away from existential responsibility. And as the relationships between keys in the First Symphony and *Falstaff* seem to demonstrate, Elgar has an almost Sartrean belief that owing to our (inescapably?) inauthentic Being-with others (always viewing them as means to an end) what we find in the final analysis, understanding Sartre properly, not as he is commonly and superficially misprised, is that hell is other people. And from that hell not even a God who breaks through into our world with the eucatastrophic joy of his grace can save us.

We could scarcely be further from embracing all human beings as brothers and sisters and giving one kiss to the whole world.

[18] Mention of *Beowulf* is not entirely off the point. Elgar's Scandinavian ancestry was pointed to as early as the second sentence of his first biography: 'His surname, of Scandinavian origin, is a modernised form of "Ælfgar", or "[elf]-spear"' (Robert J. Buckley, *Sir Edward Elgar* (London: The Bodley Head, 1905), p. 1). If 'ælf' is right, then a similar form of that name, 'Gandálfr' ('staff- or wand-elf'), which Tolkien borrowed for his fiction, appears in the Elder Edda. But if the first part of the name is not 'ælf' but 'œl', then 'Elgar' might mean 'eel-spear', from Old English 'œl' (eel) + 'gar' (spear), or Flemish 'aalgeer' or 'elger', from which the *OED* believes the obsolete English 'elger', eel-spear, may be derived. Its pronunciation –'ɛlgə(r), *not* 'ɛlgɑː – is probably the correct one for Elgar's name. I consider Beowulfian resonances in both the structure and meaning of the Second Symphony in 'Elgar's deconstruction of the *belle époque*'.

[19] In *Hugh Selwyn Mauberley* ([London]: The Ovid Press, 1920), 'E. P. *Ode pour l'election de son sepulchre*', part 4.

Glossary

This book makes frequent use of a number of terms which may be unfamiliar to readers. This glossary provides working definitions of the most important of these terms, of which 'Dasein' is perhaps the principal one, appearing in virtually all of the definitions. It is in the nature of a glossary that definitions be gnomic, but it is hoped that they will serve as reminders of longer and more nuanced definitions in the text, to which the reader will be led by the index. References are arranged alphabetically according to the form (whether German or English) in which they are most often used in the text. For a more comprehensive and detailed account of Heidegger's language, the reader is directed to Michael Inwood, *A Heidegger Dictionary* (Oxford: Blackwell, 1999), which has aided in the creation of this glossary.

(a) Heideggerian terms

anticipation

see temporality

anxiety (*Angst*)

A basic mood of Dasein which discloses Dasein's responsibility to choose its own destiny, and reaffirms its basic 'unsettledness' in the world.

Augenblick, der (the moment of vision)

The authentic mode of the present; the moment of resolution in which Dasein decides how to shape its future in the light of its past and present 'situation'.

authenticity (*Eigentlichkeit*) and inauthenticity (*Uneigentlichkeit*)

Derived from the adjective *eigen*, 'own', authenticity and inauthenticity characterize Dasein's capacity either to make existential choices which are in accord with its 'ownmost' Being (authentic) or, contrarily, to accept the choices offered by 'the They' (inauthentic).

Being

The most general feature of everything that is. Different beings have a different kind of Being. The most distinctive element of the Being of Dasein is its temporality.

Being-alongside (*Sein-bei*); concern (*Besorgen*) Being-in-the-world (*In-der-Welt-sein*)	Dasein's mode of Being towards things in the world (pencils, tables, animals, etc.). Dasein and the world are indivisible and complementary; Heidegger considers the theoretical separation of humans and the external world to be 'the scandal of philosophy'. As Being-in-the-world, Dasein approaches the world with concern and involvement, treating it as an inter-referential whole which is essentially involved with Dasein's projects.
Being-with (*Mitsein*); solicitude (*Fürsorge*) forgetfulness-of-Being (*Seinsvergessenheit*)	Dasein's mode of being with other Daseins. In misconceiving the Being of things – for instance as being present-at-hand (with properties) rather than ready-to-hand (with use) – Dasein is guilty of forgetfulness-of-Being. This leads to Being (and with it 'truth') getting 'covered up' and hidden from view. On Heidegger's view it was the essential feature and failure of the philosophical tradition from Plato to Heidegger; as the 'enframing' it is also the defining characteristic of modernity.
potentiality-for-Being (*Seinkönnen*)	Used in many connexions with the character of Dasein, potentiality-for-Being refers to Dasein's freedom to choose between personal existential possibilities. Its potentiality-for-Being means that Dasein is essentially its possibilities, not its actuality.
care (*Sorge*)	A tripartite structure, containing concern (Being-alongside) and solicitude (Being-with) but overarched by 'care', Dasein's involvement with things and other Daseins in-the-world. Dasein's involvement is not primarily cognitive or theoretical, nor is it merely practical: Dasein's relationship with the world and with others is 'care' because Being itself is an issue for Dasein.
Dasein	Literally, 'Being-there'; Heidegger's term for the way of Being typical of humans,

	for whom alone of all beings, Being is an issue.
destruction (*Destruktion*)	For Heidegger, 'hermeneutics is destruction'. Working from presuppositions and prejudgements inherent in all Dasein, the hermeneutic project works by acknowledging, analyzing, and 'destroying' them, before rebeginning the hermeneutic circle.
disclosure	Truth, for Heidegger, is disclosure, the unveiling of hidden aspects of Being. Disclosure of anything depends on Dasein and is in fact an essential part of Dasein's Being. As a being which discloses Being, Dasein is the primary locus of truth.
ecstasis, ecstases, ecstatic temporality	*see* temporality
enframing, the (*das Gestell*)	Sometimes the enframing (*Gestell*) is, for Heidegger, the framing of the 'rift' between 'earth' and 'world' in the form or figure (*Gestalt*) of the work of art. Later (and this is its use in this book) it becomes the framing of all things, including Dasein, within a technological form which reduces everything to 'standing resource' and covers over or denies the individual Being of entities. It is related to forgetfulness-of-Being, and has been present (initially in a productive way) in all human thinking, but has become a destructive blight of modernity.
equipment, equipmental being	Things which are ready-to-hand and are used by Dasein 'in-order-to' do something are equipment; their essential Being (until they cease to operate) is as equipment.
Ereignis (event, happening, occurrence)	The 'happening' (for instance, in a work of art) which re-sacralizes the world and reveals the awesomeness of Being. In music I call this the 'mimetic hermeneutic window'.

everydayness	The state, distinct from the philosophical or scientific attitude (among countless others), in which Dasein ordinarily finds itself.
existence (*Existenz*)	Existence is, uniquely, Dasein's mode of Being. Unlike all other entities, Dasein has no 'essence': its nature lies in its existence; it is as it is through individual choice, not preordained nature. Dasein 'stands out' (ek-sists) from or transcends the ordinary flow of time to create itself. Unlike Sartre, Heidegger holds that Dasein's self-defining choices are limited by its 'situation'.
horizon (*Horizont*)	A horizon is for Heidegger a point of view which is independent of a thing or concern under discussion, and allows for objective scrutiny of it. *Being and Time* suggests that time is the horizon of Being.
phenomenology (*Phänomenologie*)	On Heidegger's idiomatic definition, phenomenology does not concern itself with entities that show themselves (which is the classic Husserlian definition), but rather with aspects of the Being of entities, especially ones which are normally hidden from view but can be disclosed or discovered by Dasein.
present-at-hand (*vorhanden*) and ready-to-hand (*zuhanden*)	Two modes of Being of things in Dasein's world. Put crudely, entities which are ready-to-hand have use; those present-at-hand have properties. Things are ready-to-hand because they are part of one of Dasein's projects, as 'equipment'. Entities denuded of their equipmental use are merely present-at-hand, objects of scrutiny.
repetition	*see* temporality
resoluteness	A distinctive mode of Dasein's nature as a disclosive Being, specifically in the context of disclosing or discovering itself *as itself.* In the *Augenblick*, Dasein *resolutely* 'runs ahead' to its own death

situation	and makes self-defining (self-disclosing) decisions in the present for the future. Dasein is 'thrown' into a particular historical and social 'situation' which defines and delimits its existential possibilities. Awareness of its situation enables Dasein to make authentic decisions.
temporality	A defining characteristic of Dasein, and in Heidegger's usage quite different from time as ordinarily understood. It is intimately bound up with Dasein's Being-in-the-world as 'care', and involved with Dasein's activity – as 'time to do things'.
ecstatic temporality	Dasein's temporality is ecstatic, *ekstatisch*, because it 'steps outside itself'. Temporality is split into three 'ecstases', and Dasein's essence lies in 'extemporizing' within the unity of the ecstases – typically, in the authentic attitude, by creating a present in the light of the future which is grasped in the *Augenblick*. But the ecstases each have both authentic and inauthentic modes.
past: repetition (*Wiederholung*); having-been-ness (*Gewesenheit*)	Inauthentic Dasein experiences the past as the 'having-been', a time gone and no longer accessible. Authentic Dasein 'repeats' the past by recognizing and seizing the opportunities it presents for choice.
present: *Augenblick* (moment of vision); waiting-towards (*Gegenwart*)	Inauthentic Dasein experiences the present as a 'waiting-towards' the future; in this mode Dasein is irresolute, subject to 'the They'. Authentic Dasein experiences the present as a moment of vision, an *Augenblick*, which it uses to bind together the three ecstases in a Self-forming unity.
future: anticipation; coming-towards	Inauthentic Dasein lets its future 'come towards' it; authentic Dasein 'anticipates' its future by resolutely 'repeating' its past.

They/One, the (*das Man*)	The They or the One (*das Man*) is the set of all Daseins. They restrict the freedom of individual Dasein by offering predesigned scripts for a way to live. Inauthentic Dasein is in the thrall of 'the They' insofar as it chooses a course because 'one does this', or 'they want me to do that'. Authentic Dasein is constructed largely in opposition to 'the They'.
thrownness (*Geworfenheit*)	Every Dasein finds itself in a situation into which it has been 'thrown'; thrownness bears the past as a burden. There is no warning that existence will begin, nor can there be any preparation for the specific situation Dasein will find itself. Being 'thrown', there are certain aspects of its history and capability, and the range of possibilities that are open to it, which Dasein must deal with as best it can.
truth	Truth is 'disclosedness' or 'discoveredness', i.e. Being that is not 'covered up'. Dasein discloses the Being of itself and other things. Because Dasein is the only disclosive being, it is the primary locus of truth.
understanding	Dasein is always understanding. There is never a time when Dasein does not already have a prior understanding of its world and its place in it. Dasein understands itself chiefly as a set of possibilities.
unsettledness (*Unheimlichkeit*)	Not to be confused with the Freudian 'uncanny'. Dasein feels 'unsettled' in the world because, unlike trees and tables etc. it is 'natureless' – responsible for choosing and creating its own nature. Dasein's unsettledness is a boon, not a lack which makes its existence 'contingent' or 'absurd'.
Ursprung, Ur-sprung (origin [of the work of art], or 'primordial leap')	'Ursprung' in ordinary German means 'origin', but Heidegger's hyphen brings out the etymological sense, 'primordial

leap'. Art is about this 'leap' into truth, from hiddenness to openness. Art discloses truth; the origin ('leap') of the artwork is the 'unconcealment' of truth.

(b) Other unfamiliar terms

breakthrough (*Durchbruch*); the rupture between self and forms	In Adorno's reading of Mahler, the moment in which the form of the work is breached by a power reaching in from 'outside' the frame, and which changes the course of the following events.
eucatastrophe and dyscatastrophe	In Tolkien's analysis of the fairy-story, the eucatastrophe is the sudden good turn which (like the 'breakthrough') reaches in from outside the frame and changes the course of future events. Dyscatastrophe is a sudden bad turn, which has the opposite effect.
intentionality and intentional objects	An intentional object is one to which, on the Husserlian view, consciousness is directed. Heidegger's definition is different and more complex, because he rejects the subject–object distinction Husserl's definition presupposes. Because Dasein relates to things in the world in terms of 'care', intentionality is not directed at (present-at-hand) objects but at goals towards which Dasein is working (by using ready-to-hand things).
mimesis	For Plato, mimesis is the representation of something in the world; and since a thing in the world is a representation of a Form or Idea (ἰδέα), mimesis is a representation of a representation. On Gadamer's stronger view, by contrast, mimesis is more than mere representation: it is the appearance of an aspect of reality in the thing that is represented – mimesis reveals truth.
prosopon	The outward appearance of a thing (Greek πρόσπον, 'face').

prosopopœia	A rhetorical figure by which personal characteristics are attributed to an inanimate or abstract thing; personification.
retention and protention	In Husserlian phenomenology, time-consciousness depends on the past being 'retained' in consciousness and the future 'protained' – i.e. predicted with some confidence through extrapolation from the past. Together 'retention' and 'protention' make the present 'longer' than a mere 'now' or instant.
supratemporality	In Ingarden's ontology of music, the temporal form which is on the one hand not bound to the specific time of a given performance, but on the other hand is clearly dependent on temporal organization of a high order, can be described as 'supratemporal'.
telos	Greek τέλος, 'end': signifying, in musical discourse, the point to which all activity (melodic, harmonic, motivic, etc.) is directed; the goal of the structure.

Bibliography

Abbate, Carolyn, *Unsung Voices: Opera and Musical Narrative in the Nineteenth Century* (Princeton, NJ: Princeton University Press, 1991).

Adams, Byron, 'Elgar's later oratorios: Roman Catholicism, decadence and the Wagnerian dialectic of shame and grace', in *The Cambridge Companion to Elgar*, ed. Daniel M. Grimley and Julian Rushton (Cambridge: Cambridge University Press, 2004), pp. 81–105.

'The "dark saying" of the Enigma: homoeroticism and the Elgarian paradox', *Nineteenth-Century Music* 23 (2000), pp. 218–35.

Adorno, Theodor W., *Mahler: a Musical Physiognomy*, trans. Edmund Jephcott (Chicago and London: University of Chicago Press, 1992; orig. edn 1960).

Philosophy of Modern Music, trans. Anne G. Mitchell and Wesley V. Bloomster (London: Sheed and Ward, 1973).

Agawu, Kofi, 'Extended tonality in Mahler and Strauss', in *Richard Strauss: New Perspectives on the Composer and His Work*, ed. Bryan Gilliam (Durham, NC: Duke University Press, 1992), pp. 55–75.

'Prolonged counterpoint in Mahler', in *Mahler Studies*, ed. Stephen E. Hefling (Cambridge: Cambridge University Press, 1997), pp. 217–47.

Allis, Michael, 'Elgar and the art of retrospective narrative', *The Journal of Musicological Research* 19 (2000), pp. 289–328.

Altick, Richard D., '*Hamlet* and the odor of mortality', *Shakespeare Quarterly* 5 (1954), pp. 167–76.

Anderson, Andrew, 'A phenomenology of music analysis', Ph.D. thesis, University of North Texas (1996).

Anderson, Robert, *Elgar* (London: Dent, 1993).

Elgar in Manuscript (Portland, OR: Amadeus Press, 1990).

Auden, W. H., 'Dingley Dell & the Fleet' in *The Dyer's Hand and Other Essays* (London: Faber and Faber, 1963), pp. 407–28.

'The quest hero', in *Tolkien and the Critics: Essays on J. R. R. Tolkien's 'The Lord of the Rings'*, ed. Neil D. Isaacs and Rose A. Zimbardo (Notre Dame, IN: University of Notre Dame Press, 1968), pp. 40–61.

Bailey, Robert, 'An analytical study of the sketches and drafts', in *Richard Wagner, Prelude and Transfiguration from 'Tristan und Isolde'* (New York and London: Norton, 1985), pp. 113–46.

'Musical language and structure in the Third Symphony', in *Brahms Studies: Analytical and Historical Perspectives*, ed. George S. Bozarth (Oxford: Clarendon Press, 1990), pp. 405–22.

'The structure of the *Ring* and its evolution', *Nineteenth-Century Music* 1 (1977), pp. 48–61.

Beckett, Lucy, 'A proposed interpretation', in *Richard Wagner: Parsifal*, ed. Lucy Beckett (Cambridge: Cambridge University Press, 1981), pp. 129–49.

Bloom, Harold, *Shakespeare: the Invention of the Human* (London: Fourth Estate, 1999).

Brett, Philip, 'Britten, Benjamin', in *The New Grove Dictionary of Music and Musicians*, 2nd edn, ed. Stanley Sadie and John Tyrrell (London: Macmillan, 2001).

Brett, Philip, Wood, Elizabeth, and Thomas, Gary (eds.), *Queering the Pitch: the New Gay and Lesbian Musicology* (New York: Routledge, 1994).

Buckley, Robert J., *Sir Edward Elgar* (London: The Bodley Head, 1905).

Burnham, Scott, *Beethoven Hero* (Princeton, NJ: Princeton University Press, 1995).

Caldwell, John, *The Oxford History of English Music – Volume II: From c.1715 to the Present Day* (Oxford: Clarendon Press, 1999).

Carpenter, Humphrey, *Benjamin Britten: a Biography* (London: Faber and Faber, 1992).

Child, Francis James (ed.), *English and Scottish Ballads* (London: Sampson Low, 1861).

Clifton, Thomas, *Music as Heard: a Study in Applied Phenomenology* (New Haven, CT: Yale University Press, 1983).

Cohn, Richard, 'Maximally smooth cycles, hexatonic systems, and the analysis of late-romantic triadic progressions', *Music Analysis* 15 (1996), pp. 9–40.

Dahlhaus, Carl, *Between Romanticism and Modernism: Four Studies in the Music of the Later Nineteenth Century*, trans. Mary Whittall and Arnold Whittall (Berkeley, CA and London: University of California Press, 1980; orig. edn 1974).

Foundations of Music History, trans. J. Bradford Robinson (Cambridge: Cambridge University Press, 1983; orig. edn 1967).

Nineteenth-Century Music, trans. J. Bradford Robinson (Berkeley, CA and London: University of California Press, 1989; orig. edn 1980).

Richard Wagner's Music Dramas, trans. Mary Whittall (Cambridge: Cambridge University Press, 1979; orig. edn 1971).

Dahlhaus, Carl, and Deathridge, John, *The New Grove Wagner* (London: Macmillan, 1984).

Darcy, Warren, 'Bruckner's sonata deformations', in *Bruckner Studies*, ed. Timothy L. Jackson and Paul Hawkshaw (Cambridge: Cambridge University Press, 1997), pp. 256–77.

Wagner's 'Das Rheingold' (Oxford: Clarendon Press, 1993).

Dipert, Randall R., 'The composer's intentions: an examination of their relevance for performance', *The Musical Quarterly* 66 (1980), pp. 205–18.

Dowden, Edward, *Shakspere: A Critical Study of His Mind and Art* (London: Henry S. King, 1875; 20th edn London: Kegan Paul, Trench, Trubner & Co., n.d.).

Dreyfus, Hubert L., *Being-in-the-World: a Commentary on Heidegger's* Being and Time, *Division I* (Cambridge, MA: MIT Press, 1991).

'Heidegger on the connection between nihilism, art, technology, and politics', in *The Cambridge Companion to Heidegger*, ed. Charles Guignon (Cambridge: Cambridge University Press, 1993), pp. 215–39.

Dunsby, Jonathan, 'The multi-piece in Brahms: *Fantasien*, op. 116', in *Brahms: Biographical, Documentary, and Analytical Studies*, ed. Robert Pascall (Cambridge: Cambridge University Press, 1983), pp. 167–89.

Elgar, Edward, *Edward Elgar: Letters of a Lifetime*, ed. Jerrold Northrop Moore (Oxford: Clarendon Press, 1990).

Elgar and his Publishers: Letters of a Creative Life, 2 vols., ed. Jerrold Northrop Moore (Oxford: Clarendon Press, 1987).

'Falstaff', *Musical Times* 54 (1913), pp. 575–9.

'A Future For English Music' and Other Lectures, ed. Percy M. Young (London: D. Dobson, 1968).

Letters to Nimrod: Edward Elgar to August Jaeger, 1897–1908, ed. Percy M. Young (London: D. Dobson, 1965).

Eliot, T. S., *The Sacred Wood: Essays on Poetry and Criticism*, 2nd edn (London: Faber and Faber, 1997; reset from 1928 edn).

Evans, Peter, *The Music of Benjamin Britten* (London: Dent, 1979).

Ferguson, Niall, *Empire: How Britain Made the Modern World* (London: Penguin, 2003).

Ferrara, Lawrence, 'Phenomenology as a tool for musical analysis', *The Musical Quarterly* 70 (1984), pp. 355–73.

Forster, Michael, 'Hegel's dialectical method', in *The Cambridge Companion to Hegel*, ed. Frederick C. Beiser (Cambridge: Cambridge University Press, 1993), pp. 130–70.

Freud, Sigmund, *The Interpretation of Dreams*, trans. James Strachey (London: Pelican, 1976).

Gadamer, Hans-Georg, 'The relevance of the beautiful: art as play, symbol and festival', trans. Nicholas Walker, in *The Relevance of the Beautiful and Other Essays*, ed. Robert Bernasconi (Cambridge: Cambridge University Press, 1986), pp. 3–53.

Philosophical Hermeneutics, trans. David E. Linge (London: University of California Press, 1976).

Truth and Method, 2nd edn, rev. trans. J. Weinsheimer and D. G. Marshall (London: Sheed & Ward, 1989).

Golding, William, *The Hot Gates, and Other Occasional Pieces* (London: Faber and Faber, 1965).

Gorner, Paul, *Twentieth Century German Philosophy* (Oxford: Oxford University Press, 2000).

Gould, Corissa, 'Edward Elgar, *The Crown of India*, and the image of empire', *Elgar Society Journal* 13 (2003), pp. 25–35.

Greene, David B., *Mahler, Consciousness and Temporality* (New York: Gordon and Breach, 1984).

Temporal Processes in Beethoven's Music (New York: Gordon and Breach, 1982).

Grimley, Daniel M., "'Falstaff (tragedy)": narrative and retrospection in Elgar's Symphonic Study', unpublished paper delivered at the Elgar Conference, University of Surrey, 2002.

'Modernism and closure: Nielsen's Fifth Symphony', *The Musical Quarterly* 86 (2002), pp. 149–73.

Grondin, Jean, 'Gadamer's basic understanding of understanding', in *The Cambridge Companion to Gadamer*, ed. Robert J. Dostal (Cambridge: Cambridge University Press, 2002), pp. 36–51.

Habermas, Jürgen, *The Philosophical Discourse of Modernity: Twelve Lectures*, trans. Frederick Lawrence (Cambridge, MA: MIT Press, 1987).

Hall, Harrison, 'Intentionality and world: Division I of *Being and Time*', in *The Cambridge Companion to Heidegger*, ed. Charles Guignon (Cambridge: Cambridge University Press, 1993), pp. 122–40.

Harper-Scott, J. P. E., 'Elgar's deconstruction of the *belle époque*: interlace structures and the Second Symphony', in *Elgar Studies*, ed. J. P. E. Harper-Scott and Julian Rushton (Cambridge: Cambridge University Press, forthcoming).

'Elgar's unwumbling: the theatre music', in *The Cambridge Companion to Elgar*, ed. Julian Rushton and Daniel M. Grimley (Cambridge: Cambridge University Press, 2004), pp. 171–83.

'Henry and the *Gräfin*/Grinder: Elgar and *The Starlight Express*', *Elgar Society Journal* 13/4 (2004), pp. 15–23.

Harrison, Daniel, 'Nonconformist notions of nineteenth-century enharmonicism', *Music Analysis* 21 (2002), pp. 115–60.

Hasty, Christopher, *Meter as Rhythm* (New York: Oxford University Press, 1997).

Heaney, Seamus, *The Haw Lantern* (London: Faber and Faber, 1987).

Heidegger, Martin, *Being and Time*, 7th edn trans. John Macquarrie and Edward Robinson (Oxford: Blackwell, 1962; orig. edn 1927).

An Introduction to Metaphysics, trans. Ralph Manheim (New Haven and London: Yale University Press, 1959; orig. edn 1935).

Nietzsche, vol. I: The Will to Power as Art, trans. David Farrell Krell (London: Routledge and Kegan Paul, 1981; orig. edn 1961).

Ontology: the Hermeneutics of Facticity, trans. J. van Buren (Bloomington: University of Indiana Press, 1995; orig. edn 1988).

'The origin of the work of art', trans. Albert Hofstadter, in *Martin Heidegger: Basic Writings*, ed. David Farrell Krell (London: Routledge, 1993; orig. edn 1949), pp. 139–212. Also printed as 'The origin of the work of art', trans. Albert Hofstadter, in *Poetry, Language, Thought* (New York: Harper and Row, 1971; orig. edn 1950, 2nd edn 1960), pp. 15–86.

'The question concerning technology', trans. with some editorial changes by William Lovitt, in *Martin Heidegger: Basic Writings*, ed. David Farrell Krell (London: Routledge, 1993; orig. edn 1949), pp. 307–41.

'What are poets for?', trans. Albert Hofstadter, in *Poetry, Language, Thought* (New York: Harper and Row, 1977; orig. edn 1946), pp. 89–142.

Hepokoski, James A., 'Back and forth from *Egmont*: Beethoven, Mozart, and the nonresolving recapitulation', *Nineteenth-Century Music* 25 (2001–2), pp. 127–54.

'Beethoven reception: the symphonic tradition', in *The Cambridge History of Nineteenth-Century Music*, ed. Jim Samson (Cambridge: Cambridge University Press, 2001), pp. 424–59.

'Beyond the sonata principle', *Journal of the American Musicological Society* 55 (2002), pp. 91–154.

'Elgar', in *The Nineteenth-Century Symphony*, ed. D. Kern Holoman (New York and London: Schirmer, 1997), pp. 327–44.

'Fiery-pulsed libertine or domestic hero? Strauss's *Don Juan* reinvestigated', in *Richard Strauss: New Perspectives on the Composer and His Work*, ed. Bryan Gilliam (Durham, NC: Duke University Press, 1992), pp. 135–75.

'Sibelius', in *The Nineteenth-Century Symphony*, ed. D. Kern Holoman (New York and London: Schirmer, 1997), pp. 417–49.

Sibelius: Symphony No. 5 (Cambridge: Cambridge University Press, 1993).

'Structure and program in *Macbeth*: a proposed reading of Strauss's first symphonic poem', in *Richard Strauss and His World*, ed. Bryan Gilliam (Princeton, NJ: Princeton University Press, 1992), pp. 67–89.

Hepokoski, James A., and Darcy, Warren, *Elements of Sonata Theory – Norms, Types, and Deformations* (New York and Oxford: Oxford University Press, forthcoming).

Holloway, Robin, 'The early choral works', in *The Cambridge Companion to Elgar*, ed. Daniel M. Grimley and Julian Rushton (Cambridge: Cambridge University Press, 2004), pp. 63–80.

Ingarden, Roman, *The Work of Music and the Problem of its Identity*, trans. Adam Czerniawski (Basingstoke: Macmillan, 1986; orig. edn 1958).

Inwood, Michael, *A Heidegger Dictionary* (Oxford: Blackwell, 1999).

Johnson, Julian, *Who Needs Classical Music? Cultural Choice and Musical Value* (New York and Oxford: Oxford University Press, 2002).

Jung, Carl Gustav, 'On the nature of dreams', in *Dreams*, trans. R. F. C. Hull (London: Routledge, 1985), pp. 67–83.

Keller, Hans, 'Elgar the progressive', *The Music Review* 43 (1957), pp. 294–7.

Kennedy, Michael, *Elgar Orchestral Music* (London: BBC, 1970).

The Life of Elgar (Cambridge: Cambridge University Press, 2004).

Portrait of Elgar, 3rd edn (Oxford: Clarendon Press, 1987).

Kent, Christopher, '*Falstaff*: Elgar's symphonic study', in *Edward Elgar: Music and Literature*, ed. Raymond Monk (Aldershot: Scolar, 1993), pp. 83–107.

Kinderman, William, *Beethoven* (Oxford: Oxford University Press, 1995).

'Dramatic recapitulation and tonal pairing in Wagner's *Tristan und Isolde* and *Parsifal*', in *The Second Practice of Nineteenth-Century Tonality* (Lincoln, NE: University of Nebraska Press, 1996), pp. 178–214.

Kinderman, William and Krebs, Harald (eds.), *The Second Practice of Nineteenth-Century Tonality* (Lincoln, NE: University of Nebraska Press, 1996).

Kramer, Jonathan D., *The Time of Music: New Meanings, New Temporalities, New Listening Strategies* (New York: Schirmer, 1988).

Kramer, Lawrence, *Music as Cultural Practice, 1800–1900* (Berkeley, CA and London: University of California Press, 1990).

Lerdahl, Fred, and Jackendoff, Ray, *A Generative Theory of Tonal Music* (Cambridge, MA: MIT Press, 1983).

Lewis, Christopher, 'The mind's chronology: narrative times and harmonic disruption in post-Romantic music', in *The Second Practice of Nineteenth-Century Tonality*, ed. William Kinderman and Harald Krebs (Lincoln, NE: University of Nebraska Press, 1996), pp. 114–49.

Tonal Coherence in Mahler's Ninth Symphony (Ann Arbor, MI: UMI Research Press, 1984).

Macquarrie, John, *Principles of Christian Theology*, 2nd edn (London: SCM, 1977).

McCreless, Patrick, *Wagner's 'Siegfried': its Drama, History, and Music* (Ann Arbor, MI: UMI Research Press, 1982).

McGuire, Charles Edward, *Elgar's Oratorios: the Creation of an Epic Narrative* (Aldershot: Ashgate, 2002).

'Functional music: imperialism, the Great War, and Elgar as popular composer', in *The Cambridge Companion to Elgar*, ed. Julian Rushton and Daniel M. Grimley (Cambridge: Cambridge University Press, 2004), pp. 214–24.

McVeagh, Diana M., *Edward Elgar: His Life and Music* (London: Dent, 1955).

Maine, Basil, *Edward Elgar: His Life and Works*, 2 vols. (London: G. Bell & Sons, 1933).

Marston, Nicholas, *Beethoven's Piano Sonata in E, Op. 109* (Oxford: Clarendon Press, 1995).

'Schubert's homecoming', *Journal of the Royal Musical Association*, 125 (2000), pp. 248–70.

'Trifles or a multitrifle? Beethoven's Bagatelles, Op. 119, Nos. 7–11', *Music Analysis* 5 (1986), pp. 192–206.

Matthews, David, 'The Sixth Symphony', in *The Mahler Companion*, ed. Donald Mitchell and Andrew Nicholson (Oxford: Oxford University Press, 1999), pp. 366–75.

Meikle, Robert, 'The symphonies and concertos', in *William Walton: Music and Literature*, ed. Stewart R. Craggs (Aldershot: Scolar, 1999), pp. 67–108.

'"The true foundation": the symphonies', in *Edward Elgar: Music and Literature*, ed. Raymond Monk (Aldershot: Scolar, 1993), pp. 45–71.

Mitchell, Donald, 'Some thoughts on Elgar', in *An Elgar Companion*, ed. Christopher Redwood (Ashbourne: Sequoia, 1982), pp. 279–90 (reprinted from *Music & Letters* 38 (1957), pp. 113–23, and reprinted in Mitchell, *Cradles of the New: Writings on Music, 1951–1991*, selected Christopher Palmer, ed. Mervyn Cooke (London: Faber and Faber, 1995), pp. 255–68).

'Some observations on William Walton, I', *The Chesterian* 26 (1952), pp. 35–8.

Moody, A. David, *Thomas Stearns Eliot, Poet*, 2nd edn (Cambridge: Cambridge University Press, 1994).

Moore, Jerrold Northrop, *Edward Elgar: a Creative Life* (Oxford: Oxford University Press, 1984).

Morgann, Maurice, *An Essay on the Dramatic Character of Sir John Falstaff* (London: T. Davies, 1777).

Newcomb, Anthony, 'The birth of music out of the spirit of drama: an essay in Wagnerian formal analysis', *Nineteenth-Century Music* 5 (1981), pp. 38–66.

The New Grove Dictionary of Music and Musicians, 2nd edn, ed. Stanley Sadie and John Tyrrell (London: Macmillan, 2001).

Nordin, Irene Gilsenan, 'Nihilism in Seamus Heaney', *Philosophy and Literature* 26 (2002), pp. 405–14.

Nuttall, A. D., *A New Mimesis: Shakespeare and the Representation of Reality* (London: Methuen & Co., 1983).

'The argument about Shakespeare's characters', in *Shakespeare's Wide and Universal Stage*, ed. C. B. Cox and D. J. Palmer (Manchester: Manchester University Press, 1984), pp. 18–31.

Why Does Tragedy Give Pleasure? (Oxford: Clarendon Press, 1996).

Paddison, Max, *Adorno's Aesthetics of Music* (Cambridge: Cambridge University Press, 1993).

Philipse, Herman, *Heidegger's Philosophy of Being* (Princeton, NJ: Princeton University Press, 1998).

Pike, Alfred, *A Phenomenological Analysis of Musical Experience and Other Related Essays* (New York: St John's University Press, 1970).

Porter, Bernard, 'Edward Elgar and empire', *The Journal of Imperial and Commonwealth History* 29 (2001), pp. 1–34, reprinted as 'Elgar and empire: music, nationalism and the war', in *'Oh, My Horses!': Elgar and the Great War* (Rickmansworth: Elgar Editions, 2001), pp. 133–73.

The Absent-Minded Imperialists: Empire, Society, and Culture in Britain (New York: Oxford University Press, 2004).

Prince, Gerald, *A Dictionary of Narratology*, rev. edn (Lincoln, NE: University of Nebraska Press, and Chesham: Combined Academic, 2003).

Prior, A. N., *Formal Logic* (Oxford: Clarendon Press, 1962).

Richards, Jeffrey, *Imperialism and Music: Britain 1876–1953* (Manchester and New York: Manchester University Press, 2001).

Rosen, Charles, *Sonata Forms*, rev. edn (New York: Norton, 1988).

Rupprecht, Philip, *Britten's Musical Language* (Cambridge: Cambridge University Press, 2002).

Rushton, Julian, *Elgar: 'Enigma' Variations* (Cambridge: Cambridge University Press, 1999).

The Musical Language of Berlioz (Cambridge: Cambridge University Press, 1982).

Said, Edward W., *Orientalism* (London: Routledge and Kegan Paul, 1978).

Schopenhauer, Arthur, *The World as Will and Representation*, 2 vols., trans. E. F. J. Payne (New York: Dover, 1966).

Scruton, Roger, *Death-Devoted Heart: Sex and the Sacred in Wagner's 'Tristan und Isolde'* (New York: Oxford University Press, 2004).

Sheldon, A. J., *Edward Elgar* (London: Office of 'Musical opinion', 1932).

Shippey, Tom, *J. R. R. Tolkien: Author of the Century* (London: Harper Collins, 2000).

Solomon, Robert C., *Continental Philosophy Since 1750: The Rise and Fall of the Self* (Oxford: Oxford University Press, 1988).

Smith, F. Joseph, *The Experiencing of Musical Sound: Prelude to a Phenomenology of Music* (New York: Gordon and Breach, 1979).

Taruskin, Richard, 'On letting the music speak for itself: some reflections on musicology and performance', *The Journal of Musicology* 1 (1982), pp. 338–49.

  The Oxford History of Western Music (Oxford: Oxford University Press, 2005).

Thomson, Aidan J., 'Elgar and chivalry', *Nineteenth-Century Music* 28 (2005), pp. 254–75.

  'Re-reading Elgar: hermeneutics, criticism and reception in England and Germany, 1900–1914', D.Phil. thesis, University of Oxford, 2002.

Tolkien, J. R. R., 'On fairy-stories', in *The Monsters and the Critics and Other Essays*, ed. Christopher Tolkien (London: Harper Collins, 1983), pp. 109–61.

Tomlinson, Gary, *Music in Renaissance Magic: Toward a Historiography of Others* (Chicago: University of Chicago Press, 1993).

Tovey, Donald Francis, *Beethoven* (London: Oxford University Press, 1945).

  Essays in Musical Analysis, 6 vols. (London: Oxford University Press, 1935–9).

  '"Falstaff", symphonic study, Op. 68', in *Essays in Musical Analysis vol. IV, Illustrative Music* (London: Oxford University Press, 1936), pp. 3–16.

Trowell, Brian, 'Elgar's use of literature', in *Edward Elgar: Music and Literature*, ed. Raymond Monk (Aldershot: Scolar, 1993), pp. 182–326.

Vendler, Helen, *Seamus Heaney* (London: Harper Collins, 1998).

Whittall, Arnold, *Musical Composition in the Twentieth Century* (Oxford: Oxford University Press, 1999).

  'The later symphonies', in *The Cambridge Companion to Sibelius*, ed. Daniel M. Grimley (Cambridge: Cambridge University Press, 2004), pp. 49–65.

Young, Julian, *The Death of God and the Meaning of Life* (London: Routledge, 2003).

  Heidegger, Philosophy, Nazism (Cambridge: Cambridge University Press, 1997).

  Heidegger's Later Philosophy (Cambridge: Cambridge University Press, 2002).

  Heidegger's Philosophy of Art (Cambridge: Cambridge University Press, 2001).

  Nietzsche's Philosophy of Art (Cambridge: Cambridge University Press, 1992).

Index